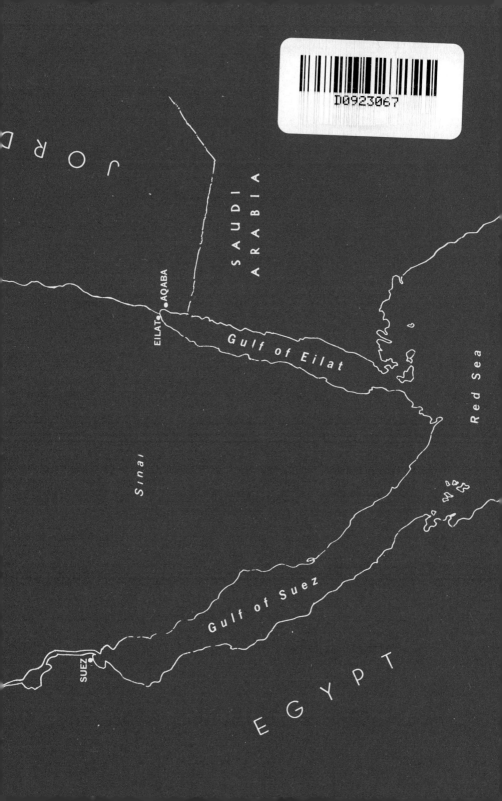

The Israelis

HARRY
GOLDEN

The Israelis

PORTRAIT OF A PEOPLE

by the author of ONLY IN AMERICA

G. P. Putnam's Sons
New York

Copyright © 1971 by Harry Golden

Library of Congress Catalog Card Number: 77-136790

PRINTED IN THE UNITED STATES OF AMERICA

for John Goldhurst, my grandson, who visited Israel before he was two, rode a camel in Jerusalem, survived three stitches in Tel Aviv, and found the axle grease on the kibbutz

Acknowledgments

First to Joe Lapid, Israeli newspaperman, one of the best in the world, who advised, counseled, and aided these efforts; then to Richard Goldhurst, another newspaperman, my son and collaborator.

Contents

9

Introductory

Everybody says *shalom!*

Shalom means "hello" and "good-bye" and it means
"peace." *Shabat shalom* is the tender salutation between Jews
on the eve of the Sabbath. The breathless *shalom-shalom* means
"I'll see you later." There are probably as many variant meanings
to the word *shalom* as there are Israels.

Indeed there are many Israels.

There is the land of Israel which Jacob received from God
in Shechem, the present-day Nablus, for him and his descendants
forever and ever. Israel is still the Palestinian Holy Land, adored
by Christians, the place where Jesus Christ was born, crucified,
died, and ascended. There is the Israel from one of whose Judean
hills Mohammed, in a fiery chariot, rode to heaven. There is
Israel, the new homeland for nineteenth- and twentieth-century
Jewish refugees from Europe, and there is Israel, the industrial
society from which another people fled in this century to become
the Arab refugees. There is the Israel of the tourist, 100,000 of
whom scamper through its streets and mountains, almost all of
them outfitted in the pastel-colored *temble*, which was borrowed
from the kibbutz and which looks like a sailor's hat pulled down.
And there is Israel, the political integer in the power struggle
between the Soviet Union and the United States.

It is a complex land whose password is *shalom.*

Most importantly there is Israel, the country populated by a
people trying to survive, to make a living and, now and then on

15

the weekends, to have a good time on a Mediterranean beach with the family. Half of them spend their day near the water batting a little black ball over a nonexistent net with outsized ping-pong paddles, and God protect the innocent bather who walks between the volley. Vendors, burdened by white, square boxes slung from their shoulders, trudge through the sand stepping over lounging sweethearts, shouting, "Mish-mish, mish-mish." Mish-mish is an apricot confection. In the Israeli argot, "Count the mish-mish tomorrow" translates as *Hubba hubba*.

This is the Israel with no fewer than 1,000 clinics, 400 hospitals, 500 mother-and-child health centers. For a population of 2,500,-000, there are almost 5,000 doctors, one doctor for every 420 inhabitants, by far the highest ratio in the world. It is the one country in the Middle East free from the ravaging epidemics of its neighbors—malaria, typhus, typhoid, tuberculosis.

It is a country with a small standing army, which over a weekend can swell to almost 1,000,000, still commanded by the same 16 generals, by far the lowest ratio of generals to men in the world. It is probably the only country in the world with two trained pilots for every plane, which explains why, when war comes, its Air Force can fly sorties for twenty-four hours at a stretch.

In this little country on the southern curve of the Mediterranean Sea there are at least a dozen different climates. Jerusalemites can huddle in their overcoats against a chilling December rain while less than a morning's drive away kibbutzniks harvest avocados under a broiling sun. Mount Hermon, which rises 9,000 feet in the north, is snowcapped the year round, while to the south the citizens of Beersheba will hurry from the city after a rare shower to see desert flowers bloom momentarily in the Negev.

This was my fourth trip to Israel. I came first in 1959, when my book *Only in America* earned me enough money to take a two-month vacation. I came again in 1961 to cover the trial of Adolph Eichmann for *Life* magazine. I returned in 1964, when my seat companion on the El Al flight was the poet Robert Frost. I know now that it is not hard to see all of Israel, nor is it hard to meet a representative number of its people.

Before the Six-Day War, Israel measured some 8,000 square

miles, which is about the size of New Jersey, and its population did not exceed that of Massachusetts. From the kibbutzim in the north, under the shadow of the Syrian Golan Heights, to Eilat on the tip of the Negev, the port in the south on the Red Sea, Israel was 270 miles long. It had the geographical shape in those days of a bulging paring knife, the Negev the blade, with a tight belt around the middle of its handle.

After the Six-Day War in 1967, Israel added 26,000 miles of territory to its jurisdiction. It took on the steep Golan Heights and the flat plateau, which stretches almost to Damascus; in the middle of the country, it let out the tight belt by swallowing the West Bank of the Jordan River; and to the south it occupied the Gaza Strip and the Sinai, another desert it needed like a hole in the head, but it needed artillery and infantry escarpments along the Suez Canal. Now Israel resembles the profile of the jawbone of an ass with which Samson flailed the Philistines.

Jerusalem is Israel's soul. It has a population of 260,000—Jews, Arabs, and Christians. The stone windmill, built by Sir Moses Montifiore for the first Zionists in the 1800's, still stands beside the old Walled City of the Ottoman Turks.

Tel Aviv, with a population of over 500,000 Jews, sits on the Mediterranean. It is the heart of Israel. There are more violinists in its ensembles and orchestras than there are in Chicago.

Two hours north of Tel Aviv along the shoreline is Haifa, the country's principal port, a city of 225,000. It is the muscle of Israel. The Israelis say the man who wants to study lives in Jerusalem, the man who wants to play lives in Tel Aviv, and the man who wants to work lives in Haifa.

The Scandinavians and the hippies love Eilat, where it's always nice and warm and the curious stone formations make the sea red at sunset. There are Scandinavians who for years have gotten off jets at Lydda, taxied to the small airport outside Tel Aviv, and two hours later are in their bathing suits sunning themselves. And that is all they know of Israel. And, they insist, all they need to know.

In between my last trip, when I first thought of writing a book about Israel, and my present one, the country had won an incredible military victory. The Six-Day War, I knew, hadn't changed the land, and I wondered how it had changed the people.

Not as much as I suspected.

The first words I heard in Lydda Airport issued from an old friend trying to attract my attention from behind the customs gate. "*Shalom*, Harry," he was shouting as he waved his hands. "*Shalom.*"

Coffee in Bet Sokolow

I WAS having nescafe, as the Israelis call all instant coffee, in the cafeteria of Bet Sokolow in Tel Aviv. This building, adjacent to the Israeli Army and Government Press offices, takes its name from the Polish journalist who was an ardent and early Zionist and whose daughter, Anna Sokolow, was the well-known American choreographer. For foreign newsmen, Bet Sokolow is the nearest thing in the Holy Land to a press club.

Across from me was Joe Lapid, always called Tommy, who is a magazine editor and columnist on *Ma'ariv*, the biggest newspaper in Israel. Tommy, thirty-seven, promised to open doors for me.

The last time I had seen him was several years ago when he had produced a flap of cyclonic proportions in the Israeli Tourist Ministry and among the public relations corps of the Sheraton Hotel chain. The occasion then was the opening of the Tel Aviv Sheraton. The public relations office distributed to the Israeli newsmen, among other gifts, a copy of *Mr. Sheraton*, purportedly the autobiography of one Mr. Henderson, who happens to own the Sheraton Hotel chain. The book is centrally located in each and every Sheraton Hotel room for the edification and amusement of paying guests.

For reasons of his own, Tommy read the book and discovered therein a page filled with what can charitably only be described as anti-Semitic sentiments. Sensing a story, Tommy hastened to reproduce these paragraphs, along with some suitable corrective comments.

"How the devil," he exclaimed, "was I supposed to guess the

story would make every newspaper in the United States and England?"

"How did you get out of that one?" I asked.

"Ben-Gurion came to the rescue. He said anyone who builds a hotel in Tel Aviv is a friend of the Jews. But I notice the books aren't in the rooms anymore." He put his big curly head back and laughed.

Thoughtfully then, Tommy stirred his Turkish coffee, as thick as molasses with sugar and sediment. Coffee, either Turkish or nescafe, is so uniformly bitter in Israel that unless the drinking of it is accompanied by pointed, artful, and intelligent conversation, all the sugar in the world makes no difference. Since Tommy had used only one spoonful, I suspected the story he had just told reminded him of something else.

"I had a letter today," he said, cradling his cup, "from a friend of mine, Arnold Wesker, the English playwright. He wrote me that as a Jew he is increasingly distressed by rumors of the Israelis torturing Arab terrorists in the Nablus prison. I feel in some way I should answer him."

"I understand," I said. Now it was my turn with the coffee.

"My first impulse was to say to him, '*Lech laazazel,* a Biblical phrase directing a man to hell. But that was too easy. I was letting him off. Instead I shall write him that I am doing everything in my power to bring a halt to this execrable practice. What about that for irony?"

"A curious coincidence," I said, wanting to let the coffee cool. "I received a letter this very day, too, from the president of a prestigious Jewish organization. He begged me to be sure to include in my book how the Israelis have turned the Nablus prison camp into a university where they teach the terrorists English and philosophy."

"'*Lech laazazel* won't do for him," said Tommy.

"No, it won't," I said. "His Hebrew isn't that good. I told him the truth. I wrote him that the Israelis do not have enough English and philosophy teachers to take care of the returning soldiers, let alone the terrorists who plant bombs in supermarkets which blow the legs off shopping housewives."

"We are worrying two decent men who are filled with hopeless good will," said Tommy.

"They are both worrying about the same thing," I said. "They are worrying what the Christians will think."

"And that doesn't make any difference anymore," said my friend.

So I am writing this book to unworry these two fellows, the Englishman and the American. Israelis neither think nor behave as much of the world wishes or insists they should. In fact, the Israelis are fond of saying that world opinion is what kept Hitler and Kosygin from occupying Czechoslovakia. Since Israelis are unworried about world or Christian opinion, they indulge in little duplicity in their public statements. They are as direct as Ezer Weizman, formerly the Air Force Chief of Staff and now a member of the Cabinet, was direct when he remarked: "The Jewish state was formed to solve the Jewish problem, not the Arab problem."

This may well not be the wisest response, but it is a typical response. Israelis feel they offer the world the first chance to see if a people can overcome a long and pitiless history.

Perhaps that is why American and English Jews indulge their representative misconceptions. American and English Jews are, after all, Yanks and Britons, descended from a people who chose their own history, elected it, did not have it thrust upon them by God and Hitler. It may be these Jews experience an atavistic envy at not participating in the effort to see whether or not a people can have a history.

Eric Hoffer, the longshoreman turned philosopher, wrote that if Israel did not succeed then history can have no meaning. I think that is the way to understand Israel and its Jews—as a land and a people devoted to history. Everything they do and touch and see, whether they are laughing or crying, is colored by a historical sense of themselves and their mission.

It is no coincidence that archeology is the national hobby in Israel. Abba Eban, Israel's Foreign Minister, once pointed out that there is no other place in the world where a child can dig up in the garden a stone 3,000 years old and read and understand every word on it.

Part **I**

Meanwhile, Back at the Kibbutz

Farmers, not peasants

ONE OF the beguiling characteristics of the Israelis is
that, whether they like or dislike you, they will still tell you what
to do and exactly how to do it. They are, they admit, a pragmatic
people. They cannot help themselves.

In my devoted pursuit of the new and the novel, I wanted
to tour some of the kibbutzim once more. An Israeli turned to
me in indignation and said, "For goodness sake, at this late date
do not discover the kibbutz. Do not waste a reader's time telling
him a sabra is a fruit prickly on the outside and sweet on the
inside."

But I must.

The sabra, a fruit which grows on a cactus all over Israel, is
the name also given to native-born Israelis. As a fruit, the sabra
is more trouble than it is worth. You cannot buy it in fruit stores
nor are you served it in restaurants. Along the roads now and
then you see little kids with a tin pail at the end of a long pole
trying to dislodge the sabra from the cactus. But as a symbol,
the sabra is something else again. There is a sabra generation, a
sabra vote, and a sabra milieu. It is something in Israel to be
a sabra.

A kibbutz is a communal farm, of which there are 224 in Israel.
It is the invention of the Russian and Polish Jews who came to
Israel in the second aliyah. Aliyah, which means "ascent" in
Hebrew, refers to the successive waves of Jewish immigration
into Israel. There have been seven aliyah in all, two of which

have been crucial, the second and the fifth. The Germans came in the fifth aliyah in the 1930's—the architects with the Bauhaus behind them, the doctors already specialists, the professors with PhD's. The fifth aliyah came with the skills and sciences without which there is no such thing as a modern industrial state; but the second aliyah came with the idea that the land belongs to him who will work it, without which there could be no Israel.

In fact, when the United Nations decided upon partition in 1947, it accepted the recommendations of the Sykes-Picot Commission, which urged that the borders of Israel be determined by the extremities of the kibbutzim.

The kibbutzniks developed the land to a point where in the 1970's there is no more left. They gave Israel its aristocracy. The kibbutz remains one of the unique social phenomena of the twentieth-century world.

A kibbutz is a social unit in which the members distribute among themselves all of the labors needed to sustain life but do not apportion shares in the profits their labor earns. The profits belong to the kibbutz. The kibbutzniks direct how these profits may be reinvested or spent, but they claim no equity in them. A kibbutznik, in short, does not own property. He does not own the land he works, the home in which he lives, or the convenient small refrigerator which helps him entertain his guests; sometimes he does not own his clothes.

At Ein Hashofet I inspected a huge wardrobe filled with expensive suits and natty sports jackets and pretty dresses and party gowns. These clothes are at the disposal of a kibbutznik who needs a dark suit for a funeral or a chic gown for a wedding. From this wardrobe the couple choose clothes they want for a European vacation. These clothes are new and stylish and, when a kibbutznik returns from the funeral or the wedding or the trip abroad, the clothes go back into the communal wardrobe.

What kibbutzniks do have is the guarantee that the kibbutz will provide food, housing, education, medical care, clothes, leisure, and work—dignity—for as long as they live on it. And the kibbutz will provide all these when they are too old or unable to work and will provide the same for their children if their children choose to live there.

There are only two kinds of people in the world who walk

around without money—millionaires and kibbutzniks. And millionaires are notorious for borrowing small change.

Nor is the kibbutz exclusive. Almost all kibbutzim will consider the applications of new members, whether these applications come from returning grandchildren of founding members or new immigrants. Sde Boker admitted David and Paula Ben-Gurion as members when both were in their seventies.

Those immigrants of the second aliyah who started the kibbutz movement in the Jordan Valley around the Sea of Galilee did not realize they were founding a communal institution which would have a profound influence on the Jewish state. These early settlers were sure that once the land was settled, they would all own their farms or plantations one day. Necessity compelled them to form the kibbutz where all the labor and property were shared.

First of all, there was no work in Palestine for these immigrants of the second aliyah. The Jews of the first aliyah in the 1870's had started the citrus plantations and the distilleries with money advanced by Baron Rothschild, but they hired Arab and Bedouin laborers who worked longer for lower wages. One of the catchy folk songs still popular in the schools is "Who Will Give Us Work?" To survive, the new immigrants had to work together.

The land is intractable. No one could work it alone. The American pioneer worked his land alone because he had water. If he could not sink wells, still he had accessible rivers, streams, and brooks; if he lacked these, he had rain. There is not even dew around the Sea of Galilee. Irrigating took many hands.

The Jews could not do it alone because their neighbors, Arabs and Bedouins, were hostile. The kibbutzniks had to band together to protect themselves from marauders who murdered them for their livestock and sometimes for their shoes.

The first kibbutzniks knew they had to till the land together, because none of them knew anything about tilling at all. They had to depend on each other for newly acquired skills, for experience.

And in the beginning, they did not want to do it alone. They were Zionists who believed the Jews had to return to the soil to reclaim the homeland; they were Socialists who believed in setting upright the pyramid of Jewish society turned wrongside down centuries ago. They wanted a pyramid with a base of farmers and laborers instead of intellectuals.

They were missionaries. They believed a farmer need not be a peasant, and indeed in Israel a kibbutznik is not. They believed one man should not exploit another, therefore they would not depend on hired labor (an idea they have noticeably violated in recent years because industrialization made it an economic necessity). They believed the kibbutz was a family, that there was no qualitative difference in the labor each member of the family contributed.

Because of these ideals, these Jews of the second aliyah introduced the singular difference between the kibbutz and communal and cooperative villages throughout the world and down through history. That difference is that the children are reared communally in separate dormitories. Children are the responsibility of the whole kibbutz, not solely of the parents. Admittedly, the idea is an old one, at least as old as recorded philosophy, for Plato outlined the same program in the *Republic*. But the kibbutz put it into action. Not only did the mothers not want to leave their work in the fields, often they could not be spared. A few members of the kibbutz, therefore, took charge of all the children. Children are not divorced from their parents, but they are separated from their mother after six, seven, or eight weeks of infancy. Their home is a dormitory filled with children their own age, with whom they live during their childhood and school years. Parents see their children for four hours every day and enjoy them on the Sabbath. Parents always tuck in their infants and toddlers at night, but the worry over the children's health and schooling and future is the worry of the whole kibbutz, if indeed it is a worry. Some kibbutzniks are the nursemaids and some are the teachers, just as others are truck drivers or reapers.

I have met Americans who believe the separation of children from parents is universal throughout Israel, which it is not. It is not even universal on the kibbutzim, but it is a way of life, say, on 210 of the 224.

It is a system which has occasioned a great deal of study. One of the recent critical commentaries came from Dr. Bruno Bettelheim. In *Children of the Dream*, Dr. Bettelheim says that in the kibbutz he foresaw a way of salvaging the children of the slums and backward countries, but he felt also that the kibbutz experience generated a shallowness in children, turning them away from art and cultural refinements. *Children of the Dream* led one kibbutznik to ask me, "How many concert pianists a year are you turning out in New York City?"

Kibbutzniks are the first to admit their way of life is not a way of life for everyone. Few kibbutzim have been started by immigrants who came to Israel after World War II, though many joined existing ones. Most of the kibbutzim grow organically from the children raised on them, if they grow at all. Among the relatively few enthusiasts I met for the kibbutz life were young American immigrants.

Still, the kibbutzniks are proud, sure their way will endure. They are especially proud of three statistics. They number roughly 100,000, just 4 percent of the total Israeli population, yet they produce half the food Israel consumes. Out of this same 4 percent came 25 percent of the casualties in the Six-Day War, a stunning statistic. The kibbutzim produces a disproportionately large number of officers. Like their British and American counterparts, Israeli line officers never say "Forward" but "Follow me." And last, the kibbutz is second only to the United States in farm technology.

If it is not a way of life for everyone, still it has compensations few people elsewhere ever realize. "What amazed my children most on their first visit to town," said a kibbutznik "was not the Shalom Meyer Tower, Israel's skyscraper. What amazed them most was the sight of a beggar. The skyscraper they could understand. The beggar they could not."

I thought Israel was a rich uncle

AT DEGANIA I met Yosl Gartner, who came to this kibbutz from Poland in the early 1930's.

"We were well-to-do," he told me, "and the family were all Zionists. I had heard a lot about Israel. I pictured the country as a rich uncle. I landed at Jaffa and came straight to the Jordan on a day that the heat broke all records. I didn't know we were

700 feet below sea level, that it is always hot here. Two women had to help me from the road to my bunk, because the men were too busy with their work. Israel might be a rich uncle, but you cannot convince him easily about your inheritance."

Ain Zivan

RED TRIANGLES on a yellow background (the international symbol for mine fields) line the road that twists to the crest of the Golan Heights. These precipitous slopes are still dangerous years after the end of the Six-Day War. In the summer, when the thistles turn to tinder, soldiers set fire to the hills to make some of the mines explode.

The Golan Heights are a steep mountainous range which stretches along the Jordan frontier, rings the east shore of the Sea of Galilee, and curves toward Lebanon. Once they formed the natural borders between Israel and Syria. From the lip of these Heights, the Syrians often fired mortars onto the homes and the fields of the kibbutzim below. Kibbutz Gadot is still ringed by rusting barbed wire from those days. Near this kibbutz is a memorial built of eight concrete pillars on which are inscribed the names of kibbutzniks who lost their lives at work.

In 1967, the Israelis took not only the Heights, but the broad plateau which pancakes for several miles into Syria. Looking from the desolate Golan at the cultivated fields of the kibbutz below, I felt like an astronaut looking from the moon at some green patch on earth. Stiff winds often beat across this flat, lonely land. In many places the plateau is treeless. Living on the plateau could make a man brood. It is conceivable that Israel could grow here all the wheat she now must import.

An Israeli road sign, a green and white steel flag, points the way to kibbutz Ain Zivan, named after the grains it grows, the second oldest of twelve new kibbutzim established on the Golan Heights since the cease-fire of June, 1967.

Two powerful floodlights mounted on poles and an armored sentry cage mark the kibbutz's entryway. In the middle of the compound is the air raid shelter, carved out of solid rock, the concrete not yet poured. Surrounding this pit stand several new concrete bungalows and a congeries of old Arab sheds.

Sholem and Avram, two of the kibbutzniks, showed me around. Kibbutzniks have little use for last names and Sholem and Avram were no exceptions. Last names are extraneous, they say, if nicknames will do. If there are two Moshes on a kibbutz, the older might be called Moshe Aleph and the younger Moshe Bet; if there is a third Moshe, fair-skinned and light, he becomes Moshe Hablondi (Blond Moshe); if there is a fourth who is left-handed, he is Moshe Smoli. The children of the kibbutz, like children everywhere, identify parents by the names of their playmates. Yitzhak is *Abba shel Miryam* (father of Miryam); Shmuel and Rachel, a childless couple, are *Abba Veima Shel af echad* (father and mother of no one).

Sholem was dark-haired, green-eyed, and wore a beautifully trimmed beard. He was raised on a kibbutz near the Sea of Galilee and, like most native-born kibbutzniks, he was reserved, almost remote, thoughtful and, when he chose to answer, always direct. Avram, the son of a Haifa factory owner, was freckled, red-headed, barefoot, and wore a beard that looked like fireworks going off. Avram said he was just a gardener, while Sholem was the expert, a member of the kibbutz secretariat who spent his day meeting big shots.

At the government's urging, Sholem and Avram were two of five young men who scouted the Heights for suitable land. Once they staked out their 6,000 *dunam* (about 1,880 acres) they recruited sixty other kibbutzniks—all under twenty-five—through the Army Nahal movement and Israeli youth organizations.

Kibbutz Ain Zivan borrowed one million Israeli pounds from the Jewish Agency at three percent interest for twenty years with which the kibbutz bought its heavy farm equipment and built the communal dining hall.

At first, the kibbutzniks lived in the deserted Arab dwellings, small square blocks, with only a doorway to admit light, the floor hard-packed dirt.

"Do you know what these homes are made of?" Avram asked, peeling away at one of the walls. "They're made out of shit."

Indeed, he was right. They were cloacal homes, the interior plaster made of dung and excrement, covered over by sheets and sheets of paint. Half of the kibbutzniks still lived in these and living in them cannot be comfortable. They are small, dark, impossible to heat, without any conveniences, although they are sturdy enough.

Hardship wasn't a surprise, Sholem said. They knew they would have to sink wells and it took a year before the kibbutz had running water. They knew the land had never been tilled and that life would be frugal.

The climate! Over the first winter, they had a five-foot snowfall. None of these Israelis had ever seen snow before. Fortunately, the sun dissipated it quickly. And the fields were agony. They were filled with boulders. Clearing the fields, a task still unfinished, usurped more time than Sholem had imagined. To speed up the work, two of the kibbutzniks invented a machine by attaching the teeth of a clamshell shovel via hydraulic pumps to a huge steel cart.

"What is that?" I asked. "A stone scrounger?"

"We didn't have a name for it until you came," said Avram.

"Americans are so technical," said Sholem, marveling.

"We had to make it," said Avram, "because a bulldozer costs a lot of money plus eleven percent interest."

"It will take us six or seven years to become self-sustaining," added Sholem. "The weather is bad. We need houses more than machines."

The first houses Ain Zivan built were of cinder blocks. The Army advised the kibbutz to make future homes of reinforced concrete to withstand Syrian shelling. Eight of these houses are completed.

Avram offered to show off his room. But he was single, he explained. His room was a mess. Sholem lived with a girl. His room was neater.

"My room is worse than yours," said Sholem.

I saw both.

There were two beds in Avram's room, at the foot of each was an Uzi, the small automatic rifle Israeli soldiers carry. Avram was right: his room was a mess. Sholem's room was bigger, his bed neatly made, and on a small, round end table was a homemade cake. There were bric-a-brac on the shelves. Sholem flicked one with his fingers and said, "You know how women are."

Avram kept referring to the women on the kibbutz as the "younger generation." He pronounced it "yonker." When I met the "yonker" generation, I discovered all of them were eighteen. The winters are long and dark, I thought, but they can't be too lonely.

Because of the winters, however, Ain Zivan harvests only one crop of barley, wheat, and potatoes. In partnership with another nearby kibbutz, Ain Zivan has invested in a plastic machine which manufactures sandals. All of the kibbutzniks not barefoot wore them. The black plastic, imported from Italy, is fed into a blue and white machine resembling a huge butter churn which dispenses sandals; then the kibbutzniks pack them by sizes. A television set entertained the workers—the reception in the factory was better than in the dining hall.

Produce from the kibbutz is handled through Tnuva, the central marketing board of all the kibbutzim which establishes prices. Ain Zivan must go to the competitive marketplace, however, to sell its industry.

There are eight married couples on Ain Zivan and three children, all still nursing. "There's going to be a fourth," said Avram, "but they're not telling anybody."

When I asked if the rabbi ever came up this way, Sholem said, "If you like religion, this is not the place for you."

Kibbutzniks generally are irreverent. The first kibbutzim were in part established to enable Russian Jews to divorce themselves from the old-time religion. Sholem told me there were three new kibbutzim on the Heights which kept the Sabbath. "That's their business," he said.

As I was leaving Ain Zivan, I met a young American girl named Emily Steinberger, from Great Neck, New York, who had joined the kibbutz eight months ago.

Emily worked in the kitchen and she was attired in sweater, apron, slacks, and plastic sandals.

"My obvious question, Emily," I asked, "is why have you chosen to live here on a kibbutz on the Golan Heights?"

Emily thought a minute and said, "Now that you ask, tell me who in America would lend someone under thirty, three hundred thousand dollars for anything?"

Ghost town

FIVE MILES into the Administered Territory of the Golan Heights is the town of Quneitra, once populated by 50,000 Syrians. It is a ghost town. Canvas pulled taut over the windows, now torn, flaps vainly. Weeds grow in the streets. The wind echoes through the deserted alleys. Fifty thousand people ran away from this town.

The Israelis did not have to fight for Quneitra. The Syrians gave it to them. When the Syrian High Command realized the Israelis might indeed win the fight for the Heights, they grew desperate for a cease-fire to save what they had. To lend urgency to this appeal to the pro-Arab bloc in the United Nations, for which read Russia, the Syrians announced Quneitra had fallen. The Russians believed it. So did the Syrians in Quneitra.

Druse village

A FEW miles past Quneitra is a Druse village. The Druses stayed on, though the Syrians fled. The Druses are a splinter sect of Mohammedanism. They have always refused to explain to outsiders either the details of their worship or their theology. Three or four times in their history, the Druses have been slaughtered by the Syrians.

That is one of the reasons, I suppose, these villagers on the Golan remained.

Another reason is that the Druses in Israel are completely integrated. They not only pay taxes but serve in the Army as both noncommissioned and commissioned officers. Many Israeli Druses are in the border police because they are experts at detecting infiltrators. Compare them, if you will, to the Ghurkas who fought in the British armies. The Syrian Druses thought they had nothing to lose.

In the village was a Druse school and the teachers offered me tea. In Arabic, they begged me to wait until the principal, who spoke English, arrived.

He was a tall, lean, athletic man with high cheekbones and, like all Druses, a polite manner. But he had been giving his colleagues a story about his linguistic ability. His English consisted of "yes," "no," and "thank you."

"We stayed," said the principal through our interpreter, "because we always worked this land, we live on this land, we own this land. We still work it, we still live on it, we still own it. We are either teachers or farmers in this village."

What about the students? When they leave this school, where will they go to become doctors or teachers?

The principal said quickly it was not a problem this year. Next year it would be. From this village, students had gone on to the schools and the university in Damascus. Now Syrians do not allow commerce back and forth across the border. The principal said he guessed Druse students would have to go to Haifa. In the meantime, they would continue to farm and teach, six thousand of them, along with several hundred kibbutzniks, in sole command of the Golan Heights.

This problem, if it was a problem, was solved for the Druses by the end of the week when the then Israeli Attorney General, Meir Shamgar, announced that Israeli civil law would prevail along the Golan Heights from 1969 on. An Israeli magistrate's court held its first sessions in deserted Quneitra in October, 1969. At the time of the announcement, Shamgar said the extension of civil law did not in any way imply that Israel would annex the Heights, but if b-u-r-d don't spell "bird," what the hell does it spell?

The kibbutz bartender

A DECADE or so ago the kibbutzniks discovered the tourists. About the same time the tourists discovered the kibbutz. As a consequence there are twenty or so kibbutzim which maintain tourist guest cottages, which is a euphemism to describe an incipiently growing chain of Howard Johnson motels in the Middle East. From the display cases in the lobby, the tourist can buy Chanel No. 5 or No. 22, along with lacquered olive-wood camels and T-shirts which spell out Kibbutz Ayelet Hasha-har. At these cabins, the tourist can also enjoy the usual pot roast dinner (which, for historical reasons beyond all explanation, the Israelis call roast beef), sleep in an air-conditioned room, and imagine he is roughing it like the kibbutzniks out back, in their concrete bungalows, munching raw vegetables for dinner washed down with citrus juice.

A visit to one of these kibbutzim introduces the tourist to a problem the Israelis have not only failed to solve but failed even to consider. That problem is the kibbutz bartender.

The kibbutz bartender is obviously a malcontent who becomes surly if a tourist wants a drink before 6 P.M. Ordering a second drink transforms him into a glint-eyed Dr. Caligari considering whether to clamp the drunk into the cabinet. He is incapable of comprehending that there are people who want three drinks. Nor can he believe that here in the Middle East people would ask for ice (but in this he is no different from El Al steward-esses). The kibbutz bartender can conserve the gin of a martini with the discipline of a Captain Bligh conserving the water in the longboat.

Unfortunately for the tourist, cosmopolitan world traveler, and wet, the kibbutz bartender is typical of all Israelis.

"We would give up drinking tomorrow," they insist, "if other nations would quit. We do it only to keep company with the Gentiles."

I have traversed every street in Tel Aviv trying to track down one bottle of bourbon, which the Israelis, for all the languages they boast of speaking, have never heard of. There is not a liquor store in Tel Aviv. That's the handwriting on the wall for the thirsty visitor. Liquor can be purchased from the topmost shelves of grocery stores.

On my first visit in 1959, I gave a friend on a kibbutz a bottle of Carmel brandy, good stuff. He still had half of that bottle in 1969.

"What are you doing with it," I asked, "saving it for the Smithsonian?"

The sad truth is that the Israelis do not drink. They refuse to understand that other people do. Tommy Lapid, who feels no shame in ordering a second steak after he has polished off the first plus a plate of humus and techina, a square of mousaca, and a bowl of soup, still puritanically condemns a Scandinavian editor he met who was blotto at four in the afternoon.

"Really, Tommy, blotto?"

"At four in the afternoon."

"That early, eh?"

"Blotto, Harry, absolutely blotto. I give you my word."

The drinking habits of the Israelis, which are as nonexistent as their drinking manners, is a subject to which I must return again and again and again. In short, to poeticize: "I have seen much here to love, little to forgive, but in a world where drinking is dead or gone, I have no wish to live."

The lottery winner

LET'S SAY this young man's name is Asher, which it is not, but he does live on Mishmar Ha'emek, a kibbutz in the Jezreel Valley. Asher was nineteen years old when the kibbutz provided him with six pounds for bus fare back and forth to a doctor in Haifa. At the foot of the hill, he hitched a ride on a passing truck.

What to do with three pounds? Asher bought a lottery ticket. Why not? After all, the government sponsors the lottery and uses the profits to build schools and hospitals. Then you can never tell.

It won. The ticket entitled its owner to 100,000 pounds. Israelis think of pounds as we think of dollars; 100,000 pounds is a lot of money. It was also the first time a kibbutznik had ever won the first prize.

What should he do with the money? All Israel inundated Mishmar Ha'emek with advice. People win in the lottery every week and no one ever before dared or bothered to advise them. But a kibbutznik was different.

Since Asher was a kibbutznik, he didn't need the money, he ought to give it back, said some. He ought to take the money and live in Tel Aviv, he won it fair and square, said others. He ought to give it away to people needier than himself was a third school of thought.

Tommy Lapid interviewed Asher on the radio. "What will you do with the money?" asked Tommy.

"I haven't received it yet," answered Asher. Typical.

In the end, Asher gave the money to his kibbutz, which set aside 30,000 pounds for the veteran's convalescent hospital and used the remaining 70,000 pounds to finance European vacations for members, half of the vacationing couples old-timers, half young folks.

Among the letters Asher received was one from a young girl on a neighboring kibbutz. She wrote that in her opinion he and only he ought to decide what to do with the money.

It was the only sage advice he received, and Asher wrote to thank her. And soon they were married. It was the best three pounds he ever spent, said Asher, better than giving it to a bus driver.

Hagshama

KIBBUTZNIKS ARE NOT at all reticent about describing the quality of their life. They tell me that while day-to-day existence is not cushy, it is always meaningful. The Hebrew word which best describes the motivation of those who choose life on a kibbutz is *hagshama,* which translates as "dedication" or, more metaphorically, as "putting ideals into action."

Hagshama does not mean that kibbutzniks cannot make trouble for themselves. Take the case of Mrs. Ada Feinberg-Sereni, the school principal of Kibbutz Yir-on. With the approach of the national elections in October, 1969, a political party nominated Mrs. Sereni as one of its candidates for the Knesset. At first reluctant, Mrs. Sereni accepted the endorsement. All she needed was the kibbutz's permission to serve if elected—which up to now kibbutzniks unfailingly granted. Yigal Allon, the Deputy Prime Minister, comes from a kibbutz, so did the late Levi Eshkol, and so do many other important government officials. As a matter of fact, there are several government officials who have not seen their kibbutz in years; they reserve their visits for the chance to escort a foreign dignitary over the grounds and say proudly, "This is my kibbutz," as though they spent every night of their life on that cot instead of in a comfortable Jerusalem apartment. The kibbutzniks, however, figure it's still good publicity.

On the occasion of Mrs. Sereni's nomination, however, Kibbutz Yir'on said no. The kibbutzniks argued that a school principal was more important than a member of the Knesset. The kibbutzniks are on record as declaring that politicians are a dime a dozen while school principals are expensive. *Hagshama* for Mrs. Sereni meant declining the nomination.

Party bosses made their way up to the kibbutz on the Lebanese border with impassioned rhetoric for the Appeals Committee of Yir'on, who still said no. There was strong sentiment against mobilizing Mrs. Sereni for politics.

There's an obverse and reverse to all coins. There was equally strong sentiment insisting it was unfair to deprive Israeli women and Israeli kibbutzniks of the chance to serve. Which proves that life, even on a kibbutz, is one damned thing after another.

When I asked Tommy Lapid how he thought this impasse would be resolved, he thought a long while before his face lit up like a menorah. He said, "Leave it to Golda."

Mrs. Sereni, by the way, won election. Happy landings, Mrs. M.K. (Member of Knesset).

Christmas balls from Israel

KIBBUTZ GAN-SHMUEL exports shiploads of Christmas decorations to Europe every year.

The decorations are Nazareth and Bethlehem fruits.

Nazareth fruit looks like a collection of small tomatoes which grow on a vine often reaching fifteen feet in length. The vines are cut and dried, after which the leaves fall off, and then the fruit turns a brilliant red and orange. In Switzerland a stalk costs one dollar.

Bethlehem fruit looks like one of Al Capp's shmoos. It has a roly-poly shape with what looks like four stubby toes. After drying, it turns yellow. It is also called Fox-face, and Pig-face. It, too, grows on a stalk which reaches five and sometimes six feet in height.

The Bethlehem and Nazareth fruits are indigenous to South America. Both plants blossom in the autumn and are preserved in water for a full year.

That's what you call your Jewish know-how.

Gesher

GESHER IS on the Jordan River above the Sea of Galilee.

In the War of Independence in 1948, Gesher's defenders withstood the Arab attackers, although the battle decimated the kibbutz.

After the cease-fire, Gesher moved its living quarters a half mile to the west because they were so close to the Jordanian border.

"For nineteen years," said Arie Eitan, a member of the Gesher secretariat, "this kibbutz was a sea of tranquility. We had 200 working members. We grew fruits, vegetables, made artificial palms, and started a gypsum factory. Several times we won first prize in the competition for the most beautiful landscape gardening. Visitors always commented on how clever we were to have located our kibbutz in such a lovely park. An old joke. No more."

The landscaping of Gesher is now honeycombed with trenches six and eight feet deep which lead to the newly constructed air raid shelters. The children no longer sleep in their dormitories but below ground. In the infant's shelter, double-decker cribs line the concave cement walls. The entryway to the shelter, one side of which is camouflaged by dirt, is gaily decorated on the other with paintings of clowns, elephants, balloons, and hobby horses.

Terrorists nightly shell the kibbutz from the nearby mountains. Often the terrorists cross the river and plant mines in the fields. All of Gesher is within rifle range and snipers open up unexpectedly.

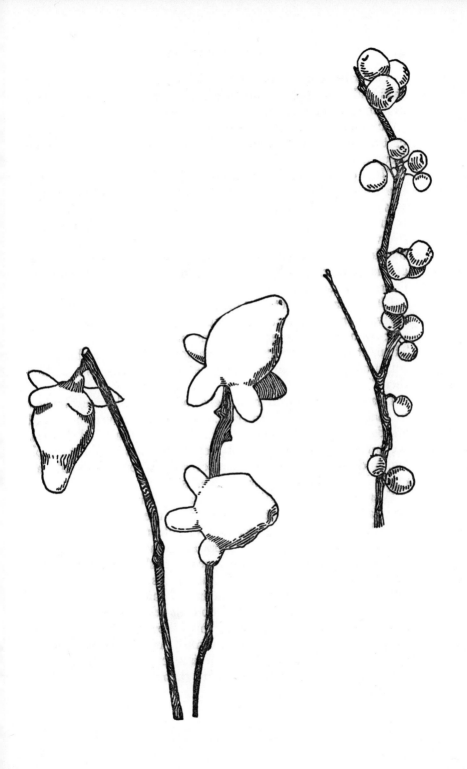

The kibbutzniks plow these fields in tractors armored by steel and protected by bulletproof glass. Army units walk guard as men spread out the irrigation pipes every morning.

Six tractors have hit mines and been destroyed, two members of the kibbutz have been killed, and several more have been wounded.

"It is catastrophic," Arie Eitan said. "Not the terror, not the fear of death, we can live with that. Everyone sooner or later gets used to that. We pretend nothing is happening. But this is the catastrophe—every man and woman in this kibbutz loses two working hours every morning. The Army will not let us into the fields until they have cleared the mines and that is 8 A.M. at the earliest. That's 400 hours a day, almost 3,000 working hours a week—lost."

Eitan, a tall, bespectacled man, talked under an obvious strain. He went on, "The heat in this valley makes it impossible to work past noon. The fields are an inferno until the sun begins to set. Then, at three in the afternoon, we lose time disassembling our irrigation pipes, because otherwise the terrorists will destroy them."

Eitan is the man who must make ends meet, who must budget so that profits exceed expenses. Though the government will one day reimburse Gesher for the building of its air raid shelters, the immediate expense for beds, generators, fans is almost crippling. And sometimes the shelling keeps the kibbutzniks awake all night; in the morning they are exhausted.

Were it not for the Histadrut, Eitan explained, Gesher would have failed in its harvest. The Histadrut, the union to which all the kibbutzniks belong, recruited volunteers in the cities who gave up a week's vacation to work at Gesher. These volunteers built the trenches and constructed the shelters so that the kibbutzniks could keep up with their fields.

"What makes us despair sometimes," said Eitan, "is that in 1948 we fought against much more hopeless odds. We know how to fight. A lot of men on this kibbutz, myself included, spent five and a half years in the British Army. The government won't send the Army after the terrorists across the river and they won't let us go ourselves to secure them because Jordan is a pro-Western ally."

It is this political situation which makes Gesher's problem a static one. The Israeli government encourages as many young people as it can to start kibbutzim on the Golan Heights, which once belonged to Syria, and spends just as much time chasing would-be kibbutzniks from settling on the west bank of the Jordan River, which once belonged to Jordan.

While there is a certain unanimity among nations that Israel has a right to exist, there is no unanimity that Israel has a right to win wars.

Nor is Gesher alone. There are many kibbutzim who operate under enemy guns. Across the Sea of Galilee, a half hour's drive from Gesher, is Tel Katzir, a kibbutz of 60 members who grow bananas, grapefruit, artichokes, and manage a small dairy on their 2,500 *dunam*. For 19 years, the Syrians shelled Tel Katzir from the Golan Heights. The Heights secured to the north, the Jordanians started shelling from the south. Tel Katzir is geographically more fortunate than Gesher because half its fields are out of rifle range. Tel Katzir works these fields in the morning and the more dangerous fields in the afternoon, when the Army has cleared them.

Of the two enemies, Tel Katzir preferred the Syrians because the Syrians never shelled at night.

Help

THERE ARE eleven Orthodox kibbutzim which observe all of the dietary laws and obey every one of the religious prescriptions. One of these is Sa'ad in the south, two miles from the Gaza Strip.

In 1947, when a group of Orthodox Jews from South America, the United States, and Israel wanted to establish their own kibbutz, the Minister of Agriculture sent them here to help the other kibbutzim defend the road from Gaza, which one way stretched along the shore to Tel Aviv and another way across the desert to Beersheba. Thus the name: *Sa'ad* means "help."

Yad Mordechai, the kibbutz just across the border from Gaza, fell in 1948 after six fierce days of fighting; Sa'ad and a neighbor held the road, however, and the Egyptians never broke out. It was from Sa'ad that the tanks moved into the Sinai in 1956.

"And in the Six-Day War," I asked my host, Naftali Armon, "what did you do?"

"I was in the paratroops," answered Naftali. "We were supposed to bottle up the Egyptians at the Mitla Pass. But the tankers took it, so they sent my regiment to Jerusalem. We got to Jerusalem the day the Jordanians surrendered, so they sent us to the Golan Heights. We got there just in time to hear Richard Tucker sing."

Naftali Armon is a burly man, with a russet beard and a face reddened by the sun. He is a New York City boy who was graduated from City College and, as an ardent Zionist, immigrated to Israel seventeen years ago when he was twenty-two, expecting to teach school. To learn the language, he worked for a while on Sa'ad, met a girl, married her, and today oversees the orchards of plum, peach, and pear trees. Two days before my arrival, Mrs. Armon had given birth to a baby girl, who was expected home by the weekend.

"I have to think of a name," worried Naftali. The Israelis dig into the deepest recesses of the Old Testament to find a suitable ancient name with modern nuances.

As we walked across the compound, Naftali claimed his five-year-old son, Eliahu, from the nursery group, and we sat in the kibbutz playground while he told me about Sa'ad.

A kibbutz playground is an exercise in ingenuity. Two of the mechanics at Sa'ad had constructed a spaceship, outlined by old piping through the center of which was a slide. A dozen worn tires, set halfway into the ground, formed a tunnel maze. There were the stripped remains of two tractors with refurbished seats on which preschoolers climbed. Supports for the swings and the chinning bar were made from discarded irrigation pipes.

"That's the way we test our tanks," said Naftali, pointing to the shouting children. "We park the brand-new ones in a kibbutz playground and let the children play on them. If they still start at night, we certify that they are combat ready for the Sinai."

The Jews of the second aliyah believed that the traditional values of middle-European Jewry had helped to build ghetto walls as much as did the anti-Semitism of Gentiles. No place could they turn their back more obdurately on these values than on a kibbutz. Yet thirty years later, there were Jews who thought only on a kibbutz could they realize the laws of their forefathers.

One of the principles which animate the kibbutzniks at Sa'ad is the hope that their obedience to Orthodox laws and regulations will help breach the difference between observant and nonobservant Jews in Israel.

Keeping this law imposes a great many inconveniences. The kitchen of the communal dining hall must be twice as big as others because it is divided: one half for the preparation of meat and the other half for the preparation of dairy meals and dishes. The kibbutzniks must stock two sets of cutlery and two sets of china. They must stock a third set used only for Passover.

The Sabbath is scrupulously observed from the appearance of the first star on Friday night to sunset on Saturday. It is a day of complete rest. But the roses in the greenhouse need attention seven days a week. Those near bloom must be picked. Because of keeping the Sabbath, the gardeners at Sa'ad anticipated a 15 percent loss every year from plants which bloomed unpicked. But a scientist at the Hebrew University School of Agriculture developed a fertilizer which gave plucked roses an extra day of growth. As a consequence, Sa'ad loses only 8 percent of its flowers.

Naftali Armon was hard pressed how to start a new pear orchard, for the Talmud prohibits grafting the wood of one tree onto another. Again, the scientists at the School of Agriculture developed a pear stock which grew without grafting.

Cows must be milked daily. On the Sabbath an automatic machine milks the herd at Sa'ad. If the machine breaks down the Talmud provides that a Jew must show pity for dumb animals. Therefore, the cows can be milked by hand.

I found a great deal of skepticism among the other kibbutzim. They took a jaundiced view of how rigorously Sa'ad obeyed all the laws. One kibbutznik charged, "The Talmud says you must have pity on dumb animals. That is true. The Talmud also says you must pour out the milk you get on the Sabbath. I wonder how many times an observant Jew at Sa'ad has milked the cows and let the milk stand until another observant Jew comes along and picks up the pails?"

Other kibbutzniks tease Sa'ad about its synagogue—a beautiful building with stained glass windows and blue and gold mosaics on the walls. They tease Sa'ad because the kibbutz has yet to find a rabbi who wants to be a kibbutznik. Yet the neighboring kibbutzim all use the synagogue for Bar Mitzvahs and weddings.

Years ago the circuit rabbi used to tour the kibbutzim and ask, "Who got married in the last three months?" and then sign all the marriage licenses. Today, the boys and girls wait for the ceremony performed by the circuit rabbi.

And many of the neighboring kibbutzim, observing Sa'ad's example, have come to the conclusion that six days of work a week are still enough to gather the harvest.

I could not help noticing how neat Sa'ad looked. As I listened to its history and aspirations on the playground bench, lawn mowers glided across the grass. Shrubbery disguised the sharp outlines of the concrete buildings. All the walks were paved. The switchboard was automated.

I told Naftali Armon I was sure he would select the perfect name for his daughter and I hoped the kibbutz would find an amiable if weak-willed, strong-backed rabbi.

Cornflower

THE MAN who most compelled me had been dead for over a decade. He was Joseph Baratz who came to Palestine at the time I came to the United States. Before I worked on Wall Street, Baratz had helped found the first kibbutz. What we have in common, however, is that both of us wrote our first book when we were in our late fifties. Mine was *Only in America*; Baratz's was *A Village by the Jordan*. It is the history of that first kibbutz, Degania.

Jews have been wanderers for two thousand years. But in the twentieth century, America and Palestine made Jews into something more than wanderers; it made them into immigrants, a political entity. Because they were immigrants, they became, after the respective fashion of America and Palestine, pioneers.

From Jaffa, Baratz went to Rishon le Zion. He writes that as he approached this Jewish village, he expected it to look like the villages he knew in Russia: hens pecking in the road, children shouting by the river, peasants in the fields. Instead he found a row of neat brick houses and heard the tinkling of a piano. People strolled up and down the street in finery. He learned straightaway that the Jews had become the managers of the plantations and the Arabs did the work. Young immigrants got jobs only when these rich farmers felt sorry for them.

The Zionist Organization asked Baratz to go to Jerusalem. A new city was springing up outside the walls. Christians were building monasteries and charitable institutions and Jews were building hospitals and schools. All these buildings were constructed from Jerusalem stone, which up to now only skilled masons from Italy had cut. If some Jews could learn stonecutting, perhaps other young immigrants would find in it a trade.

Baratz squatted in the white hot dust all day, chipping away at the stones, until at night his hands were so torn from the pick he couldn't hold a piece of bread.

The Zionists paid him a small subsidy which hardly covered the expense of his food. He and two other young *halutzim* (the Hebrew word for pioneers) lived in a grove of olive trees. At night, Baratz often crawled from his tent to sit under the trees and cry, afraid he could not hold out against the work and the hunger.

He heard there was work in Hadera. Baratz and his two friends went. They found living conditions primitive, the farm work hard, and the pay meager. Yet they began to learn something about farming. Each worked for a different farmer, but to ease their lot they lived together in a little community, a *kvutza*, pooling their earnings with other young immigrants who joined them.

In 1908, the Palestine office of the Jewish National Fund acquired two tracts of land called Kinneret * around the Sea of Galilee. One tract of land was on the east of the Jordan River

---

* The Sea of Galilee is also called Lake Kinneret after the Hebrew word for violin which it resembles; and it is also called Lake Tiberias after the resort city which sits on its west bank.

and the other on the west. This second tract, which was offered
to Baratz and his *kvutza*, was called Um Juni, after an Arab
village nearby. It measured 3,000 *dunam*—750 acres—and would
cost them 50 percent of the net profits they made farming.

They were twelve, ten men and two women, working in cruel
circumstances. When the Jordan flooded it was sometimes impossible to reach the farm from Um Juni. Arabs often attacked
them. The soil was unyielding.

"For what had happened," writes Baratz, "was the land had
lost its fertility and it seemed to us that we ourselves, divorced
from it, had become barren in spirit. Now we must give it our
strength and give it back its creativeness."

Six men did the plowing and planting, two acted as watchmen,
one served as a secretary-accountant, and one was in reserve—the
pekak of the kibbutz, the "cork" who fills in wherever needed.
The two women did the housework and the cooking. One of
them became Mrs. Baratz.

At first they planted only grain, tilling with primitive tools.
They owned six mules and two horses, which carried water for
irrigating. The Jewish National Fund advanced them seed and
in the beginning paid them 50 francs a month as wages, all of
which went into the kibbutz. Soon the women began complaining. They had come to Palestine to work and live with nature;
sewing and cooking on the kibbutz they were worse off than their
mothers in the Pale of Settlements in Russia.

The men bought them two cows, the beginnings of the kibbutz's dairy herd.

Two years later they were able to move from the village onto
the land itself, which they called Degania after the blue corn-
flowers which bloomed on the surrounding hills.

A member of the group then proposed that the kibbutz enact
an ordinance in which all agreed not to marry for five years.
"Living as we do in this climate," the young man argued, "in
danger from the Arabs, how can we have children?"

"But," writes Baratz, "a young girl came out from Russia
and within a few weeks the young man fell in love with her.
Theirs was the second marriage on the kibbutz and their third
child was Moshe Dayan."

It took ten years to understand the land. The kibbutzniks of

Degania made a great many mistakes. They started with tomatoes and potatoes, neither of which would grow in this soil. They had to survive an epidemic of hoof and mouth disease. There was only a short rainy season and no dew. They had to learn a system of mixed farming to restore the soil's richness.

Gideon Baratz was the first child born on Degania, the first Jewish boy in the whole of the Jordan Valley. Two years later the Baratz's had a daughter, and the kibbutzniks faced up to the problem of what to do with the children if the mothers were to do their share of the work.

Joseph Bussell, the accountant, who later drowned trying to save refugees in World War I, argued that the children must belong to the parents but all must share the responsibility for their welfare. The community must bear the cost of education. Degania consequently did not hire a nurse but chose one girl to attend the children, and the kibbutz put aside a house where the children and their keeper could spend the day while the mothers were at work. As Degania developed this system, it was eventually adapted by all of the kibbutzim. Degania, however, is one of the exceptions to the usual practice, for the children spend the night in their parents' quarters.

Within a decade, these Jews had established not only a large Jewish community, but an even larger Jewish family. A lot of them gave their lives for it. Moshe Barsky was killed by nomads while he defended one of the mules the kibbutz owned. A young boy named Zvi committed suicide after the Germans and Turks invested the kibbutz and the cattle epidemic had decimated the herd. Another young girl named Elisheva committed suicide after her brothers were killed in World War I.

On a kibbutz, observes Baratz, there is a breaking point, there is always some disappointment and then grief and worry. There is often a disillusionment with the way of life and there is often a loss of belief. Visitors to Degania are often shocked that the inscriptions on some of the gravestones describe the suicides, ". . . but after all, it is the truth. It is the truth about them, good children though they were, and it is the truth about those times."

Baratz came to America several times to meet Jewish working people who might contribute money to Israel. What the kibbutzniks didn't realize was that nearly all of the big Jewish organizations and trade unions in the 1920's and 1930's were controlled by anti-Zionists. Baratz tried to raise money in Rochester, New York, then one of the centers of the Jewish needlework industry. He was escorted by some American Zionists who had rented a large hall in the downtown area. But the anti-Zionists hired an even larger hall and stewards directed the working-class audience to it.

Only 35 people showed up, and Josef Swirkin, the leader of the American Zionist Labor Party, rose to address them. He berated the few people in the audience. Baratz pulled him by the sleeve and asked, "Why are you attacking the people on our side?" Swirkin whirled and hissed, "There's nobody else to attack."

On his last visit to the United States in 1954, Baratz met the same anti-Zionists who had turned their backs on him twenty years before. But this time he sat with them on the same dais, Israeli flags displayed behind them, and all rose to sing the "Hatikva" with equal fervor.

A Syrian battalion advanced on Degania on May 11, 1948. With settlers from other kibbutzim, the defenders of Degania met the attackers on the road. The Syrians beat them back. The kibbutzniks retreated. They had lost 60 people, one a woman. Two hundred yards from Degania, the Syrians halted to regroup. The kibbutz used the respite to evacuate the women and children to Haifa. A delegation hurried to Tel Aviv that night to ask Ben-Gurion for help. Ben-Gurion told them he had no weapons. If Degania wanted, said the Prime Minister, he would fight with them at the kibbutz, but he had no arms to send. The kibbutzniks had one machine gun, some Molotov cocktails, which one of the kibbutzniks who had fought in Russia knew how to make, and some rifles.

Three Syrian tanks advanced the next day, the infantry following. The machine gun stopped one tank. A Molotov cocktail exploded under another, killing the two officers inside. The third tank and the infantry battalion retreated. The war was over around Degania.

The tank the kibbutzniks exploded still sits in the garden. The government once sent soldiers to remove it, but the children said they didn't want to give it up. Today it has sunk halfway into the soil.

Not this Pesach

IN THE old days, if you wanted any excitement over the Sabbath, either you went to Jaffa, which had a large Arab population, or to the kibbutz. Everything else closed down from Friday afternoon to Sunday morning.

The city slickers knew the kibbutzniks were generous to a fault and, besides, their kitchens serve the best food in Israel.

Then there was always all that fresh air. Going to a kibbutz became a Sabbath custom.

Not wanting to be rude, the kibbutzniks devised a harmless tactic to deter the freeloaders. Prior to the Sabbath or Pesach or Simchat Torah, the joyous holidays, the kibbutzniks used to announce in the newspapers, "Atid has just suffered an epidemic of hoof and mouth disease," or "Ein Hashofet reports fourteen cases of measles."

For a while it worked. The city slickers, however, got wise, and you can see them still roaming the fields filling their lungs with the fresh air and their bellies with the good food every Sabbath.

Last year before Pesach, a kibbutz put an advertisement in one of the leading newspapers: "Tel Atid requests its friends and relatives not to plan on visiting the kibbutz over Pesach. There is only room in the shelters for the kibbutzniks."

And everybody knew they were playing it straight.

The Jew tree

MANY YEARS ago, the kibbutzniks in the valleys of the north discovered the gum tree from Australia. The gum tree is a eucalyptus with deep roots, just the tree to help suck up the water from the swamps. The gum tree has provided more land for cultivation and it helped banish malaria. The Israelites have imported so many of these trees that now the Australians call the gum tree the Jew tree.

Singles weekend

THERE IS virtually no privacy on the kibbutz; consequently there is little adultery and less divorce. But there are also fewer pressures attending marriage. A kibbutznik in love does not have to worry about the quality of his education or will his profession provide her a living to which she can become accustomed or in what kind of house they will live.

Obviously, it is rare that a boy and a girl who grow up on the same kibbutz marry each other. The girl next door is probably an American invention. Kibbutzniks marry from their school and Army experience (Israeli boys serve three years, Israeli girls twenty months).

Still there are spinsters and bachelors on the kibbutz. The kibbutz does its best. Each kibbutz yearly must send a proportionate number of its members to different organizations in Haifa, Tel Aviv, or Jerusalem which manage the affairs of all the kibbutzim. Many of these volunteers are unmarried. Each kibbutz has to volunteer teachers for the schools. There is a great deal of interkibbutzim travel and it always involves a large percentage of eligible maidens and youths.

And still there are bachelors and spinsters.

There is, lastly, a resort hotel on the Mediterranean near Natanya which is jointly owned by all the kibbutzim. That is where the kibbutzniks go for their vacation. Two weeks out of every year the hotel accommodates only unmarrieds—the longest singles weekend in the world.

And still there are bachelors and spinsters on the kibbutz.

Harry, I ate half an egg!

AFTER THE Arab riots of 1936, it wasn't easy for Jews anyplace in the world to enter Palestine, but my good friend Moshe Barzilai, an ardent Zionist, made it from Brooklyn in 1939. The British would admit only a limited number of unmarried pioneers, young men able to work; or tourists with capital; or married couples with no children. Moshe, who had recently married his sweetheart, Shoshana, applied for a visa under the last category. Suddenly the British said no, they weren't admitting childless couples. Moshe and Shoshana persevered. Finally Moshe came as a pioneer and Shoshana as a tourist with capital. They suffered one deprivation: on the ship which took them to Haifa they could not share a cabin.

"What cities we saw then!" Moshe told me. "Cairo, Alexandria, all the Middle East, places we may never see again."

The Barzilais came to Ein Hashofet, a kibbutz founded by American Jews two years before. One of the Zionists who sponsored this settlement was Supreme Court Justice Louis Brandeis and the kibbutz is named in his honor—Ein Hashofet means "fountains of justice." It is on the east side of Mount Carmel, midway between Haifa and Megiddo—Megiddo, the Biblical Armageddon, where if the world comes to an end, it will come to an end where President Shazar received Pope Paul VI.

There was almost nothing at Ein Hashofet in those early years. The kibbutzniks lived in tents and makeshift dwellings. The land was barren. The Turks had stripped the entire country of trees. The hills were bald rocks. Moshe Barzilai spent almost two years planting trees as a start toward reclaiming the soil and halting erosion. Today, the long entryway up the mountain to Ein Hashofet is as densely and beautifully wooded as an American national park.

Food was sparse, the dining spartan. The cooks knew how to apportion proteins and calories to maintain a minimum balanced diet. One fact that every kibbutznik still remembers is that seven olives have the same nourishment as one egg. Moshe told me about going to a neighboring kibbutz for dinner. The settings were laid and on each plate was a pat of oleo, a roll, four olives, and half a hard-boiled egg.

Ein Hashofet had rescued much of the land by 1942, when Moshe volunteered for the Jewish Brigade the British were recruiting in Palestine. A private's pay was low but married soldiers qualified for an allotment. Since Moshe had torn up his marriage certificate to get into Palestine, he and Shoshana asked a rabbi to marry them again.

"Married?" asked the recruiting sergeant when Moshe reported for duty ten days later.

"Yes," answered Moshe.

"Date of marriage?" asked the sergeant.

"Just a minute," said Moshe, trying to count back. "It was nine or ten days ago."

"Nine or ten days ago?" asked the incredulous sergeant. "And you can't remember? I don't give you and your missus 'arf a year."

The British also tried to recruit an Arab brigade. They put the Jews in even-numbered companies and the Arabs in odd-numbered companies. The Jewish companies numbered to thirty-two, but the Arab companies stopped at one. Moshe remembered watching the Arab company drill. Some of the Arabs were so ill-coordinated they couldn't remember with which hand to salute. The British colonel solved this dilemma by ordering them to carry a rock in their left hand so they would remember to salute with the right. "Even at that," said Moshe, "some of the Arabs still knocked themselves out now and then."

The brigade was stationed first in the Latrun Valley, transferred to Egypt, and then fought up the Italian peninsula, by which time Moshe was a sergeant major. He was offered a commission, which he declined for two reasons. His colonel shamed him by asking, "Would you desert this regiment for a pair of pips?" and the Haganah, the Jewish underground army, said he was more valuable as a sergeant major forging travel orders to transport Jews from Europe to Israel.

After he was discharged, Moshe started the poultry houses at his kibbutz. Moshe is a renowned expert. The hens at Ein Hashofet lay 2,000,000 hatching eggs and produce 700,000 chicks a year. Eggs and chicks are sold to other kibbutzim as well as exported to Italian and Persian hatcheries.

In between was the Israeli War of Independence in 1948. There was a British airfield near Ein Hashofet. In 1948, the kibbutzniks suspected the British would inform the Arabs on exactly what day they were pulling out. Two days before the British left, the kibbutzniks sent out a false report on their own wireless. The message said the British were leaving immediately.

The Egyptians assumed the Jews had occupied the airfield and sent over a bombing mission. British Spitfires zoomed up to chase off the Egyptian planes, downing one which crashed into Ein Hashofet. The kibbutzniks pulled an Egyptian major from the wreckage, who kept repeating in amazement, "I can't understand it. The British sent us up and the British brought us down." The airplane was divided equally between the playgrounds of Ein Hashofet and its neighbor, Kibbutz Dalya.

As soon as the British left, the kibbutzniks flocked to the airdrome, hoping to replenish their meager food supply from the stores the British left behind. They discovered in dismay that the departing British had poured kerosene over everything, especially the sugar which was in short supply and severely rationed during those war years. I asked Moshe what else had happened to the kibbutz during the War of Independence, and he said one of the things he did was to lead an intrepid band of kibbutzniks into a deserted Arab village, where they spent several days picking olives. "Picking olives is the worst job in the world," said Moshe. "Pick and pick all day to fill maybe two or three bushels. You can't shake olives off the tree or you'll bruise them. Then they're only good for olive oil. Oh, do your fingers ache picking olives."

This is a response typical of kibbutzniks. On the subject of the War of Independence or the Sinai Campaign or the Six-Day War they clam up like agents entrusted with a supersecret.

Over the years, Ein Hashofet prospered. It made 7,000,000 pounds in 1969 ($2,000,000). The kibbutzim in Israel always invested a portion of their profits in research. But the kibbutzniks say that while God stopped making land, he kept right on making people. Ein Hashofet, with a population of 600 and only 7,500 *dunam*, began to consider establishing a medium industry in the 1950's, one of the first of the kibbutzim to take this step. Industry usurped less land, offered more work, and promised large profits. This kibbutz sells $1,000,000 a year worth of pre-cision-tooled screws. Ein Hashofet manufactures screws which are sold to the largest American supplier and also to the Israeli Army and aircraft industry. Moshe gave up his chickens for three years to help the industry get on its feet.

"We import tons of rolled steel from the United States," Moshe said, "from which we turn out screws which we ship right back to the same place. I asked the supplier one time, 'How come?' and he said, 'All I know is I gotta have inventory.' "

Ein Hashofet chose to manufacture screws through circum-stances dating back to the Nazi era in Germany. In the early 1930's, if a Jew wanted to escape Germany he had to leave his money behind, though he could take out personal property. One man managed to bring to Israel two lathes which could manufacture screws. For twenty years these lathes gathered dust in a warehouse in Nes Ziona, but when Ein Hashofet was casting about for equipment to start an industry, someone remembered them. The C & D Chocolate Company, the largest confectioner in Israel, started in similar fashion, with machinery a German confectioner salvaged from the Nazis.

Sixty lathes in three factories turned out screws in 1970. Since the French embargo, Ein Hashofet cannot keep up with the orders from the Israeli defense industries. The factory is manned by kibbutzniks, from the manager and the accountant to the foreman and the truck drivers.

Nor is this Ein Hashofet's only industry. An accomplished sculptress—a pretty English girl named Jean Mayer—with three assistants operates a ceramics studio boasting two kilns, the larger of which can bake fifty or sixty statuettes at once. These exquisite statuettes are sold to Tel Aviv gift shops and exported to England and America. Her studio, with its new all-glass annex, occupies what was once one of Moshe's chicken houses.

Moshe is proud of his kibbutz, proud of the fields which yield cotton, peanuts, and fruit, proud of the extensive dairy herd and the chicken houses. There are facilities for both a dentist and a doctor at Ein Hashofet. And there is a museum which contains a personal record and mementos of everyone who has lived in the kibbutz and died there. There is a high school on Ein Hashofet which accommodates students from several kibbutzim in the area. These students can only return to their kibbutzim on Tuesdays and Saturdays because of the distances involved. Because they thought their proximity to home gave them an unfair advantage, the children from Ein Hashofet voted to visit *their* families inside the kibbutz only on Tuesdays and Saturdays as well.

Yet Moshe is worried. Life on the kibbutz is changing perceptibly. Precision-tooled screws for a jet fighter demand the skills, say, of a quality control engineer.

"Does it pay us," Moshe asked, "to turn a kibbutznik into an engineer and then ask him to take his turn in the kitchen?"

The answer is, it doesn't, which means the kibbutznik who once was available for any job now has a specialty. Shoshana, who is Ein Hashofet's postmistress, and Moshe still take their turns in the kitchen, a job most kibbutzniks hate, but they are motivated by an earlier ideal. A managerial class is emerging in the kibbutz. Skills are not learned naturally and to waste the expense of learning them may dissipate profits. Only by profits does a kibbutz support itself.

I looked at Moshe Barzilai, still trim and hard in his fifties, his gentle face creased with worry because life will not be the same for sons and grandchildren as it was for him. But Ein Hashofet was once a desert, and as the kibbutzniks survived the arduous work of turning barely arable land into a garden, as Moshe survived meals which consisted of half an egg, and as the kibbutzniks survived the incursions of the Arabs, I am sure Ein Hashofet will survive a managerial class. ✓

Everybody can live on a kibbutz

"WHAT IS a worry to the fathers," explained Dr. Y. Plevler, an economist on the faculty of Hebrew University's School of Agriculture, "is a fact to the sons. What your friend and his friends worry about, my students take for granted. They have to. Fifty percent of the income of the kibbutzim derives from industry. In the coming decade, the percentage will be even higher."

Dr. Plevler knew whereof he spoke. Not only has he taught young men and women from the kibbutz for the last eight years, but he himself was born on a kibbutz. He spent a morning trying to put the complexity of the kibbutz into perspective.

On many a kibbutz there are three generations working side by side. Where this situation once obtained throughout the world, it obtains less and less. Only in Israel does it obtain more and more. No longer can these generations preoccupy themselves with agriculture and animal husbandry. Agriculture and husbandry have been mechanized and rationalized, and now only a small number of the kibbutz is needed to carry on production and make it increase. The kibbutzniks who find time on their hands cannot move on to other farms because all the arable land is already developed.

There is, of course, the Negev, dear to the heart of David Ben-Gurion, but Plevler pointed out there are areas in the Negev which can never be made arable. Nor is it always economically feasible to pump water from the Galilee when desert land can be reclaimed. The atomic-powered desalinization plant that would make great quantities of brackish or sea water available for irrigation or industry is a long way off.

Even where water can be pumped from deep wells, there are still certain restrictions on what a kibbutz can grow. The Ministry of Agriculture, together with a board of appointed kibbutzniks, has already established quotas on certain crops—tomatoes for instance. For citrus, Israel's number one export, government regulations insist on a certain quality and size.

There are no restrictions on cotton, which the Californian Sam Hamburg taught the Israelis to grow ten-odd years ago; and no restrictions on grain. But grain will not grow in the Negev and cotton is not profitable, although one sees it wrapped in gigantic plastic bales all over. Which leaves only innovating farming—greenhouse products, crops grown under plastic, or new stocks which will grow in sand. This type of produce does not need many hands. A singular success is the Israeli avocado. So kibbutzniks may well develop the Negev, but it will be for industrial not agricultural use.

The future of the kibbutz is not in agriculture but in industry. In a complex of nearly 170 factories, kibbutzniks now produce over ten percent of the nation's manufactured goods. One kibbutz has a factory which cans the produce from the surrounding kibbutzim. There are a dozen kibbutzim in the Jezreel Valley raising, in man-made beds, the fresh carp, which is as dear to the heart of the Israeli housewife as the Negev is to Ben-Gurion.*

Fifteen hundred kibbutzniks are in college or taking part-time courses ranging from sciences to the arts. "They are there," he said, "because they have not only taken into account the changes in the world but the changes in their midst. The fathers will have to realize that because a boy is born on a farm is no guarantee he will take to farming."

This is the substance if not the tenor of what Zvi Brenner told me. Zvi Brenner is one of the top administrators of the kibbutz movement on loan from his own kibbutz, Afikim. He is in charge of the kibbutz labor department.

Brenner knows Moshe Barzilai. "Moshe is an old-timer," he said. "Old-timers talk about the good old days. I was one of the forty-three Palmach officers the British arrested in 1939. And when we get together we, too, talk about the good old days. But eighteen months in the Acre prison was not pleasant. Planting trees on Ein Hashofet for two or three Palestine pounds a month doled out by the Jewish Agency was not pleasant. The old days weren't so good and now the old days are gone. The young have changed the kibbutz. And if you want my opinion, they have changed it for the better. Their idea is that *everybody* can live

---

* Fresh carp, of course, becomes gefilte fish. The orthodox Jewish housewife prepares it on Friday, because she cannot cook on the Sabbath. The great virtue of gefilte fish is that it is delicious served cold, with a dollop of red horseradish. In the rear of every Israeli supermarket, called "Super Sol," is a huge tank in which hundreds of delectable carp swim. On Friday, housewives congregate around the tank and point out which fish they want. The monger nets it, weighs it, stuns it with a club, and drops it into a plastic bag. The process literally transported my two-year-old grandson, John. He thought there was nothing better in this world than endlessly to watch a Yiddish fishmonger bang a wriggling fish over the head with a big stick. His antics so delighted the monger that he netted John a small live carp and gave it to him. The family naturally called the fish Gefilte and kept him in a basin. Poor Gefilte, however, did not survive one of the Goldhursts' trips to Jerusalem and went the way of all fresh fish.

on a kibbutz. And everybody *means* everybody, no matter what you do."

Brenner, who is perhaps sixty and as trim and hard as Moshe, talked to me in his office at 123 Hayarkon Street, in an old building on top of the bluff overlooking the beach. From his window, I could see the dusk settling and the lights beginning to go on in the spanking new Hilton Hotel which commands the Mediterranean. On the wall was a map of Israel. Different colored dots marked each kibbutz to indicate out of which movement it came, whether Social-Democrat, Socialist, religious, or Nahal, this last Army-inspired. There was one kibbutz with no color—Sde Boker, Ben-Gurion's kibbutz, in the middle of the Negev. The kibbutzniks of Sde Boker were not animated by a political ideology, they just wanted to farm in the middle of a desert, where it is so hot the visitor can see camels running the other way, looking for water.

Because I had been to Sde Boker, I understood immediately what Brenner was telling me about the younger kibbutz generation. On the perimeter of Sde Boker stands a collection of colossal statuary, the work of a kibbutznik. That is his job on the kibbutz, just as Ben-Gurion's job is serving in the Knesset. Collectively, the kibbutz has decided that politics or art is as useful as harvesting lettuce. Work has become that which provides value for the kibbutz and expression for the worker. What the young mean to say is that the kibbutz can accommodate any aspiration, any creativity.

"And," Brenner added, "they have set about proving it. There is a choir from the kibbutzim touring six countries in Europe and at Kibbutz Afikim there is a computer. The kibbutz makes room for singers and technologists."

Offhand, he could think of only two professions whose practitioners have difficulty adjusting to the kibbutz. One are the doctors, because the kibbutzniks are so healthy that medicine becomes routine; and the others are writers, because while they are thinking they see other men working and are filled with guilt.

Night had fallen. Brenner bid me good-bye and said, "When you see Moshe, remind him he is a grandfather as I am. Tell him last Sabbath I saw my sons at the kibbutz with all my grandsons. Then ask him when in history could a Jew see all his generations in the same place, not on one Sabbath but on every Sabbath. Tell him the kibbutz as a way of life has changed. Remind him the kibbutz has become more than a way of life. The kibbutz has become home, a place where we will see our great-grandchildren."

Part *II*
Jerusalem: Arab, Christian, Jew

Up to Jerusalem

ON FRIDAY noons and Sunday mornings, before and after the Sabbath, the bus shed at the big intersection outside of Tel Aviv is crowded with soldiers, young men and women hitching rides to and from their posts. Their pay is low and no one in Israel with space refuses a military passenger. The road to the right leads to Ashkelon, Ashdod, and Beersheba; the road straight ahead, to Jerusalem. We picked up two young soldiers, both armed with Uzis, and drove straight toward Jerusalem.

Past Ramle, the road curves sharply and narrows, so that only one car can traverse the crossing which lets traffic into the Latrun Valley, perhaps the greenest valley in the world—not with the green of an American forest, but with the green painters use, a deep green. This is the place where Joshua bid the sun stand still. Part of the Latrun is lined with eucalyptuses, which stand like sentinels along the roadside. They give way to the fields of a kibbutz, water spraying in smooth arcs from the grid of the irrigation pipes.

A mile away is the Abbey du Silence. To the left of the Abbey is the old stone police barracks from which the Jordanians commanded the valley until the Six-Day War. Again the road turns sharply, this time to the left, and we begin our ascent up the Judean Hills, the bluffs and steep slopes lightly bearded with thousands of young trees. The road corkscrews through the hills. To the right is Abu Ghosh, an Arab village. Again a descent,

63

again a rise. The hills and slopes are formed by the outcroppings
of Jerusalem stone, yellow in the daytime, but as dusk begins
to fill the valleys between the hills becoming gold, almost lumi-
nous, shining against that background of deep green in which
now purple and blue begin to play, making the hills magical.

Then the city, Jerusalem, the Golden, glowing in the early
twilight. On the terraces of the apartments above, the housewives are taking in their laundry. Laundry always waves from
Jerusalem homes like the ensigns of a gigantic fleet entering port.

Teddy takes a walk, or whatever happened to Ruhi el-Khatib?

THE MOST cordial relations I have ever enjoyed with a
mayor anywhere are those with Teddy Kollek, the mayor of
Jerusalem. To say we're fast friends is presumptuous, but I know
enough about him to realize he is a consummate art expert whose
taste and knowledge of contemporary art history could easily
qualify him as the director of the Museum of Modern Art. In
1965, I sent off to the Israel Museum the only statuary I have
ever owned, Stankiewicz's "The Secretary" and for my gener-
osity received a letter of appreciation from Teddy Kollek, who
explained to me for the first time the artistic values inherent
in the work.

Teddy is stout, has massive shoulders, and looks six feet tall.
He speaks with a clipped British accent. He is humorous and
considerate. But he wasn't going to talk to me. I had spent nine
whole days in Tel Aviv before coming to Jerusalem. Anyone who
would prefer Tel Aviv to Jerusalem exhibited a deficiency of soul.

I explained I had no choice. My son and collaborator was in
Tel Aviv with his wife and my twenty-two-month-old grandson.
They couldn't get an apartment in Jerusalem.

When I said that the Israelis thought he was a shoo-in for
reelection as mayor of Jerusalem, he softened. He produced a
box of Havana cigars with the comment, "These are hard come
by in the United States," and then he whipped out a bottle of

Jack Daniels bourbon and said, "And this is even harder come by in Jerusalem."

You can see I liked the man. So it is sad to report that on our next meeting Teddy and I parted company rudely arguing over Ruhi el-Khatib, the last Arab mayor of East Jerusalem, whom the Israelis expelled, and Menahem Porush, the Orthodox rabbi who wanted to succeed Teddy as the mayor of reunited Jerusalem.

It all started after the Six-Day War, when the only Arab territory the Israelis formally annexed was old Jerusalem and its 60,000 Arab inhabitants. The Israeli government conferred citizenship upon these Arabs, conferring as well their fair share of taxation.

The Israelis have yet to deal with the problem of the Arab population in the conquered areas, the so-called Administered Territories. In fact, the only influentially placed Israeli who has tried and is still trying to deal with this problem is Hizzoner, Teddy Kollek. Teddy started to deal with the problem in August, 1967; the Golda Meir Cabinet did not get around to it until December, 1969, when Shimon Peres was appointed as minister without portfolio and charged with coordinating plans and programs for the Arab refugees as well as initiating policies to facilitate interaction between the economies of Israel and the territories.

The issue of what to do with these Administered Territories was not even raised in the last election—except by the minuscule Communists who wanted immediate withdrawal and Israeli hardliners who wanted immediate annexation. Everyone else was for peace, which, though it means "get out to find it" in the United States, means "stay in until it comes" in Israel. Even the hippies in Tel Aviv, known locally as the Dizengoff group, were wholeheartedly for the latter peace—peace and the legalization of hashish.

Jerusalem was different. A modest and tentative start toward integrating the New City Jews and the Old City Arabs was under way. Arab and Jewish boys meet in sporting competition at the YMCA where they behave as good Christians should, there are Hebrew and Arabic language programs, Arabs and Jews go abroad for study together, and everyone in Jerusalem has access to every part of the city.

Menahem Porush, Kollek's opponent, charged such programs
would dilute the quality and vigor of the Jewish state. He said
Teddy Kollek curried favor with the Arabs to insure reelection.
He said mixing was bad, to which Teddy Kollek replied, "We
should be the last ones to say so."

On that preelection Sunday when we were last pleasant, Teddy
confided that he faced the same aggravating problems every
mayor faced: the city was almost inundated by an avalanche of
garbage, there was no parking for the autos of the affluent, the
municipality needed a larger staff, the housing shortage was a
nightmare, and all the electorate worried about was 60,000
Arabs, only 3,000 of whom had ever voted before.

"There are reasons for everything," Teddy explained. "Jews
and Arabs are strangers. They eat different foods, they dress
differently, and they walk with different gaits. Strangers do not
always like one another. And over one-half the Jews in Jerusalem
are Oriental Jews, from Syria, Yemen, Iraq—Arab countries—
who were more or less forced to leave for Israel in 1948. These
Jews, too, were uprooted, refugees, and they regard Arabs with
suspicion. They are not going to be happy with Arabs for neighbors."

The Jerusalem constituency returned Teddy Kollek. His party
won an absolute majority of 16 out of 31 seats on the City
Council. Eight thousand Arabs swarmed to the voting places,
so many appearing suddenly at some of the polls that all could
not be accommodated. The ballot is secret, but they sure weren't
voting for Menahem Porush.

Voting moderators were unprepared for the large Arab turnout. They had difficulty identifying Arab names. They also had
difficulty verifying the identity of each voter. The large turnout
surprised observers and reporters. Some said the Arabs came to
vote to have their identity cards stamped, which would prove
them cooperative citizens (identity cards are stamped so a man
cannot vote twice). Others said the turnout was due to the
realization that Jerusalem has been reunited. The city's religious
community had actively supported Kollek. Clergymen were
among the first to cast their ballots, especially at the poll outside
the Jaffa gate. Arabs enjoy municipal services far superior to
what they knew in the past. They are no longer villagers.

It didn't all go off peacefully. Some Arabs waited in line so long they gave up and went home. When Kollek's car passed through the city, Jewish youths shouted, "Fifth column!" Rabbi Porush charged that Kollek used buses from his campaign headquarters to transport Arabs.

John Lindsay of New York sent Teddy a telegram reading, "Congratulations from one *meshugganah* to another."

Four days later I met Teddy Kollek for dinner at the King David Hotel. He was happy, no question about it. He looked like a combination Spencer Tracy and Brian Donlevy as he darted here and there across the lobby to confer with pals, wave hello to friends, and sign autographs in Hebrew for the tourists. But he said that he was tired, awfully tired, that he had been up three nights forming a coalition.

Here I must interrupt: putting together a coalition for an Israeli politician is as protracted a process as picking a new Cabinet is for an incoming American President, except the President-elect has nothing to worry about save whether his best bib and tucker will still fit him for the inaugural ball. While an Israeli puts together his coalition, he dare not make controversial political decisions.

Teddy and I were joined at the table by my son and colleague, Richard Goldhurst. Goldhurst asked the reelected though tired mayor about the future of his city.

"What about the future of my city?" Kollek replied sharply. I suddenly detected no trace of fatigue in his voice.

"What about your city vis-à-vis its new Arab population?" Goldhurst pursued like a college-educated reporter at a Senatorial press conference. I had a feeling it wasn't the right tack.

"Menahem Porush raised the issue. What does the issue portend for Jerusalem? For Israel? In other words, does Ruhi el-Khatib have a political future in this town?"

"These are naïve questions," said Kollek, waving his big hands as though brushing away flies. "Why not," he continued, "ask the mayor of Belfast when he will solve *his* problems? Or the mayor of Montreal? The people of Brussels lived together for five hundred years before they found out they didn't like each other. People with differences often do not get along. Here in Jerusalem we have managed English, a third language, more than any other city has ever managed, but we may not get along either."

During the week I met twenty American newsmen on a junket sponsored by the United Jewish Appeal. Several of these men were from papers in the South and I had known them for twenty and thirty years. They told me they had interviewed Golda Meir the day before, and I asked if they had better luck with the Prime Minister than I had with the mayor of Jerusalem.

They were treated tactfully, they said, but all they got out of administration officials were position papers. Golda had confided to them what she confided last summer to Ted Sorensen: Israel is the best friend Jordan's Hussein has. (He may not be around by the time this book appears.)

So you see I got more from Teddy Kollek.

The Arabs do not engage my sympathy for obvious reasons. I do not believe they understand that it is territorial politics which is the first principle of nationhood. The Arab countries call themselves nations, but they are nations with only a foreign policy and a narrow foreign policy at that, namely to annihilate Israel, a threat the Israelis for good reasons take literally. That foreign policy is a failure, not only in its stated goal, but in its ability to inspire a discipline among the majority of the people by which nations achieve stability.

The Israelis were naïve when they thought they could coax the Arabs into responsible statehood. Naïvely they expected the Arabs in the Administered Territories to regard them as benevolent conquerors. The Israelis came with the hopes of insuring their own territorial integrity, for which they guaranteed their captives a longer life expectancy and a diminished infant mortality rate. But the Arabs do not want to brush their teeth or sit at a conference table. In their disappointment, the Israelis blow up houses in Hebron when they find a weapons cache and the Arabs, in vengeance, blow up apartments in Haifa when they find unsuspecting tenants.

And Teddy Kollek is naïve when he compares Brussels, Belfast, and Montreal to Jerusalem. No matter how these cities devastate themselves, their destruction will not set off a world conflagration. If the fire that the crazy Australian Michael Rohan set in the Al Aksa Mosque provoked a riot in Jerusalem, the direction of life might change for millions. For Jerusalem is a pressure point between East and West.

Similarly, if one of the rockets fired by the Al Fatah from the Golan Heights hits a schoolroom filled with Israeli kids, the Jews might bomb Amman.

American newsmen know that the trouble spots of this world are the underdeveloped areas—the Congo, the American slums, the Middle East. The United States chose not to challenge the building of the Berlin Wall and the Soviet Union chose not to challenge the dismantling of the missiles in Cuba. Had the Israelis, however, crossed the Suez and made for Cairo, perhaps neither of these great powers would have had the time for the judicious exercise of self-restraint.

One thing in favor of a peaceful settlement in Jerusalem is this oversensitive though remarkable organizer and adminis-trator, Teddy Kollek. During World War II, Kollek gathered hundreds of young people out of the Nazi death camps and brought them to England to study farming while they awaited the day they could go to Palestine. And during the 1948 War of Liberation, Kollek was in the United States buying arms for the Haganah. It has been said that Kollek had the entire Atlantic seaboard of Irish longshoremen working for him shipping arms to Israel. Kollek might very well make this Arab and Jew con-frontation of day to day living in Jerusalem come out all right.

By the way, Ruhi el-Khatib is one of Jordan's occasional dele-gates to the United Nations, where he is notorious for his anti-Jewish propaganda.

Playing ball with the Vatican

WHEN THE Israeli Army appointed him military governor of Jerusalem, General Vivian Herzog mused about the special irony destiny had reserved for him. General Herzog is the son of Yitzhak Halevi Herzog, once the Chief Rabbi of Ireland, the most Catholic country in the world. "I should have known," remarked General Herzog, "that as a soldier in the most Jewish army in the world, I would become protector of the Church of the Holy Sepulchre, the Stations of the Via Dolorosa, and the Cenaculum, the scene of the Last Supper." The father became Chief Rabbi of Israel, leaving behind him a Jewish lord mayor in Dublin.

Israel found itself in an ironic situation. The most venerated shrines in Christianity were suddenly within the borders of the Jewish state. Israel had become the stepfather to sanctuaries revered throughout the world. Like most stepfathers, Israel encountered responsibilities it never anticipated.

For example, Israel was now responsible for preventing the minor riots which erupted from time to time in Bethlehem when tens of thousands of pilgrims tried to squeeze into a church which could accommodate only a small fraction of their number. On Christmas Eve and Easter there was often bloodletting in front of the Church of the Nativity, ugly episodes the Jordanians somehow could not prevent. Under its single roof, the Church of the Nativity houses four churches—Greek Orthodox, Armenian, Syrian, and Coptic.* Israel brought peace to these warring Christians by seeing to it that they observe a strict schedule of services for each of these churches, and the Jews also installed open-air television on Manger Square for those who could not obtain a pew inside.

As Israel had doubled its Christian population after the Six-Day War, so it doubled religious contention. Suddenly there were two Russian Orthodox churches, each insisting it represented the true faith. Before the Revolution of 1917, White Russian Orthodoxy founded churches, convents, schools, and hospices in Palestine. The Red Orthodox Church, an ecclesiastical mission dependent upon the Russian Orthodox Patriarch of Moscow—and the party line—operated in Jordan. Each of these wants to swallow up the other on the absolutely logical grounds that one must be heretical.

But under Israeli law, religious minorities enjoy autonomy not only in personal rights but in liturgical practice. The law itself is old, first promulgated by the Ottoman Turks in 1757

---

* St. Catherine's, the Roman Catholic Church in Bethlehem, is only an annex of the Church of the Nativity. Nevertheless, it is to St. Catherine's that an Italian monsignor, an Arab mayor, and a Jewish military governor lead a procession of pilgrims on Christmas Eve from Jerusalem.

and called the Statute of Sublime Porte, conferring on every community or nation, then called millets, its rights and obligations.

The British, under their mandate, continued the practice and, when Israel declared its independence in 1948, it made the Statute of Sublime Porte the law of the land. Essentially the Statute of Sublime Porte defined the status quo when the Turks let the various Christian churches divvy up the holy places.

This law is implemented and interpreted by the Israeli Ministry for Christian Affairs, whose head is Dr. Shaul Colbi, an Italian-born Jew who is the only expert on Roman Catholic canon law in Israel. Dr. Colbi is a commander of the Order of St. Gregory the Great. Catholic priests in Israel jokingly call him "Monsignor."

"How come?" I asked him.

"They make exceptions," he said.

Colbi's ministry on King Solomon Street is the most anachronistic in Jerusalem. In his office wait Italian monks who look as though they stepped from the pages of Boccaccio's *Decameron* and Russian archmandrites who look as though they stepped from Gogol's *Dead Souls*. Colbi, one of the world's foremost authorities on Christian shrines, has headed this department for twenty-two years. His ministry has helped Israel develop continually improving relationships with its Christian community. Hebrew has become the *lingua franca* between clergymen of different nationalities and denominations; at their own insistence, the former Greek Catholic Archbishop Georges Hakim and all his clergy joined the Histadrut, Israel's universal labor union; and—and hereby hangs the tale—Pope Paul came to the Holy Land.

This visit was of crucial significance for *de facto* and *de jure* recognition from the Vatican. Because it was crucial, the Israelis wanted the Pope's short visit to be a happy one. Pope Paul wanted to see the Cenaculum, access to which was only by a narrow, tortuous flight of stone steps; the Israelis built a new road to make the Pontiff's approach more convenient. In the Pope's entourage were three elderly cardinals, one on a salt-free diet, one on protein-plus, and one on a diet heady with boiled foods, the preparation of which taxed the Israeli cuisine. And, of course, the Israelis wanted to give Paul a memento of his visit, something which the Pope and the Jews valued commonly; the Israelis minted a gold medal embossed with the injunction, "Love Thy Neighbor as Thyself."

There is no question that the visit was a success. Prior to Paul, only two cardinals had come to the Holy Land, both on private visits. In the last five years, thirty cardinals and other prominent members of the hierarchy have made state visits. During my visit, the Archbishop of Cologne, Joseph Cardinal Hoeffner, toured Nazareth, Jerusalem, and Bethlehem and then asked Dr. Colbi to show him a kibbutz.

Israel works hard to secure the Vatican's good will and, happily, the Vatican plays ball. The Pope subscribes to the notion of *realpolitik*. The Vatican has interests in the Holy Land and the way to protect those interests is realpolitically.

Historically, the Greek Orthodox Patriarch holds preference among the spiritual leaders of all the Christian Churches, and the Greek Orthodox Church holds preference in the main Christian sanctuaries. In trying to preserve its Hellenic character, however, the Greek Orthodoxy has often shamefully neglected its pastoral duties toward its followers, who are mostly Arabs. A shortage of priests has also weakened the church's prestige. And saddest of all, the church has run out of money. For generations the faithful in the Balkans and in Russia supported it. The Soviets put an end to this.

The Monophysites—which include the Armenian, Coptic, Syrian-Jacobite, and Ethiopian Churches—have the oldest links with the Holy Land. Some of these churches were founded in the fifth and sixth centuries. These Christians were always few in numbers. Even adding the adherents who live in the Administered Territories, there are probably only 3,000 in Israel. With the Greek Orthodox Church, however, the Monophysites exercise condominium in some of the most important sanctuaries from which the Roman Catholics are excluded.

The Protestants came last to the Holy Land; when they first began coming, they were for the most part German Lutherans. Kaiser Wilhelm II, anxious to establish German interests in the Middle East, built many churches in Palestine. At the beginning of World War II, the British took these churches and land into vested custody. After the war, for obvious reasons, the German Lutherans chose not to resume their work in Israel. For a nominal fee, the Germans sold these properties to the Jews. There are still many Anglican churches throughout the country founded during the British mandate. Almost every Protestant denomination is represented here, but in the main their work is missionary, which the Jews neither understand nor like.

Protestants were never overly interested in establishing shrines. They regarded the whole of the land as the cradle of Christianity. One can still see Protestant divines filling empty milk bottles with water from the River Jordan.

The reaction of worldwide Protestant organizations to Israel's victory in the Six-Day War was negative and anti-Jewish—not the wisest way to seek favors from your host.

Lastly, the Protestant presence in Israel is diminished by its very variety. In America alone, I believe, there are over 200 Protestant denominations and almost as many in Israel. Anyone who knows anything about *realpolitik* knows, after all, there is only one Pope. His influence and his friendship can prove decisive factors for a small country.

Take Nazareth, a town of 35,000 Arabs. There is no room in Nazareth even for the Jews who live in Nazareth Elit, up on the hills (which gives them a tactical advantage in case of Arab unrest). Yet there was room in Nazareth for the Great Basilica of the Catholic Church of the Annunciation, which has just been completed. While this monumental church run by the Franciscan Order was designed by the Italian architect Giovanni Muzio, it was built by Solel Boneh, the construction company owned by the Histadrut.

This kind of economic muscle is enough to make the Vatican a pal for life.

"There are numerous signs," writes Dr. Colbi in his monograph *Christian Churches in Israel*, "that the Catholic Church is appraising realistically a new situation in which the Israel factor must not be underestimated. In the theological field, that situation appears more acceptable in view of the change in attitudes toward Judaism resulting from the memorable decisions arrived at by the recent Ecumenical Council. Israel's presence in east Jerusalem and throughout the Holy Land is a

74   THE ISRAELIS

fact which cannot be ignored; the church adopted a posture of
remarkable correctness in its day to day *de facto* relations with
Israeli authorities."

In December, 1969, Lawrence Cardinal Shehan, the Archbishop of Baltimore, made public a document approved by the
Vatican secretariat which recommended: that Catholics should
recognize the significance of the state of Israel for the Jews;
that the Jewish religion should not be seen as a stepping-stone
to Christianity; and that the Catholic view of the Jewish religion should recognize that it is not one of "justice alone," thus
implying that only Christianity possesses the law of love and
freedom.

This is a big league trade which helps both clubs.

Tell it to thy son

STUDENTS AT Hebrew University in Jerusalem ask the
question, just as well-intentioned Christians in America ask it:
"Why? Why bring up the subject of six million murdered Jews?
What good will it do?" Israelis also add, "Since the state executed Eichmann, isn't that an end to it?"

Young Israelis cannot comprehend the conditions under which
almost all of European Jewry walked into the gas chambers.
Three times in the last twenty years, they and their fathers, who
number only 2,500,000, have saved their country from the incursion of 100,000,000 Arabs. What can heroes and martyrs have
in common, save in this instance they were both Jews? The one
fought and the other didn't and that is the difference between
life and death.

"I start with the uprising of the Warsaw Ghetto," explained
Dr. Yehuda Bauer. "Almost all the students at the university
are veterans and they relate to this readily. Then I go back and
forth until we have covered all the work. But Holocaust Studies
is not the most popular course at the university."

Dr. Bauer is the head of the Department for Holocaust Studies
in the Institute for Contemporary Judaism. Tall, dark-haired,
probably not forty, he has a facility of expression which makes

his views seem artless and casual when they are, in fact, ordered, precise, and logical.

He is one of the few historians who are holocaust specialists. In his own research he is concentrating on the typology of Nazi round-ups and exterminations which differed from place to place and time to time.

What struck me as unusual about Dr. Bauer was neither his specialty nor his sophistication but that he is a kibbutznik who lives with his family on Kibbutz Shoval in the Negev. Dr. Bauer teaches three days a week at Hebrew University and three at the kibbutz.

Psychologically and morally the holocaust has had a profound effect upon Diaspora and Israeli Jewry. Historically, the hope of a worldwide aliyah dates from this time. Until anti-Semitism spread to Germany, one of the most advanced countries in the world, well-informed Zionists thought it was Israel's destiny to solve the Jewish problem in Eastern Europe. The fear of the impending holocaust led to the first political compromise by the Jews over the land. David Ben-Gurion and other Zionists begged the British for a state into which they could accept German refugees.

In 1937, the Peel Commission, headed by one Lord Peel no less, came to the conclusion that Palestine could not accommodate both Jew and Arab and, therefore, it ought to be divided. Accordingly, Lord Peel gave the Jews one plot of land from Tel Aviv to the Galilee and another smaller plot from south of Jaffa to Ashkelon.

But the British already foresaw war with Nazi Germany and thought the Arabs would become important allies. Britain never implemented the Peel Commission's recommendations. Instead, it steadily clamped down on immigration and halted it completely in 1939 when European Jews needed a refuge more than ever.

The Israelis, too, saw the handwriting on the wall. With Rommel approaching Alexandria, the Jews correctly assumed the British would not waste troops in the Middle East when Africa itself was at stake. They devised the Plan of the Masada, in which they fortified Mount Carmel and planned to use Haifa as a headquarters to fight against the Germans.

Israeli paratroopers joined the ghettos in Rumania, Bulgaria, and Estonia to help organize resistance, but they had relatively little effect. Three hundred thousand Rumanian Jews were exterminated; forty paratroopers could hardly be considered an effective force.

Holocaust studies have given the martyred Jews a more heroic role than the world suspected. Dr. Bauer and other experts have proved there were Jewish resistance movements which often preceded national resistance movements against the Nazis. But what happened to the Jewish partisans in Poland was that the Poles killed them before the Nazis got around to it, just as Lithuanians killed the Jewish partisans in Lithuania.

"What these discoveries add to our knowledge of the holocaust," said Dr. Bauer, "is that the description painted by Bruno Bettelheim, say, or Hannah Arendt, or Raul Hilberg, is poorly focused because these authorities consulted only German records. The Germans naturally did not record, say, the activities of the Jewish partisans in Russia, but in Israel there is a veterans organization which numbers 2,000 of these men."

"What other records are there?" I asked.

"There are the Jewish records. There are the diaries, the histories, the descriptions offered by the victims themselves. At the university, we have become experts in the art of taking oral depositions. Other records are stored at the museums, on two of the kibbutzim and, of course, in the archives at Yad Vashem."

Yad Vashem is the Memorial to the Martyrs and Heroes, a large compound on the Mount of Remembrance in Jerusalem. It consists of a Hall of Remembrance, a large rectangular building of basalt boulders and uneven concrete, purposely re-creating the appearance of a Nazi gas chamber. Within, on a floor of inlaid tile, are inscribed the names of the 21 largest concentration camps. A shaft of sunlight, admitted through a skylight, illuminates the eternal flame contained in the hollow of a colossal broken bronze urn.

Beside this hall is a large square where thousands gather annually for the ceremonies on Martyred and Heroes' Remembrance Day in April (the date of the Warsaw Ghetto uprising, which changes according to the Hebrew calendar). To the left of the hall is a double-storied museum; on the top floor are kept the names of those who perished in the camps, and on the bottom floor is a photographic re-creation of the history of Nazi anti-Semitism.

Guarding the museum is an anguished statue of Job by the sculptor Nathan Rapoport.

Ringing these buildings is a small forest called the Avenue of the Righteous Gentiles, which honors Gentiles who risked their lives to save Jews.

"A strict judicial procedure determines this selection," said Katriel Katz, chairman of the Yad Vashem directorate. "If our jury finds a man acted in the hope of recompense or reward, we are grateful he saved a Jewish life but we cannot call him righteous and we do not plant a tree bearing his name."

Mr. Katz, a burly man in his late fifties, wearing rimless spectacles, proceeded to show me the archives, which were down a long flight of stairs to our left. Here, in bound copies and on microfilm, are not only the German records, which from America alone filled seven boxcars, but the files of the rescue activities of Jewish organizations, the documents captured in Germany and satellite countries, the work of the Jewish Historical Committee set up immediately after the Allied liberation and, most importantly, the diaries, histories, notes, and attestations made by the Jews in the ghettos and concentration camps.

Among these, for example, are the Ringlebloom Diaries. Ringlebloom was a Jewish professor of history who was herded with other Polish Jews into the Warsaw Ghetto. In the ghetto, Ringlebloom set up a historical bureau which kept a complete record of every order posted by the Nazis, every underground publication printed or mimeographed by the Jews, and a day to day description of everything which transpired within the walls.

Ringlebloom died in the ghetto, but he preserved this history by burying it in hermetically sealed milk cans which were exhumed after the war, although the Polish government evinced no enthusiasm about their publication.

Among these archives are the attendance records of the ghetto yeshivas and clandestine universities the Jews established. Not only holocaust experts but governments have availed themselves of these histories.

"Just recently," said Mr. Katz, "a prosecuting attorney from

Austria found all the police records of wartime Vienna while he was searching for evidence to convict a war criminal."

Katriel Katz has a background as interesting as Yehuda Bauer. Mr. Katz was formerly the Israeli consul general in New York and later the ambassador to Russia. After the Six-Day War, Israel was overcrowded with ambassadors sent home from the Communist countries. The chairman of the Yad Vashem directorate holds ambassadorial rank and Mr. Katz has served here since 1967.

Over coffee in his study, Mr. Katz showed me a well-worn book—a novel entitled *Les Vrais Riches* by Françoise Coppée. On flyleaves and margins of this novel a young Jew kept a running account of what happened in the Lodz Ghetto from May until August, 1944. By the end of August there were only a few hundred Jews left in Lodz out of 61,000. The remarkable fact about this diarist is that he used four languages to record his entries: English, Hebrew, Yiddish, and Polish.

The diary was preserved by Avraham Benkel, a survivor of Auschwitz, who returned to Lodz to find his home and all the others vandalized by Poles looking for "Jewish treasures." This discarded diary was all that remained in a neighboring flat, and Benkel carried it with him to Israel, where recently he turned it over to Yad Vashem. The Diary of Lodz has been the subject of several monographs and a popular essay, this by Michael Bernet which appeared in the October, 1969, issue of *Hadassah Magazine.*

"But I disagree with Mr. Bernet," said Katriel Katz. "Bernet says the diarist wrote in four languages to keep secrets from his little sister. In one of his entries he confessed he stole his sister's ration of bread. But I do not think this is the answer. I am sure this diarist knew exactly what he was doing, he was leaving a record he wanted read. He wrote in four languages to enlarge upon the chances that whoever found the diary could understand it. That is why he chose a French novel, so a Frenchman would open it. He didn't know French or he would have used five languages for his entries."

As I took my leave of Dr. Katz, back in the sunshine he introduced me to two young girls, both Israeli Army corporals. These girls were escorting new immigrants through the memorial.

These immigrants were Oriental Jews from Syria, Iraq, Morocco, and Tunisia. Many of them had never heard of the holocaust.

"We teach them it happened," said Dr. Katz. "We think it is important that they learn it."

Going out of Yad Vashem, I passed the Pillar of Heroism, a simple severe triangular shaft of stainless steel which rises 70 feet high on this Judean hill. Deeds of Jewish valor are carved into the surrounding stones.

One million seven hundred thousand Jews of varying nationalities fought the Germans in World War II. If young Israelis, or the world for that matter, think this effort was not enough, then both should also remember that among the 6,000,000 martyred there were still those who in their agony kept the Biblical command: "Tell your children of it and let your children tell their children and their children another generation."

Baal Shem Tov, the Polish Jew who founded the Hassidic movement, wrote that "The secret of redemption is remembering and exile is the price of forgetting."

That is the succinct reason for holocaust studies.

Part *III*
Pipe Clay and Drill

War stories

IN THE time I spent in Israel, only two Israelis ever volunteered a war story. To be sure, they will talk about the Six-Day War or the Sinai Campaign or the War of Independence, but not what they did during any of them. Americans go to great extremes to re-create a war story, we have even had a television series about a happy prisoner-of-war camp; and the British are still sympathizing with poor old Bertie, a dear chap, RAF ace y'know, having a terrible time of it back in Mayfair since the war ended. But not the Israelis.

It may be that war is a concomitant of life in the Middle East. Yoram Matmor, the Israeli playwright and novelist, told me that as he enjoyed his first meal in Jerusalem after escaping from Europe, a bomb went off in the street and disturbed no one's table manners. And it may well also be that the soldiers who die daily on the Suez Canal diminish the exploits of old heroes.

The first war story I heard came from a graduate student at Tel Aviv University. He had been a noncommissioned officer in the tank regiment which took Nablus, an Arab stronghold to the north of Jersualem. As the regiment rolled into the city, guns swiveling the turrets, treads chewing up the stones, the entire Arab population came out cheering and waving flags. The Nablusians had been listening to the Arab radio which had just announced that Tel Aviv was in flames, its streets red with flowing blood. What also deceived these people was that the Israeli tanks did not invest Nablus from the east but from the west, the rear of the city. The Nablusians thought these tanks belonged to an Iraqi expeditionary force.

"They kept cheering," said this serious student, "until they saw the Mogen David. Then they stopped cheering and went home."

Tommy Lapid told me the other war story. I have known and admired Tommy for the last decade, but this was the first time I learned he was a corporal in the Army. I expressed my profound amazement that the Israeli military apparatus could waste his abundant talents. I told him I thought he was at least a captain, probably a major, maybe even a colonel.

"The Army doesn't work that way," said Tommy. "When I came to Israel I couldn't speak Hebrew so the Army made me a mechanic in the motor pool."

"And you're still in the motor pool?"

"No, I'm not in the motor pool," said Tommy. "I'm in the Army Public Relations. For three days during the war I showed Mr. Saul Bellow around. He came here as a war correspondent. I just don't wear my stripes so that Mr. Bellow and other A-Number One novelists shouldn't think the Army is shortchanging them with enlisted men. Besides, Mr. Bellow wasn't interested in war, only in human suffering."

There are some apocryphal stories, the most repeated of which concerns the tank colonel who reached the canal in '67 and told Defense Minister Moshe Dayan he thought he could have his regiment across by nightfall and into Cairo by morning.

Dayan ordered the colonel to stop at the east bank of the Suez.

The colonel persisted. He was sure of his flank. He knew his men could cross and not even get their knees wet.

Just as insistently Dayan repeated the orders. The colonel would turn left and his men would dig in on the east bank.

There was a long pause. Then the colonel said in English, "Chicken," thus becoming the only colonel ever to call Moshe Dayan chicken and live to become a general.

A similar story is told about the colonel who reached the crest of the Golan Heights. Virtually singing, he radioed his general that his tanks were on their way to Damascus.

General Eleazar, whose nickname is Dado, ordered him to halt and draw up a defense perimeter.

"There's no one in front of me," said the colonel.

"You stop your column," said the general.

"General, I cannot hear you anymore. My radio is going dead."

"You hear me very well, my colonel. I knew these tricks before you. You are not going to take Damascus."

The unhappiest Israelis of the war were the volunteers on the *Dolphin.* When Nasser closed the Straits of Tiran, he promised to sink any Israeli ship which tried to pass. The Israelis determined to call his bluff and flew twenty sailors to the African port of Massawa, where they bought and boarded a rickety old ship which they named *Dolphin.* Armed only with the captain's revolver, the suicide squad set sail for Aqaba.

Twenty knots at sea, the *Dolphin* began to ship water. Day and night these men manned the pumps. The gauge in the boiler room was always on the danger point, but the captain ordered, "Full steam ahead." They threw everything overboard to make faster time. The sun was equatorial. The water gave out. Uncomplaining, the men took twelve on and two off as they steamed resolutely forward. There they were, the straits, dead ahead. The sailors ran up the blue and white flag.

Out came an Israeli torpedo boat. Paratroopers had secured the entire area three days before.

A captain was slightly wounded in the Sinai. His pregnant wife rushed to visit him in the hospital. The excitement was too much for her. Then and there she gave birth. Captain, wife, and brand-new baby boy all went home together.

The Israelis knew war was inevitable when Moshe Dayan became Minister of Defense in Levi Eshkol's Cabinet. It wasn't that Dayan was an unbridled hawk, they explain. It was only that with Dayan at the helm, the time for hesitation was over. Interestingly enough, for a time he was supported by the doves, who thought that only he was strong enough to prevent war. Influential Israelis told me Dayan made one or two minor adjustments in the plans of General Itzhak Rabin and then the airplanes took off.

A week later, the joke made the rounds that when newsmen at the United Nations asked U Thant who started the war, the

Secretary General replied, "I don't know, but I'd like to knock his other eye out."

At the Wailing Wall

BY NOW everyone knows that the revered Wailing Wall in Jerusalem is not a remnant of the Second Temple but a retaining wall which surrounds Har Habayit, the hill on which the temple stood. Still, the Western Wall, as it is now called, is the holiest of all Judaic shrines. Throughout our history, the poignant moment of the week was the blowing of the *shofar* at the base of the wall to signal the advent of Sabbath, the *shofar* being the traditional trumpet made out of a ram's horn.

Under the Turks, however, and then under the British mandate, the Jews could not blow the *shofar* because the *shofar* distressed the Arabs. Under the Jordanians, the Jews could not even get to the wall.

Thus, when the paratroopers took the Dung Gate in Jerusalem, there was a moment of supreme elation when the Israeli Army's Chief Rabbi, Colonel Goren, blew the *shofar*.

The colonel was one of the busiest soldiers in the Six-Day War. Hardly had he arrived with the Torah at one holy place, than the Army had taken another. The colonel hoped to blow the *shofar* at the outskirts of Jericho, but this time the walls came a-tumblin' down before he arrived.

The generation gap

AVRAHAM SHAPIRA was one of the early pioneering Zionists. He was big, a giant of a man, with a handlebar moustache, fearless. He rode guard on a white horse to protect the settlers of Petah Tikvah before there was a Haganah, only *shomrim*, simple sentries. He learned Arabic. A fierce and valiant man, even the Arabs came to respect him and asked his help in adjudicating their own quarrels.

Shapira fought in all the battles and survived every one. He was Israel's Davy Crockett.

When he was in his nineties, the Israeli government decided to honor him as an example to all the newer generations. The Cabinet ordered a special medal minted that one of the ministers would present to Shapira. The officials chose the occasion of one of the athletic jamborees which take place every summer.

The day arrived. Avraham Shapira, wearing his high boots and his floppy felt hat, sat in the center of the stadium on a raised platform, as the parade entered the stadium. The gymnasts came in turning somersaults and the basketball players entered dribbling. The handball team waved their leather-covered hands and the soccer team trotted by in their heavy shoes and thick sweaters. Then came the high-breasted girls, white knees and shoes flashing in the sunshine. They assembled to pay tribute to the old hero. The band broke into the "Hatikva."

Dramatically, the Cabinet minister read aloud the citation and slowly and deliberately Avraham Shapiro walked to the microphone. He surveyed the adoring faces clustered across the green expanse of the field.

Finally, he spoke. He looked at the Cabinet minister and then at the well-drilled youngsters. He delivered and answered his own question with words which live on in Israeli memory to this very day.

"This is youth?" he asked. "This is shit," he said.

Christians and the Six-Day War

It should come as no surprise that the Israelis keep tabs on everyone. The Cabinet keeps tabs on the Russians; the Reuven Shiloah Institute keeps tabs on the Arabs; the Afro-Asian Institute, of course, on the Africans and the Asians; Dr. Shaul Colbi on the Vatican; and across the hall from Dr. Colbi, as the director for Christian Affairs of the Ministry of Religion, Yona Malachy keeps tabs on the rest of the Christians. Dr. Malachy is also a lecturer at the Hebrew University on American Church History and the editor of the magazine *Christian News from Israel.* Since the Six-Day War, Dr. Malachy says, the Christians have been bad news.

I found this statement surprising and at first not at all acceptable. But Malachy is not talking about all Christians or individual Christians but about many national and world Christian organizations. Their attitudes toward Israel after its victory in the Six-Day War were bluntly negative for some very bad but altogether interesting reasons. Those who want Malachy's chapter and verse will find it in his treatise "The Christian Churches and the Six-Day War" which appeared in the fall, 1969, issue of the *Wiener Library Bulletin*, London.*

There are historical reasons for this negative attitude. The established Christian churches, Catholic, Protestant, and Orthodox, never defined their attitude toward the founding of the Jewish state. These churches have, however, spent a great deal of effort in defining the "place of the Jewish people in Christian belief" and have all come up with the same statement: anti-Semitism is incompatible with Christianity.

Until the Six-Day War, a great many Christians thought of Israel as a place where Jews lived, a haven for refugee Jews from Europe, but not as a political entity. There was a theological reluctance to see Israel as a state with sovereignty, exercising power and applying force when that sovereignty was threatened.

This was the reality forced upon Christian churches by the war. In June, 1967, just before the war broke out, the National Council of Churches of Christ in the United States adopted a resolution, as many church organizations did at the time, urging a quick and peaceful resolution of the Middle East crisis. This particular resolution called for a disengagement of forces, the establishment of international rights in the Gulf of Aqaba, and "an agreement between Arab States and Israel concerning the rights of the Arab refugees and the recognition of the State of Israel."

Malachy quotes this resolution at length as an example of the "objective" wording used by Christian organizations to gloss over the qualitative differences between Arab and Israeli hostility. Since the blockade of the Gulf of Aqaba threatened Israel's

* The Institute of Contemporary History and Wiener Library is England's Yad Vashem.

economic existence, it threatened its sovereignty. The statement also made the solution to the Arab problem by the Israelis the prerequisite of Arab recognition of the state.

During the war, the World Council of Churches, the Synod of the Anglican Churches of Canada, the World Association of Reformed Churches, and a dozen others, called for a cease-fire.

The cease-fire, when it came, resulted in the annexation of Jerusalem as well as the capture of the land west of the Jordan, the Gaza Strip, the whole of the Sinai, and the Golan Heights— which was not what these church organizations intended at all. The church leaders thought mistakenly that a cease-fire would send everybody back to from whence they came, as the cease-fire in 1956 eventually sent everybody back (for "everybody" read "Israelis"). Christian opinion was predictably shook to see Israelis bestriding the Middle East.

In general, Christian organizations thought there were three ways to peace. The first, the Arabs must recognize Israel; the second, the Israelis must be prepared to let their frontiers be redrawn by international negotiation; and the third, Jerusalem with its holy shrines must become an international city.

These were political considerations but of a naïve order. Such considerations were doomed from the start because the Arabs would not then, and probably will not now, recognize Israel. They were doomed because, while a sovereign state may well redraw its frontiers, it itself makes that determination, not other nations—not if a state wants to remain sovereign. And the last of these suggestions simply gagged the Israelis. I doubt Jews ever entertained for a second any thought of acceding to the last one. For twenty years Christian churches all over the world had accepted Moslem sovereignty over the holy shrines. No Christian organization was ever perturbed that the Jews were denied access to the Wailing Wall.

When the Jews proved intransigent, the quarterly newsletters of these Christian organizations turned to a description of Israeli war atrocities. These simply had not happened. Two Druses are pulling a fifty-year sentence for murdering an Arab, but whole regiments of Israeli tankers cruised the Sinai for weeks trying to rescue retreating Egyptians from the desert. The atrocity charges were rebutted by the corps of correspondents

who covered the war from the Israeli side, by the Catholic
Dominicans of Jerusalem who commended the Israelis for not
having damaged the holy places in taking the Old City, and
by the Sisters of Mercy of the Order of St. Vincent who sent a
worldwide circular to their friends.

There were instances where members of world organizations
whose sympathies were for the Israelis pointed out that the
Arabs had threatened complete annihilation of the Jews. Dr.
Eugene C. Blake, the secretary general of the World Council
of Churches, undertook to publish the Arab reply in one of that
organization's quarterly newsletters. Arab spokesmen insisted
genocide was the furthest thing from their mind, that the Arab
nations would give the Palestinian Jews the option of living on
in Palestine, provided the European Jews emigrated. "Our people
do not want to kill Jews but do want a cessation of the racial
state of Israel," concluded the Arab letter.

The Prague Christian Peace Conference, which took place
immediately after the Six-Day War, connected events in the
Near and Far East. It held American intervention in Vietnam
responsible for the fighting between Israel and the Arab nations.
This is hard-line Communist propaganda. It is argument by
analogy and it is specious. Even granting that Israel is an American satellite, it is hard to see how the Arabs in any way are
analogous to the Vietnamese or the Vietcong. Yet it has persuaded many a Christian clergyman opposed to American intervention to become *a priori* an opponent of Israel. Countless
Christians have used this argument to condemn territorial ex-
pansion by force.

The latest development of anti-Israel Christians has been to
compare these Jews to the Nazis. Henry P. Van Dusen, a leading
figure in Protestant circles in America and a former president
of Union Theological Seminary, described the Six-Day War
in a letter to the New York *Times* as ". . . the most violent and
ruthless aggression since Hitler's blitzkrieg in the summer of
1940, aiming not at victory but annihilation."

There are many Christians whose sympathy tempers these
attitudes, for not all Christians subscribe to them. Even before
the war, Dr. Martin Luther King, in a published advertisement
in many newspapers signed by Protestant, Catholic, and Ortho-

dox laymen, called upon President Lyndon Johnson to honor the United States' commitment to the freedom of international waterways. King went on to ask Americans to support the integrity and independence of Israel.

German and French theologians, both Catholic and Protestant, have been critical of their world organizations' policies regarding the Middle East.

Evangelical Protestants, the Fundamentalists who take their eschatology seriously, see the fulfillment of Biblical prophecies in the return of Jews to the homeland. Zionism to the Fundamentalists heralds the Second Coming of Christ who will proclaim the Kingdom of God. These Christians accept Israel's victory over the Arabs on religious grounds, which may not make them the most comfortable of allies but it makes them better than nothing.

The most significant development which helped temper Christian reaction was the total identification of world Jewry with Israel, a total identification which surprised even the Israelis. Until the Six-Day War there had been a rift between Israeli Jews and Jews in the Diaspora. There were, the Israelis felt, two kinds of Jews—those who had returned to the homeland and those who lived elsewhere and made money or couldn't get out. The war produced a mystical growing together. It is estimated that in the month of June, 1967, American Jews alone raised $200,000,000, and the rest of the world Jewry also gathered a great deal. This response was not only material but also a morale builder, a determination that Jews elsewhere felt all Jews were in the boat together.

In Israel itself the war ended the growing antagonism between Oriental Jews and European Jews. What looked like an incipient "color" problem was laid to rest in the tank battles of the Sinai, in the street fighting of Jerusalem, and on the bluffs of the Golan Heights.

The Jews in the Diaspora, particularly the Jews in America, articulated their universal sympathy for the cause of Israel—with their money, with their political leverage, and with what community influence their temples and shules commanded. They have said their Judaism can have no meaning unless there is an Israel. Catholics and Protestants who worked for better relations between Christians and Jews realized their concentration had now to focus on the tie between the Jewish people and the Jewish state.

What made Christian world organizations anti-Israel? Dr. Malachy advanced three reasons.

The most bitter of all arguments against Israel has been published in the pages of the liberal Protestant press. Liberal Protestants reject Jewish nationalism as a chauvinistic movement. They fail to see how Jewish destiny can be linked to a specific country. Liberal Protestant churches in the past years have also identified themselves with the New Left. The New Left, which argues the cause of Asian, African, and Black nationalism, sees the world in terms of black and white. This, unfortunately, is no pun, for to the New Left it means black *versus* white.

Another reason is that the Christian world has often regarded the Jew as an object of charity, as someone whose rights need protecting, whose very being often needs safeguarding. People on the dole are expected if not to be grateful at least to be subservient. The Israelis and world Jewry have proved neither. In fact, the Israelis regard with suspicion the missionary efforts of the Protestant churches in their country. The Israelis are not sure if even the Arabs deserve conversion.

Lastly, the Six-Day War gave many Christians the chance to shed their guilt over the Nazi extermination of the Jews. For centuries, Christians had preached rejection of the Jew, and this tradition played no small part in the holocaust. The Six-Day War provided a good excuse for many to be anti-Semitic again on a "humanitarian" basis.

The point of keeping tabs on the folks is not only to find out how nasty and unreasonable they can be, the point is to make them into better people by trying to develop more rational attitudes.

The Jerusalem Rainbow Group, composed of 18 Jewish and Christian theologians, meets monthly to discuss religious and spiritual problems. Its paper, *Reflections on Reactions to the 1967 Middle East Crisis*, may not soften the attitudes of the Christian churches in the world, but it will certainly give these churches and the organizations which they sponsor something to chew over. The Rainbow Group argues:

Jewish history is characterized by an unbroken continuity, physical and spiritual, in the relationship of the people and the land.

Special attention should be paid to the peculiar bond uniting the Jewish people and the land of Israel to the capital city of Jerusalem. Jerusalem for the Jews is at once the heart of both the land and people as well as the symbol of their total, physical and spiritual existence.

We believe that one of the greatest disservices that Christians have rendered to the Arab peoples and states in the last twenty years is in not having helped them to face the comprehensive Jewish reality, particularly the Jewish link with the land. This concerns the inevitability of the continued existence of Jews in that land in terms of the contemporary State of Israel. By playing down this fact, Christians have involuntarily encouraged the persistence of belligerency and prevented the opening of talks leading to a negotiated settlement. As Christians are becoming increasingly aware of their responsibilities for promoting peace and justice in the international community it is likewise their duty to explore every possible means for achieving the same objectives in the Middle East.

Casualty lists

THE JEWS were the first people in history to publish casualty lists.

The Spartan women told their husbands, "Come back with your shield or on it." But in accordance with religious law, a Jew was buried the day after he was killed. Law forced the humanitarian impulse. The Jews told his survivors.

There are casualties daily along the Suez Canal, on the road-building gangs in the Sinai, and on the West Bank of the Jordan. Five to ten Israeli soldiers lose their lives each week and three times as many are wounded. Each day the newspapers carry the stories of the soldiers who are buried.

The Israeli casualty list differs from ours. The list of American casualties is printed usually on page two and includes only name, rank, and serial number.

In Israel the death of a soldier is front-page news. Nothing is left to conjecture. For example: "Private David Tewrik, a 35-year-old reservist from Jerusalem, was killed at half-past nine on Tuesday evening in a mortar and bazooka attack from across the Jordan in the Manrassa Bridge area."

Another: "Lt. Yoram Shanam, 23 , of Haifa, who was killed Tuesday morning near Kuneitra, was laid to rest yesterday at the Kiryat Shaul Military Cemetery. Shanam had gone to give a lift to a soldier going on leave when their vehicle set off a booby trap on the road. Shanam was a student of mechanical engineering at the Technion and was serving in the reserves. He was recently married."

What immediately struck me was that the Israelis describe battle fatalities much as we Americans describe highway casualties.

I think we concentrate on the details of a traffic victim's life because we understand it could happen to any of us. It is harder for us to relate to men who died in a Far Eastern jungle thousands of miles away. If we start filling in the way *these* men lived, it will set us to wondering why they died.

Ennui

"LUST AND LOOT are the soldier's pay," Napoleon is supposed to have remarked, "but ennui is his lot." For the Israeli who serves in the Sinai, ennui is as menacing an enemy as the Egyptians. The Sinai is a vast eternity of monotonous sand, a waste stretching into nowhere.

It was in this vast eternity of monotonous sand stretching into nowhere that Moses received the Ten Commandments from Jehovah.

Abraham's discovery that the Lord our God is one is remarkable when we consider that monotheism was invented by desert Jews and not by the wonderful Greeks who were so far ahead of the Bedouins and Hebrews in everything else. This anomaly, however, can be easily explained. In the theological beginning, every object and every phenomenon of nature was supposed to be a creature, the dwelling place of a god. In Greece there was a remarkable variety of climate, hills, groves, streams, rugged snow-covered peaks, and warm coastal lands. But in the Sinai nature may be seen in the nude. You see nothing but sand and sky, stretching into nowhere. It was as difficult for the inhabitants of such a country to believe that there were many gods as for Greeks to believe that there was only one.

Eliyahu Salpeter, one of the most facile of Israeli newspapermen, says the desert floods the soldiers with a terrible fear of strangeness. Nothing familiar interrupts the surroundings. Sun and the sand seem one.

The soldiers live in confining bunkers, which make all activity inconvenient. The food is substantial but as boring as the landscape. These soldiers do what all soldiers do who have drawn a hard assignment. The standing order is that soldiers shave every morning. Military dress is proper at all times. Everybody keeps busy. The Sinai is littered with Egyptian vehicles beyond salvage. Each of these abandoned trucks or tanks or half-tracks is gaily painted.

Ripeness is all

NAOMI SHERER is a kibbutznik from the Galilee who moved to Tel Aviv to become a songwriter, now one of the most popular in Israel. Her words and music fit the modes of the young Israeli who is a generation away from the Hassidic incantation and Russian folk songs which were the source of early Israeli music.

She deviated from this style only once, at the request of Mayor Teddy Kollek who had organized a song festival for Jerusalem. Naomi Sherer wrote an ode, "Jerusalem, the Golden," which had a moderate success.

A few weeks later came the war. Naomi was entertaining troops in the Sinai when she heard that Israeli soldiers had retaken Jerusalem. And what were the Israeli soldiers singing?

Her own lament, "Jerusalem, the Golden." Immediately, Miss Sherer rewrote the second stanza of the song, changing it from a cry of yearning into a paean of celebration. "Jerusalem, the Golden" became the anthem of the Six-Day War, the biggest hit Israel has ever known.

Shopping spree

BECAUSE OF A lower standard of living, prices in the Administered Territories are still appreciably cheaper than prices in Israel proper. Until terrorism in the Gaza Strip escalated in the fall of 1969, Jews from Ashdod, Ashkelon, and the south did a lot of their shopping in Gaza.

No prices were as attractive to the Israelis, however, as the prices in the Old City of Jerusalem when the gates were opened for the first time. Thousands of Israelis went souvenir hunting in what was formerly Jordanian domain. Jews bought up all the tourist lures—Arab shopkeepers never knew such prosperity— and when these were exhausted, Jews went on to buy up all the commodities. By then, of course, the Arabs had caught on. But the spree continued unabated, to the despair of the Jewish shop- keepers in the New City.

To prove the futility of this epidemic, the military governor of Jerusalem ordered two soldiers dressed in mufti to sell two dozen cakes of soap from a vendor's stand. The soldiers charged twice the price the same soap cost in Israel. They sold out in one hour.

The military governor made the results of the experiment public. The psychological warfare had the desired effect.

The Israelis stopped buying soap from Arab vendors.

Gunboats a-comin' in, hot damn!

FIVE GUNBOATS, evading the French arms embargo, slipped out of Cherbourg harbor Christmas night and steamed toward Israel.

Tommy Lapid said, "We got those boats, hot damn!" but that was the only measure of excitement I heard among the Israelis. The government press and Army officials went on about their business. They are always busy because Israel is a sausage out of which every foreign journalist wants a little piece for himself.

The rest of the folks in the world were inspired by this adventurous passage through the harbor and into the Mediterranean. The first intimation the Jews had of how big a story it had become was when five Italians disembarked from an Alitalia flight at Lod, unloaded several television cameras and sound equipment, and told a cab driver, "To Haifa, as fast as you can."

Subsequent flights were filled with romantic foreign correspondents in trench coats who began besieging the authorities for more information about the gunboats. All the Israelis could tell them was that the boats were expected to dock at Haifa in a day or two or three. A drenching rain swept over Haifa, the city on a hill. The trench coats came in handy.

The Israelis kept saying over and over that they didn't know where the boats were. But this is another nasty habit here. Press officers naturally cannot reveal information which touches on security. The easiest way to keep information secret is to say, "No comment," or "I don't know." Top Israeli officials worry that if a press officer gives these replies, pedestrian foreigners will think him stupid. Therefore all press officers are trained to say "I don't know" in such a way as to intimate that of course they do.

The writers from *Life* magazine hired an airplane and scouted the Mediterranean. The Associated Press started to dog *Life*. The hotels in Haifa were jammed with correspondents, all of whom were down on the wharf, getting wet. To fill space for their rapacious editors, these newspapermen described how the Haifa port area was jammed with patriotic Israelis bedecked with streamers, dancing to the martial music of Army bands. The truth was that the Israelis were dry. There wasn't a soul on the Haifa balconies until Kol Israel, the national radio station, broadcast these colorful descriptions, and then the Haifians rushed out to join their pals at the finish line. It got the photographers their pictures: rain sluicing, Israelis waving.

By New Year's Eve, when the five gunboats made port, there were so many newsmen waiting that the press office issued only 150 passes, lest the crush of intrepid reporters capsize the boats. These 150 crack news hounds crowded into the Kishon shipyard canteen to interview the commanders of the boats, only one of whom spoke English.

None of these captains could shed any light on how the boats got out of Cherbourg.

The one captain said simply, "I received sailing orders."

"Who issued the clearance?"

"They were not formal sailing orders," said the captain.

And that was about it. After a futile hour, wet and disappointed at missing the New Year's Eve jamborees in Tel Aviv, the reporters withdrew.

The next morning, while heads rolled in France, one of the Israeli newspapers commented, "But now the ships are here. The drama has ended. And the world press for whom the story was a godsend during the generally dull holiday season will be able to focus its light on another part of the globe."

The big story was, of course, in Cherbourg, where reporters soon dug it out. Admiral Mordechai Limon, head of the Israeli Defense Purchasing Commission, allegedly managed the affair, and a cloak and dagger affair it was. The only new light I can shed about the escapade is that no one remembered that Mr. Limon has a PhD in business administration, from Columbia University I believe, and is also married to the beauteous Rachel, who once won $1,000 on the television program *Name That Tune* because she knew "A Tisket, A Tasket" was not "Jeepers Creepers."

The doctors are always busy

Dr. K. J. Mann, the director of Hadassah Hospital in Jerusalem, invited me to tour the premises. The driver who picked me up at the King David Hotel was Benjamin Adin. Adin, who used to lead the convoys of doctors and nurses to the old Hadassah on Mount Scopus, is one of three people to survive the Jordanian ambush of April 13, 1948, when 77 Jewish doctors and nurses perished under a sudden hail of bullets.

The ambush enraged the underground Irgun. It attacked the Arab village of Deir Yassin and massacred 251 men, women, and children. I have talked to Israelis who to this day wonder how Jews could kill women and children.

After the War of Independence, the Israelis had to build a new Hadassah because Mount Scopus was closed to them. This new hospital boasts the synagogue with the Marc Chagall windows which depict the twelve tribes of Israel and for the first time capture dimension in stained glass. These windows make the Hadassah one of the few hospitals in the world revered as a museum.

Chagall designed the windows so they could be instantly removed in case of shelling. But when the Six-Day War began, the maintenance staff at Hadassah discovered the putty which sealed the windows had baked them into place. It took the men a day and a half to remove the windows and store them safely. When a hospital official told Chagall by telephone about this difficulty, Chagall replied he could make new windows, it was more important for Israel to win the war. According to an apocryphal anecdote, Chagall cabled Ben-Gurion, "I wish you best and hope you stand firmly in the clouds," along with some of Chagall's cows in the windows, presumably.

I met several Israeli soldiers at Hadassah in various stages of recuperation. They had been wounded in a fight with the Al Fatah in Hebron. Two of these young boys were amputees.

In an adjoining room were three Arabs who had been wounded by the Israelis in the same action. One was also an amputee, another had less grievous wounds, and the third had taken a bullet in the forehead. The neurosurgeon had saved his life, but Dr. Mann said this fellow would never be more than a vegetable. I heard the other terrorists call their nurses "mother" and the presiding doctor "brother."

Dr. Mann sighed that the wounded would keep coming in for a long time. He told me about an old hospital built one hundred years ago by the Turks in the walled city. The Jordanians had operated it for the last twenty years. Its facilities

were far below Western standards. As soon as the Israelis secured
Jerusalem, Dr. Mann had invited the physicians and nurses of
this hospital to come to Hadassah.

At the first orientation meeting, twenty-nine Arab doctors
came. At the second, only three. Now none. Threats and in-
timidation warned them off. These doctors have left Jerusalem
for Jordan. Dr. Mann said he supposed they do their best in
Jordanian hospitals and Jewish doctors do their best at Hadassah.
There are always enough soldiers to keep both busy.

Old dogs and new tricks

THE CANAAN, a breed of dog which roamed Palestine
in the time of Abraham, has a sense of smell so strong it not
only can detect hashish hidden in the clutch mechanism of a
car but can sniff out plastic land mines planted by the Al Fatah
on a kibbutz.

One of the Canaan breed is found in Africa. The British have
bred this strain into one of the elegant show dogs. The other
strain is found in Israel. This is the breed developed by spry,
seventy-year-old Dr. Rudolfina Menzel, the director of the Institute for the Orientation and Mobility of the Blind in Haifa.
The Canaan is also one of the superior seeing-eye dogs, and
Dr. Menzel trains twenty-five of them every year.

The Canaan is a short-haired dog, as big as a collie with
heavier shoulders. Usually the Canaan is white with round black
spots on the forehead and paws. As Dr. Menzel showed me
her kennels, the dogs bouncing in the cages and yelping like
wolves, I saw how tiny she was, barely a head taller than the
dogs she trains.

She explained that the Canaan is the only breed which needs
no instructions as a watch dog; it is intuitive. We traversed a
training walk that duplicated the hazards encountered by the
blind. There were pot holes and heavy objects placed in the
center of the concrete paths, a curb whose rim had crumbled,
and an intersection with traffic lights. There were stray cats all
over and, when I asked Dr. Menzel if she were also a cat fancier,

she said, "A seeing-eye dog must accustom himself to every kind of animal."

Dr. Menzel came to Israel in the 1930's from Linz, Austria, with her husband, a veterinarian and dog trainer. She saw her first Canaan in an Arab *shuk* and paid three little boys a pound to catch the stray. It took quickly to training and Dr. Menzel and her husband began to breed Canaans, finding their first customers among the kibbutzniks who needed watch dogs. The Canaan dogs are so fierce they became virtual weapons, leaping to attack marauders.

At the beginning of World War II, the British asked Dr. Menzel to supply them with dogs for their Army. The Germans had bought up all the dogs in Europe and Dr. Menzel was the only expert on canine military training in the Middle East. She asked Moshe Sharet, then a member of the Jewish Agency Executive Committee, later the Israeli Foreign Minister, whether she should accede to this request. Sharet advised her to give the British all her cooperation.

During the War of Independence, the Israelis used the Canaan like a St. Bernard, to find wounded soldiers in the desert. Now, of course, the Canaan has become an efficient sapper.

I am partial to the Canaan since I own three of them—Gaon, which means "Genius"; Dubah, "Little Bear"; and Beenah, "Wisdom." Only three people in America breed Canaans: Ursula Berkowitz on the West Coast, Harry Golden and Jay Shaeffer on the East.

Dr. Menzel's serious mission now is to succeed in registering the Canaan with the American Kennel Club, an almost endless task which exhausts her patience. The American Kennel Club registers the pedigree of new breeds, providing there are 3,000 of the species in the United States. Madame Doctor needs to recruit another 2,997 fanciers.

And there's another problem, which is the apartment house across the way. Dr. Menzel warned the tenants when they began construction that her dogs bark every time they are fed, they bark at the approach of strangers, and they have been known to howl at the moon for no apparent reason.

The tenants assured her they loved and understood dogs. There was no reason for Dr. Menzel to doubt them. The Israelis do love dogs. There are probably more dogs in Tel Aviv than in New York City. But not all of them bark like the Canaan. Now the tenants have threatened to poison the food Dr. Menzel feeds these disturbers of the peace.

In her accented English, Dr. Menzel said, "Mr. Golden, if you take care of the publicity for the Kennel Club, I will take care of those tenants."

That was some class, that class of '39

CRUSADERS CAPTURED the Mediterranean port of Acre (today called Akko by the Israelis), which is north of present-day Haifa. Eventually the Crusaders lost the city to Saladin, but before they lost it they built an imposing fortress, still standing, which they named St. Jean d'Acre. This was the fortress Napoleon besieged and could not take.

During the time of the British mandate, St. Jean d'Acre was converted into a prison for Arab and Jewish underground fighters. It was in this prison that the British started executing resistance fighters, the first of whom was Shlomo Ben Joseph.

Fierce riots erupted between Jews and Arabs during the 1930's and terrorists had taken to blowing up buses. The Arabs blew up a bus filled with Jews and the Jews retaliated by blowing up a bus filled with Arabs. Ben Joseph, captured with weapons, was charged directly with the act. There was a question of whether this teen-age boy had, in fact, accurately tossed a grenade into the Arab bus, but the British refused him a retrial. There were sympathy strikes in Palestine and pleas by the influential, but Ben Joseph still went to his death.

The Jew made famous by his martyrdom at Acre was Dov Gruner, who staged a raid on a police station in Ramat Gan outside of Tel Aviv to capture arms for the Irgun. In the melee, Gruner was wounded and captured, then tried and sentenced. Since no British policeman had been either wounded or killed in the raid, the Home Secretary promised to commute Gruner's sentence if he made an appeal. Gruner refused, arguing that he was a prisoner of war and the British had no right to try him in a criminal court. With three comrades, he hanged for his beliefs. The next night the Irgun hanged two British sergeants. Gruner has become a national hero, and a statue in Ramat Gan commemorates his courage. By coincidence, I have known his sister, Mrs. Ernest (Helen Gruner) Friedman, who has lived for many years in Charlotte, North Carolina.

The British turned St. Jean d'Acre into a veritable Alcatraz. With its small barred windows and walls several yards in thickness, it admirably served the purpose of a prison. Its interior spawned cell after cell, into each of which dozens of prisoners could be crowded.

In 1939, the British constabulary staged a surprise raid on one of the Palmach * training camps and arrested 43 officers, all of whom were packed off to Acre. There is a surviving photograph of these Jews smiling at their captors from the prison compound. In the background is a two-eyed Moshe Dayan. The charge against these men was that they were in possession of weapons and conspiring against the Crown. In 1941, however, the British released these officers to help stage an offensive into Syria. It was in this campaign that Dayan lost his eye when an exploding shell drove the binoculars he was holding into it.

St. Jean d'Acre is the scene of one of history's most famous prison breaks. A detachment of the Haganah disguised as British soldiers led by Dov Cohen blew a hole in the fortress wall at the same moment that prisoners inside blew open their cells with smuggled dynamite. Forty-one Jews made their escape and 209 Arabs, who were not apprised of the plan, followed them. The Jews lived to fight another day, for they were provided with clothes, papers, and vehicles, but most of the Arabs were rounded up.

After the War of Independence, the Jews didn't need a prison as badly as they needed a mental hospital. St. Jean d'Acre is now a sanitarium. But one wing has been reserved as a museum to record the lives and deaths and deeds of the heroes who passed through here. The cells are preserved as they were under the mandate, with the thin mats on which the prisoners slept on

* The Palmach, organized by Yitzhak Sadeh, was the kibbutz wing of the Haganah.

the stone floor. Prison garb still hangs on rusting nails. The common slop pails stand by the barred doors.

On the ground floor, the visitor can inspect the gallows. The men who were hanged here lived in solitary cells and wore red burlap uniforms. Photographs of executed Jews slant from the walls. Israel is still in a stage of photographic history, because the Jews have not had time to verbalize or make myth out of all that has happened in the last seventy years.

To illustrate the point, almost all of the 43 officers captured in 1939 still survive and recently had a reunion on one of the kibbutzim in the Sharon Valley. Among these celebrants was Transportation Minister Moshe Carmel, Army Chief-of-Staff Haim Bar-Lev, former Chief-of-Staff Ya'acov Dori, and former Haganah commander Moshe Sneh.

The moral is that it is unwise for a territorial power ever to put all its yeggs in one basket.

O beautiful for patriot's dream

At EIGHT O'CLOCK in the morning, the first of two twin-engined Nord transports began its run over the drop zone. Below, in a training camp south of Rehovot, I was about to see young Israeli paratroopers make their first jump.

A thousand feet above, out they came, leaping from the rear of the plane, their green parachutes mushrooming open with a loud bang.

Near me was an Israeli Army doctor who held a transistor radio close to his ear and intently followed the play-by-play broadcast from Sydney of the soccer game between Israel and Australia. Beside him, two kp's casually guarded a carton of sliced bread and salami.

Before the first paratroopers were down, a second Nord appeared and dropped another stick of fourteen boys. The plane flew on, static lines flapping behind it. Paratroopers began landing in the sandy field all around us. Among the observers was a Jewish family newly emigrated from Canada, the father anxiously training his binoculars on every helmeted soldier to see if it was his son. The Canadian found him far away. He pointed excitedly.

"You can't believe what a chicken kid he was," he said. "He used to make his little brother crawl under the porch for a ball because he was afraid of grasshoppers. Now look at him. An Israeli paratrooper."

Nor was the Canadian the only father there this morning. A paratrooper major led a stick which included his son. They landed, hitting the ground like cowboys thrown from bucking steers, and came up smiling. The major began a serious lecture, telling his son, I learned later, that it was a lot harder when there were people downstairs shooting up. The boy nodded, but I could see by his grin that he didn't think anything was as hard as older men always made out.

The Army doctor with the radio kept shouting to the assembling paratroopers, "The score is one to nothing. Favor us." The young paratroopers were too excited to eat, but I noticed the doctor, the other ground officers, and the kp's were making hash, as it were, of the bread and salami.

There were two young girls with us, too, who lived on the neighboring kibbutz and who were waiting for their sweethearts to land, strip themselves of the harness, and roll up the parachutes. They walked back then, arms around each other's waists.

It was utterly unlike an American experience. A newsman would have to count influential Senators as friends before the Army would let him into Fort Benning. As far as the girls go, those you leave behind you. And I am positive the American Army would not indulge a sentimental major who wanted to give a few pointers to his son or a proud immigrant who just wanted to mill around.

The young paratroopers formed their platoons with a great deal of horseplay. One of the instructors counted heads over and over again before he reported everyone present and accounted for. The soldiers ambled off to trucks which would take them back to their barracks. I remarked to the major who had accompanied me that American paratroopers never stopped dressing right and double-timing.

"We know about the Marine boot camp," said the major, "and the training there. We know how the United States Army trains paratroopers. We are just not sure that is the best way to ask a man to do a hard job."

There must be an essential truth in what he said, I thought, because here were the Israelis with battles raging on the borders still letting the folks get in the way of the war effort.

Israeli paratrooper training is informal, to say the least, and I suspect it is informal because in many ways Israel is still a frontier society. Frontiersmen, as we Americans should know, can take care of themselves and don't need authority telling them to toe the line. People who populate the frontier have a compelling sense of unity, they sense common dangers, and no one has to argue about the need for a common response.

It was impossible to think about this and not think about America. My eldest son was a paratrooper during World War II and his brother was an artillery master sergeant during the Korean War. I felt about them then much as the Canadian immigrant and the Army major felt about their sons today. I am not sure we will ever enjoy unity again.

Well, the truth of the matter is we are not a frontier anymore and we are not always unified. Perhaps we are more fortunate than the Israelis. After all, if you have to fight for your life, there isn't much sense in indulging the question of whether it is right or wrong, you simply have to. And you have to fight together.

When was the last time we were truly unified? I asked myself. World War II? Yet a year before Pearl Harbor, when everybody knew there was going to be another war, there was still a vigorous America First Committee which deplored Lend Lease, an active German-American Bund which deplored Jews, and a vocal group of Communists who deplored capitalistic warmongers—until Hitler invaded Russia. And besides these distractions, there was a huge army of the unemployed. It would be hard to argue we are any more disunified now than we were then. And over five decades ago, I remember, our most popular ditty was "I Didn't Raise My Boy to Be a Soldier."

The transports kept passing over and spilling soldiers into the sky. I could hear the troopers whooping as they came out of the planes. There was enough in Israel to keep them busy. Until Israel found peace, they would not have the time to learn, as

Americans learn between wars, that there are two sides to every question.

Later in the week, through the courtesy of an Israeli police inspector, I made a tour of the gambling and hashish hells of Jaffa with the Tel Aviv vice squad. The vice squad consisted of three tough Jews in different sweaters who, despite the disguise, could not be taken for anything but cops.

We turned into a narrow street. The driver said, "Now we are entering the underwuurld." Several well-lighted old Moorish structures lined the otherwise dark plaza. In the first of these, an emaciated Arab desultorily rolled dice by himself on a large, round, green table, while thirty other men on benches against the wall sat smoking cigarettes and drinking Turkish coffee. No one paid any attention to the three policemen except the proprietor, who graciously offered them a table and pastry to their heart's content. The policemen nodded no.

Thirty seconds before we entered, these customers had ringed the table, frenziedly betting whether the shooter would make his point or crap out. Right now, however, a library wasn't quieter. The Arab at the table rolled the bones again for his own amusement and smiled disarmingly at the vice squad as they left. I thought the dice were awfully small.

"For the suckers," said one of the cops. "A glass or two of brandy and they cannot see to count."

In another casino, several well-dressed people sat primly at a felt-covered card table playing rummy. There was no money on this table either.

"Sometimes I think they know we're coming before we do," sighed one of the vice squad.

I wanted to know what the stakes were, and the young policeman said players could gamble for pisetas, which is not quite worth an American penny, or for thousands of pounds, which is an appreciable amount in dollars. "It's like Las Vegas," he concluded, "you name your stakes and they will take your money."

On foot, we proceeded toward the Mediterranean and then turned a sharp left through a black alley. From the alley we emerged on a flat of small sand dunes on which were pitched a long series of tents. Tar-paper shacks filled out this compound.

Tethered horses whinnied nervously at our approach. A small corral contained several goats. The vice squad called this area Sixtieth Street, because in the old days Jaffa streets had only numbers, never names. It is headquarters for the dope pushers, the dope being mainly hashish. Hashish is a variety of marijuana, stronger and more aromatic. Hashish, in fact, gives us the word "assassin," for political fanatics in the Middle East smoked it before murdering their enemies.

Hashish occupies a great deal of the vice squad's attention. The producers of hashish are the Syrians and the Lebanese, and the consumers used to be the Egyptians. The Six-Day War not only disturbed the normal flow of hashish traffic but left Arab drug pushers with huge inventories which attracted smugglers from all over the world.

Pointing to the dark tents on Sixtieth Street, one of the cops said, "These people live with their animals and some of them have more money under their mattresses than Bank Leumi."

Many of the people living here were Arabs, some were Jews, some were Libyans, and some were American and Canadian hippies.

At the other end of the compound an old man, sitting on an oil drum, stamped out a cigarette.

"Hashish," said one of the squad, sniffing.

The old man trembled as the cops stared at him. Even in the darkness, I could see his eyes darting back and forth. He was afraid, but the policeman passed him by. Smoking hashish in Israel is as serious a crime as selling hashish, but the criminal has to be caught in the act.

We went back to the car and drove toward Tel Aviv, five miles distant. I learned from my guides that there is no organized crime in Israel and crimes of violence are rare. As we passed a neon-lit gas station, one of the cops interrupted to say, "But the holdup at that station was a terrible crime of violence."

Three armed punks drove in and demanded that the owner hand over the money in the cash register. To frighten this obstinate proprietor, one of the crooks began firing his machine gun. One of the bullets killed the gas station attendant and another wounded one of the holdup men. All three were caught.

"A Bonnie and Clyde crime," said the policeman. It impressed

me at that moment that the nomenclature of these Israeli policemen all descended from American jargon: "underworld,"
"sucker," "Vegas," "punk," and the rest. The only indigenous
nomenclature I heard was that the three punks had a "tough
load" to pull, where American slang would have it that they
faced a "long stretch" or a "big rap." This was a disheartening
realization, but one I could not honestly banish. On matters of
crime and violence, others unconsciously and automatically consider us experts.

I began an impassioned defense of my countrymen to the vice
squad, arguing that the majority of Americans wouldn't know
how to smuggle dope or diamonds if the police themselves helped
out.

They didn't quite believe me. They heard the opposite was so,
that Americans knew all about crime.

"What Americans know about," I said, "are their rights."

"Maybe they have to," said one of the cops.

Road spikes and glacé cakes

On the highway from Lod Airport to Tel Aviv we were
stopped by a road block. The Israelis lay two rails of four-inch-
high steel spikes on the right lane and ten yards farther down
similar rails on the left. One by one, while a policeman peers
inside, the cars traverse this narrow ten-yard alleyway.

"The police are looking for Arab terrorists," explained Tommy.
"You will be stopped frequently all over Israel. It can be quite
annoying, but one positive effect the road blocks have had on
the economy is that car thefts are way down. A young man in a
big car gets as thorough a checking as an Arab in a tin lizzie."

"How do the police recognize would-be terrorists?" I asked.

"It's enough if the terrorists recognize the police," said
Tommy.

"It doesn't sound very judicial to me," I said, as we passed
the road block.

"There is a lot we Israelis do that does not seem judicial to
liberal Americans," said Tommy.

All Americans are "liberals" to Israelis. They accuse us of putting on "holier than thou" attitudes without having to live with their difficulties.

"When the Israeli soldiers find a cache of weapons in an Arab house," Tommy went on, "they blow it up. This gives neighboring Arab homeowners something to think about."

"I suspect it leads to a great many blown-up houses," I said.

"It is better to blow up houses than blow out people's brains. Israel is at war. We are at war on the Heights, in Eilat, along the Golan, and certainly on the Canal."

Entering Tel Aviv, however, it was hard to feel this war. The country was preparing for a general election, the quietest in years. There was hardly an issue in sight. Only the Minister of Tourism, Moshe Kol, raised one. He thought the government ought to spend as much money cleaning up the beaches as it spent escorting sympathetic journalists around to erase the Israel-at-war image. Compared to Asbury Park or Coney Island after a July weekend, Israel's Mediterranean beaches are a hygienic paradise.

The avenues in Tel Aviv are dotted with dozens of open-air restaurants. In many of these you can buy eclairs and napoleons and glacé cakes. I believe these originated in ancient Rome, a Mediterranean concoction. It was the Italians who perfected these delicacies and made them world famous. The innovation the Israelis have added is refrigeration. Glacé cakes have proceeded through history and they will march delectably into the twenty-first century together, I am afraid, with the road spikes.

Part *IV*

No Drinking Fountains in
Tel Aviv Parks

God is a mayor

TEL AVIV looks like an immense Chinatown. Instead of Chinamen, however, it is populated by Jews. The sidewalks are filled with flower stalls, vegetable markets, restaurants, cafés, butcher shops, and a bookstore on every corner. The street signs are in both Hebrew and English, but the signs on the stores and on the banks are in Hebrew, an alphabet as calligraphically beautiful as Chinese ideograms.

Tel Avivians brag they live in the New York of the Middle East. Anyone who has ever lived in New York would find Tel Aviv familiar. Still, it doesn't look like New York. The streets are not laid out in the absolute grid system of major American cities. Many of the streets are heavily lined and shaded by trees big enough so that when the municipality dispatches tree surgeons to an ailing eucalyptus, its sawed branches become a traffic obstacle. Nor does Tel Aviv have distinct industrial and shopping areas. Where New York has a garment industry on the West Side around the 30's, an advertising complex on Madison Avenue, and mammoth department stores along Fifth, Tel Aviv does not have similar divisions. People live right beside the El Al Building where the advertisers do their thing. And they live right beside the Shalom Meyer Tower, which houses the biggest department store in Israel. What everyone tells you of the latter is that the tower occupies the site of the original

Herzlia Gymnasium, the first high school in Tel Aviv. In fact, the Jews built the school before they built the city.

The traffic patterns are different. The Israelis buy small cars—Toyotas, Volkswagens, Fiats. Bicycles compound the traffic problem, as do dray horses pulling wagons and the rickshaw-style motorcycles pulling large carts, their cargo protected by a weathered canvas canopy.

Tel Aviv is busy and noisy. The Israelis are always up and about, filling its streets with determined passage. These Jews work a six-day week, opening up at eight and closing at six and often seven in the evening, although many of the shopkeepers follow the continental practice of shutting down during midday between one and three.

Tel Aviv finds peace and quiet on the Sabbath.

And the Sabbath comes to Israel with a vengeance, like a prairie cyclone sweeping away whole towns as it spins over the countryside. You cannot buy a baby milk on the Sabbath unless you show up at the dining room of one of the tourist hotels waving a bottle with a nipple.

The Sabbath starts with the first star on Friday and ends with the appearance of the first star on Saturday. In practice, the Sabbath starts arriving Friday noon and does not depart until Sunday dawn. By dusk the streets are virtually empty. Then you see men in gabardine, carrying shawls, prayer books, and *tvilin,* herding their young sons in yarmulkas decorated with Yemenite silver embroidery, all making for the neighborhood synagogue.

The movies and theaters are dark. The buses are garaged. The newsstands are locked tight, for there are no Saturday papers. Water slowly dries on the florist's cement floor.

On the Sabbath it is not quiet at all along the Dizengoff, a central boulevard in Tel Aviv. Rehov Dizengoff is crowded with literally thousands of Tel Avivians promenading in their finery from the Zina Dizengoff Fountain to Keren Kayemet Street, and often beyond. Quick passage through the crowd is impossible and slow passage is tortuous. Sidewalk artists sketch on the pavement in chalk, a huge crescent of people admiring the handiwork until their swelling numbers attract the police, who tell the artist he can draw anything except a crowd. I saw the same fellow chased week after week from the department store on the corner of Dizengoff and Frishman. Week after week, before the arrival of the cop, the crowd would ask him to draw Moshe Dayan, and week after week he would reply, "I only draw women."

Vendors equipped with pumps sell gigantic balloons which the mommies buy and tie to the stroller to amuse the tots. Whole families span the sidewalk proceeding hand in hand. Young soldiers home for the Sabbath parade with their arms around their girls' necks. Here are the girls in the newest fashion —the "Liquid Look," vinyl miniskirts. There is even a sprinkling of hippies with their long hair and bell-bottom striped trousers, most of them Americans.

Only the coffee shops are open. Every chair in the sidewalk café is occupied, people blockade the entrance to the ice cream parlor, and hungry customers wait patiently at Wimpy's for their hamburgers.

Walk down Gordon Street and you can feel the holiness of the Sabbath. Reach Dizengoff and it is dissipated in a joyous response to sun and air and people and a day off. This sense of celebration is unknown to American Jews. Everybody, willy-nilly, keeps a Jewish holiday in Israel.

The long work week is also eased by the advent of Pesach, Rosh Hashana, Yom Kippur, and another dozen-odd religious holidays. Not all of these are legally a day off, but enough people act on their own initiative so that they become so. Chanukah annually produces Tel Aviv's worse traffic jam. Everyone decides to vanish around noon. But the school children who march down the wide esplanade of Keren Kayemet to the Municipality singing festival songs and carrying flags block egress to the north, which means everyone who wants to leave town has to do so by the west. From Tommy Lapid's window in the *Ma'ariv* Building on Chanukah you see a line of steel and chrome stretching to the horizon, all of it impatiently honking.

Sometimes these partial holidays come as thick and fast as saints' days in Italy. They make one suspect God must have been a mayor who gave each generation of city employees another day off to insure a vote into perpetuity.

Independence Park

THE SHERATON and the Hilton are the two high-rise hotels which dominate the Mediterranean shoreline in Tel Aviv. The distance between the two of them is one half mile, which is filled by the verdant expanse of Independence Park.

Here teen-age boys play soccer even when the temperature is in the 90's. Benches outline the paths. Every thirty yards one comes across a bevy of young mothers surrounded by a ring of perambulators, as though they were pioneers drawing up the wagon train to ward off the Indians. I have counted three separate playgrounds all equipped with sandboxes, seesaws, swings, and jungle gyms.

The unpaved, curving paths are wide, broad, and dusty. There are no cars. But there are a great many dogs. It surprised me to see so many German shepherds. No one needs protection here, even at night in a park. The Israelis are devoted to dogs, so devoted they have refused to pass curbing ordinances.

On one of the bluffs in Independence Park is a monument. A cylindrical pillar supports a soaring eagle. Off this point two Jewish pilots lost their lives flying Piper Cubs against Egyptian pursuit planes. Piper Cubs constituted the better part of the Israeli Air Force in May, 1948.

During World War II, Independence Park was a convalescent base for Royal Air Force fliers. No monuments for them.

There is no vandalism in the park, if you will except Ze'ev Edelman and David Shmidl who were arrested for pulling up plants and cacti. They told the District Court judge that they were observant Jews and they did what they did because the plants and cacti hid couples making love. The judge took a dim view of their piety and found them guilty of destroying public property.

One thing I missed in the park was a drinking fountain. The parks in New York always had drinking fountains which were paved and round which we skated, hoping to squirt a slower and unsuspecting playmate. There were none, nor did I spot any in the park at Tiberias, the park on Arnon Street, or on the huge plaza of the Municipality.

Of course! This land is practically a desert. The Israelis have
to conserve water. They don't even drink it.

Tommy Lapid said my reasoning was logical but specious.
"It's cistern water, stale, flat. We drink citrus or Tempo soft
drinks or for-two-cents plain, but not water. My wife, Shula, was
born in Tel Aviv and she rarely tasted water until we visited
Switzerland. Then she drank it only because the soda hop didn't
know what two-cents-plain was. Harry, stay away from the
water."

On my next stroll through the park, I saw a sprinkler system
keeping a large bed of petunias in bloom. An Israeli came up,
bent over, took a cup from his pocket, and let the sprinkler fill
it up. He said, "*Shalom*," and offered me a swig.

The orange groves need a great deal of irrigation, which
means costly and precious water. An Israeli agronomist hit on
an idea which had the simplicity of all great discoveries: water
the groves at night. At night, the water does not evaporate as
quickly as it does under the Middle Eastern sun. This idea has
saved Israel millions of gallons of water each season—the greatest
bounty Israel agriculture has ever known.

Crime in Israel

THERE IS no crime to speak of in Israel but, of course,
I am speaking as an American. Law and order, crime in the
streets, drug addiction, and juvenile delinquency are of such
proportions in the United States that they have become election
issues not only in the cities but on the national level. Crime is
not of this proportion in Israel.

That is not to say that there are not mischievous and criminal
elements in the country. Crimes are rarely crimes of violence.
There is relatively little murder, even though a higher proportion
of Israelis own firearms than do Americans. The crimes are commercial crimes—the police call them "Jewish crimes"—embezzle-
ment, forgery, fraud, and income tax evasion.

There are some absolutely astounding statistics about the
Israeli crime rate. For instance, the country has the highest

incidence of traffic accidents and fatalities per capita in the world—but there is no drunken driving at all, one case in the last ten years. Patriots say this disastrous statistic is the result of men learning to drive in the Army, where they are expected to take risks, but the real experts, the cab drivers, say it is because the majority of drivers have had autos only for the last few years and they learn to drive in brand-new cars with 120 horsepower.

And there is almost no juvenile delinquency. The reason for this is that Israeli boys and girls all go into the Army at eighteen, where they have better things to do.

The Israeli bad boy perforce drops out of delinquency like the American bad boy drops out of high school. Not everybody wants to go into the Army, which is natural enough, but everybody says he does. "I am the only doctor in the world," an old Rumanian physician told me at a recruiting center, "who is trying to detect sick boys who claim to be healthy."

An Israeli boy who, for one reason or another, does not enter the armed services carries a stigma it takes him a long time to erase.

Yudin Ya'acov is one of these. Last November, Ya'acov sued for induction. He contended that his draft board refused to call him up because his hearing was defective. This handicap, not apparent to others, made him the victim of malicious gossip. He further claimed that his partial deafness did not make him unfit for Army service and that his 4F status caused him unjustifiable shame and visited disgrace upon his family. He won his case. The Supreme Court ordered the Western Galilee Draft Board to induct him forthwith.

I do not mean to insist there are no crimes of violence, for I have already described one, or crimes of passion, or prostitution, for indeed there are all three.

In Tel Aviv a local resident went on trial charged with dousing his cousin with hydrochloric acid. The two men had indulged in a long dispute over the division of the family estate. The defendant hid in the bushes one night and, as his cousin came home, leaped out yelling, "Murderer! Assassin!" and hurled the acid.

But this is hardly as juicy as the Dr. Finch-Carole Tregoff

caper in Los Angeles or as scandalous as the Melvin Powell-Candy Mossler trial in Florida.

Accompanied by the vice squad, I visited a notorious clip joint, the Morris Café, off Allenby Street near the sea in Tel Aviv. As we entered, the whores scattered like crows at the sound of buckshot. The madame, a handsome, dark-haired woman in her thirties, charged forward like a fishwife, asking in Hebrew what did the cops want from her?

The vice squad explained that I was a writer "angleit" who wanted a look at the seamy side.

She turned to me and in a clipped English accent said, "Anything you want to know, sir, ask me. I am the horse's mouth." I learned the hookers spent most of the evening with the tourists pretending, like whores everywhere, that the ginger ale was champagne. Otherwise, she said, her girls were good girls. When the cops roared at this, she became angry again.

On the sidewalk, the policemen beckoned to two teen-aged street walkers. The girls said they charged twenty pounds outside, in the park, and seventy pounds inside, on a bed. "But we charge Canadians more."

"Why Canadians?" I asked.

"They mean Americans," said the cops, "but realized you were one."

One encounters delicacy in the most unexpected places.

The cops close up a brothel in a minute, but Israeli law defines a brothel as a place where two women sell themselves *at the same time.* The Israeli whores know their rights as thoroughly as any American Mafioso.

The newspapers do a thorough job in reporting crime and convictions, but one has to read the copy closely to find dramatic points of interest.

Recently a judge gave the well-known procurer Max Elkayam three and a half years for living off the earnings of a prostitute named Rina Kadosh. The reporter noted that Elkayam had expropriated Miss Kadosh's earnings for the past eight years.

She and Elkayam had lived together since 1960 and were married during part of that time (they were divorced after the girl proved unfaithful). With that kind of morality it is no wonder the judge threw the book at him.

There is crime among the Bedouin, the Arabs, and the Druses.

What threw the police for a loss one week was sheep rustling in the Negev outside Beersheba. The singular fact about the case was that two Bedouin women served as accomplices to the rustlers, an unheard-of deviation from the Bedouin way of life. The Arab women in the villages are never criminal. They are often victims of a crime, but never participants.

From time to time a brother will kill his sister because he thinks she has discovered sex before marriage and thus dishonored the family; and when village feuds flare out, the local Hatfield and McCoys do not worry particularly whether men, women, children, or brothers get in the way of the bullets.

One June, Salah Zabidat, a Druse serving in the Israeli Army, went into the streets of his village, Bosmat Tivon, and machinegunned to death Mahmud and Ahmed Sa'adi. Salah was sentenced to life imprisonment and his brother, Ibrahim, to four years as an accessory. Ibrahim's wife, Turquia, testified that Mahmud had made an indecent proposal to her. She told her husband and he told Salah, who was on leave from the Army and had his Uzi with him.

Arab terrorists are a crucial and continuing problem for the police. Occasionally, the terrorists plant bombs in jars of nescafe which they place on supermarket shelves, and they smuggle in grenades among the bushel baskets of potatoes. But the Israeli and Druse border police have great success in rounding up terrorists. They catch them by good surveillance, good detective work, and good luck. Obviously, too, the police depend upon a network of Arab informers.

Not long ago, an Arab crossed over from Jordan. Like all Arabs, he was subjected to an intensive search by the border police. The police found a small piece of paper in the Arab's knapsack on which was written a name in Arabic.

Asked, "Who is this?" the Arab came up with a lame excuse.

The name belonged to a druggist in Bethlehem. Going from that man to the next, the police eventually arrested forty terrorists in Hebron.

There are three thousand terrorists in Israeli jails right now. The reason for this high number is that when a terrorist is apprehended, he feels at a disadvantage with the other members of his cohort. To level things off, invariably he will tell the police the names of his associates, thus putting everybody at the same disadvantage for the next ten years to life.

The police call the professional Jewish criminal the *parnossah geben*, by which the cops mean the crook provides them with a livelihood. A police officer in the Tel Aviv Fraud Division told me, his voice quivering with admiration, that the Jews are absolutely ingenious in inventing tricks by which to steal money from other Jews.

One of these tricks is to steal foreign correspondence out of letter boxes. Out of one hundred letters from France, Chile, America, or Australia, a thief is bound to find two or three checks. He proceeds to a variety of different banks, opens a checking account in the name of the man to whom the check is made out, and then a week later, when the check has cleared, cashes in.

The Fraud Division maintains a collection of all check forgeries. An expert compares the handwriting on each check. Bit by bit the cops begin to winnow out those which are forged by one man. Invariably, he will be a professional criminal who has done time at "the university," as the Israelis call the penitentiary, and invariably in his dossier there will be a sample of his handwriting. Now all the police have to do is wait to catch the forger with the goods.

The head of the Fraud Division sighed and said, "Being a cop is only a little easier than being Jewish."

Another trick is for a confidence man to walk into a store and tell the proprietor he has just moved into the apartment across the street. This afternoon he and his wife are having a housewarming party. Would the grocery provide these delicacies for him by noon?

The order is ready and the confidence man returns. He apologizes. His wife has not yet returned because she went to the bank to draw out money to pay for the new appliances. Even now there's a porter in the apartment house lobby with a refrigerator. The confidence man owes delivery charges. Would the grocer lend him fifty pounds to discharge the debt? Just add this amount to his order. It works every time. When the grocer delivers the delicacies, the con man is gone and the people in the apartment have lived there for the past fifteen years. These professionals are careful. They never ask the proprietor's wife for either of these favors, because women are able to describe what someone looks like more accurately than men.

Polished diamonds and stones, jewelry, are one of Israel's largest industries. Diamond merchants and brokers have a standing arrangement with banks whereby they deposit packets of diamonds as collateral for loans. The bank will accept the broker's estimation of each packet's worth and the bank will give him access to the vault at any time to show his stones to potential buyers.

A reputable diamond broker in Natanya had a son who wanted to go big time. This young man deposited 48 packets of diamonds in the vault of a Tel Aviv bank which he valued at one million pounds. For a few months he managed the interest rates, but then he began to default. The bank insisted on its payment. The young man authorized the bank to sell packets 3, 5, and 6, which is also a customary way of relieving indebtedness.

By mistake, the bank opened packet no. 1, which was filled not with jewels but bort, the crude stones used to cut diamonds. Over the past months, this fellow had been substituting packets of counterfeit diamonds for packets of real diamonds. Bank managers are never happy about repairing to the police. By the time a banker reaches the Fraud Division, he has a super prescience of mind that the money is gone.

Said the chief of the Fraud Division: "There are two places to cry in Israel: the Wailing Wall and this office."

One of the most notorious con men in Israel is Dr. Samuel Barron, which is one of a dozen names he uses. Dr. Barron makes an appearance at an exclusive shop with the information that he is a surgeon attached to Assuta Hospital. He is one of a team of surgeons, the senior member of which is about to retire. What appropriate gift could the shopkeeper recommend?

Gold watches, of course. Or handcrafted silver cigarette cases. Or this beautiful sterling silver menorah studded with rubies.

Dr. Barron makes several visits, investigations, questioning, considering the appropriateness of the gift. At last he decides and draws out his checkbook. But he demands a ten percent discount as a member of the medical profession.

Naturally the shopkeeper believes in that ten percent. He hands over the gift, which Dr. Barron resells while the check bounces.

This doctor is a good friend of the policemen. Every time he is caught, he asks his interrogator, "In return for my friendship, what can I expect?"

"You know very well what you can expect. It is a five-year term."

"Very well," says the doctor, "I will tell you everything."

David Ellinger is another good friend of the police. At forty-six, Ellinger's record lists 72 previous convictions. The last time he came before the court, convicted on 60 counts of fraud, theft, forgery, impersonation, and drawing checks which had no cover, the judge asked him if he had anything to say.

"Could I be sent to a psychiatrist to see why I behave the way I do?" David asked.

"You have had seventeen years to look for help," said the judge sternly, and he sent him off to the prison farm at Ramle.

By far the greatest imagination the crooks exercise is in smuggling. Hashish and heroin I have discussed; a dope smuggler can realize a $2,000 profit on a $60 investment. But a diamond smuggler can realize even more. Mr. Rafael Jacobi, head of the Criminal Intelligence Division in Tel Aviv, told me how his men controlled smuggling.

"It is not an easy job," he told me. "They think of everything. They smuggle diamonds out in phylacteries, in hollowed-out crucifixes, in cans of peaches, between their toes, and in toothpaste tubes."

The Criminal Intelligence Division employs a ghost squad, policemen who never make an arrest and whose identity is not known even to other policemen but who shadow suspected smugglers, reporting to Jacobi only by telephone.

Often the smugglers of diamonds are the brokers and the merchants. The police suspected one of these men. The ghost squad followed him day and night. The ghost squad knew where he had forged his passport, where he had had his hair dyed blond, where he had bought his luggage, but what they didn't know was where he had secreted the diamonds. He did not have the diamonds when he boarded his flight at the airport. Two members of the ghost squad disguised as passengers flew with the smuggler to London, and still they couldn't detect where he had the diamonds.

But in London, the ghost squad moved. They alerted the customs and after an intensive search, customs turned up the diamonds—in the little airline salt and pepper shakers so many people carry out with them when they leave an airplane. The smuggler had bribed a stewardess to board the aircraft with the diamonds and transfer them when she served luncheon.

Jacobi came to Israel from his native Poland, where he had studied for the rabbinate. A Zionist, he wanted to serve his new country, but the only British organization open to Jews in the 1930's was the Northern Frontier Police, which guarded the Syrian and Lebanese borders. What kept Jacobi in the police was the Haganah, which said he was too valuable a recruit to waste on a yeshiva.

One night he was assigned to guard the British Headquarters in Jaffa. As soon as the colonel went home, Jacobi and other members of the Haganah stole the files and copied all of them in another part of town. In the course of examining these papers, Jacobi came upon his own dossier in which not one fact listed was true. "I had never been to Afula in my life," he insisted, "and not only didn't I read the underground newspaper, I didn't know one was published. But we did find the dossier of a double-agent whom we thought was a loyal member of the Haganah."

No one loves a cop here or anyplace. But in Israel the police profession is never thought of as one on the take. The Israeli police are incorruptible. There is no betting in Israel, which discourages organized crime. Organized crime thrives only when it can corrupt the police. Additionally, there is no money in Israel. The pickpockets have long abandoned Tel Aviv for the Cannes Film Festival or Monte Carlo or Paris in the springtime. The pickpocket who discovers one hundred pounds in an Israeli's wallet is a lucky cutpurse and he takes a chance on a five-year rap for that money which comes to $29.73.

The Israeli Police Force is a national organization, like the FBI, and like the FBI strictly supervised.

Some Israelis attribute their honest government to its Jewish character. The more objective among them say the significant reason for honesty in the administration, the police, and other branches of the government is that all were trained by the British, famed for their incorruptibility, and the British system, in which corruption is almost impossible, is still used.

No government escapes entirely. There is no corruption, but there is "influence," "patronage," if you will. A Rumanian, for example, is the director of the Israeli lottery, the profits of which go to schools and hospitals. Of the 3,000 personnel who administer the lottery, 2,500 are Rumanians.

Well, they say he who has a Hungarian for a friend needs no enemies, and the Hungarians say with the Rumanians around you don't even need Hungarians.

No life for a Jewish boy

"AN ISRAELI architect," sighed my table companion Saadya Mandel, "is no life for a Jewish boy. The Jews have no taste. They never owned the land and they never owned the house. The land and the house belonged to the landlord who was a *goy*. So did the street. Who worries about the *goyim*? Let the house fall down. Throw the garbage into the street. But now we are in Tel Aviv. Now we own the house and we own the land and we own the street. And it makes no difference."

I reminded Saadya that home for the Jews traditionally was the Sabbath table over which the *zayde* presides.

"A balcony, a terrace," he sighed, "can be a thing of exquisite beauty. Try to convince someone of that in Tel Aviv. They will buy the first apartment where the louvers work by remote control."

Saadya Mandel is a Yugoslav who came to Israel as a young boy, studied in Paris, and has practiced in Tel Aviv for the last fifteen years. He is tall, handsome, blue-eyed, and bearded. For eleven months of the year he contends with the unesthetic impulses of the Israelis, and in the off-season he serves as a reservist in an engineering battalion which devotes itself to detonating unexploded Egyptian land mines.

Much conspires against the Israeli architect. There is practically no wood in the country. Buildings must be constructed of stone or concrete. Jerusalem stone is one of the most desirable building materials in the world, but the expense of shipping and transporting make it practicable only for Jerusalem. There is enough technology to make all the concrete Israel needs, but the sand is of inferior quality. Large cracks smirk along the walls of buildings. Brick is costly.

The temperature in the Middle East is equable, which inspires home and apartment owners to do little painting and maintenance. Consequently, there are areas in Tel Aviv shabbier than they need be.

Saadya and I were enjoying luncheon in the Café Tarshish atop old Jaffa, the hill on which the world's oldest living city was built. Old Jaffa is one of Saadya Mandel's esthetic accomplishments. Old Jaffa, which to the west affords a view of the Mediterranean and Andromeda's Rock, to the north of Tel Aviv's curving shoreline has been transformed by Saadya Mandel and two fellow architects into a large Central Park for the residents of Tel Aviv and Jaffa. In this quarter are cafés, restaurants, gift shops, and artist's studios, all of their Moorish architecture integrated. Atop this hill is also the famous St. Peter's Monastery, whose steeple is the tallest object on the shoreline. To one side is the home of Simon, the Tanner, the first non-Jew to become a Christian. In front of the monastery is the newly dug excavation of a Roman atrium.

This quarter is the first successful attempt by the municipality of Tel Aviv to transform a blighted area. This is urban development, and urban development with capital letters.

Israeli architects until now never had the chance to present their ideas of what a modern city needs and should include. For almost a decade there were always new immigrants in Haifa living in tents and barracks through which the fall rains sluiced. The architect who wanted to discuss recreational areas or parking accommodations or cultural centers heard the Minister of Immigration ask, "Supposing those were your kids up there in

Haifa in the tents?" There was no argument. Israel needed housing, and it needed housing urgently, no matter how chaotically planned.

When the pressure of housing new immigrants leveled off, Mandel and his two friends were able to persuade the Municipality that what Tel Aviv urgently needed was another place for people to go.

Apartments in Tel Aviv are cramped because families have grown two and three children larger. There is no privacy. And summer evenings are hot. Consequently, Israelis spend as much time as possible out of their homes. That is why they are inveterate vacationers and movie-goers. I saw a line six deep waiting to get in to see Maximilian Schell in *The Castle*, which should go a long way toward proving my point. There is only one day on which to escape, the Sabbath, and until Old Jaffa was developed, there was only one place to escape to, the Dizengoff, which Mandel called "the Disneygoff."

Old Jaffa is as crowded on Friday and Saturday as the Dizengoff, but Old Jaffa is much more attractive. It has not only restaurants but a broad and lovely park, not only shops but also a complement of artists who live here. Old Jaffa is not at all gaudy. Mandel and his colleagues maintain a strict supervision. They determine in exactly which window a proprietor or resident can install an air conditioner, lest it offend the total scale of architectural values.

I told Mandel the Tarshish was a dandy place to eat, and he said sadly, "It will take Israelis another fifty years before they are as proud of their homes as the American Indian is of his tepee."

English with seventy accents

It TAKES time and enterprise to find someone in New York City who speaks fluent Serbo-Croatian or the Indian dialect of Coocheen. It is relatively easy to find a Hungarian, but the chances of his speaking an honest English are something else again.

You could find someone who spoke at least one of these languages on any street corner in Tel Aviv.

Employment questionnaires have five spaces in which the applicant can list the languages he speaks. If a corporation president in the United States speaks two languages, *Fortune* will devote several paragraphs to this facility.

The population of Israel is one quarter that of New York City, yet these 2,500,000 people speak seventy languages.

Everyone speaks Hebrew.

The children of European immigrants are usually also proficient in their parents' native tongue—Yiddish, German, Polish—and the children of North African immigrants are usually proficient in theirs, French. Sephardim speak Ladino, which is related to Spanish as Yiddish is related to German, and most sabras and all Oriental Jews speak Arabic.

In addition, virtually all educated Israelis speak English. English is taught in grammar school and it is a prerequisite for college, because the textbooks are in English.

English enjoys a special status in Israel. During the British mandate, mostly government employees spoke it. It was the language of the imperialist. But this dislike ended with independence. English is the *lingua franca* of international life, in diplomacy, in science, and in tourism, and American tourists are part and parcel of Israeli life.

The American paperback book, the least expensive reading available in Israel, played a great role in spreading the English language as well. So too, curiously, did *Time* magazine, which is "required reading" in the homes of the educated, more so than in the United States.

Political, economic, and family ties with America also exerted some influence.

American influence on Israel is profound. Israelis unaffectedly have adopted many of our idioms. Israelis know the names of our Senators, have memorized the "Gettysburg Address" and are unhappy about Abe Fortas.

One Israeli, disagreeing with another, said to me, "Do not listen to him. He is not the real McCohen."

I went to the village of Kfar Shmaryahu in a cab. It is a beautiful small town, filled with expansive villas all surrounded with exquisite shrubbery. As my cab driver counted out the change, he said, "This, sir, is the place where the Levys speak only to the Cohens and the Cohens speak only to God."

Naming day in the homeland

THE AHUZAT BAYIT was the name adopted by a group of sixty Jewish families in Jaffa who decided in 1909 to found a Jewish garden suburb to the north. These sixty families purchased a 600-*dunam* tract of land, whose sand dunes they leveled with shovels and camels and on which they built a brick factory.

At a general meeting in the fall of 1909, Meir Dizengoff, the president of the association, put to the membership the important question of a name for their town. The minutes of the association record their decision.

A Mrs. Sheinken proposed the name Tel Aviv, a free translation of the German word *Altneuland*, the title coined by Herzl to describe the old land new Jews would reclaim. Tel Aviv signified the mound where the ears of corn would sprout. It had an urban sound to it. *Tel* means "hill," *Aviv* means "spring."

Professor Shapiro suggested the name Herzlia.

Dizengoff opted for New Jaffa.

These early Zionists would have preferred Biblical names to remind them of their origins, just as the British colonials in America preferred naming their new settlements after the English towns and counties they had left. The Turks, however, prohibited Jewish immigrants from using Biblical names for their settlements. The early towns in Israel, like Rishon le Zion, which means "the first town in Zion," or Petah Tikvah, which means "Gate of Hope," therefore have no religious significance. Debate at the general meeting was joined. Should the association adopt a name which had hidden meanings? Would such a name endear itself to friends abroad?

It was a protracted discussion which carried over the winter into the spring of 1910, when Dizengoff ruled they needed the name forthwith. He read the list of proposed names: Tel Aviv, New Jaffa, Herzlia, and Haviva, which means "very dear." Tel Aviv received 25 out of 42 votes. The first Jewish city in modern times was thus christened, if you will pardon the expression.

The first homes had been constructed, the first high school filled with students, when the association proceeded to the naming of the streets. There was a consensus that practice should dictate principle. They had already named their rude streets after Zionist leaders—there was now a Nordau and a Rothschild Street.

An objection. What if Tel Aviv wanted to name a street after Smolenskin or Pinsker? Tel Aviv was naming streets after Zionists, but it also was naming streets after the Russian towns of Smolensk and Pinsk. Perhaps it was wiser to use Hebrew for all the street names. The motion failed when Dizengoff confided that if a street were named after him he would much prefer it be called Dizengoff than Rehov Meir ben Moshe.

The streets in Tel Aviv retell Zionist history—as long as the pedestrian knows that Jabotinsky was a militant journalist who formed the revisionist movement in the 1920's and that Ruppin was an economist in the second aliyah, whose theories were as important to the kibbutz as Keynes's theories to deficit finance.

Tel Aviv doesn't have a Main Street or a Broadway. It has a Keren Kayemet, named after the Jewish fund-raising agency, and an Allenby, named after the British general who took Jerusalem from the Turks in 1918. In its streets the city has preserved its creation.

Tel Aviv does more. There are a dozen pocket museums throughout the city located in the homes in which these early settlers lived. The Tel Aviv Museum on Sderot Rothschild is where Dizengoff lived as Tel Aviv's mayor. What a home it was! Twenty-foot-high ceilings, parqueted floors in rich colors, broad stairways.

Here are displayed the paintings and sculpture of Israeli artists. I call it a pocket museum because it simply doesn't take more than twenty or thirty minutes to move through it.

The sedate Tel Aviv Museum, with its portraits of ladies in floppy hats and long gloves, is an appropriate memorial to the handsome, vigorous Dizengoff, who proved the political axiom that a man will not make a good conservative at forty if he does not throw bombs at eighteen. Born in 1861 in Bessarabia, Dizengoff was arrested by the Czarist police in 1879 for anarchist activities. In jail, he began to speculate about his fate as a Jew. After he was released, he went to Paris to study chemistry. He met Baron Rothschild and convinced him that the distilleries the Baron financed in Rishon le Zion ought to vint wine in bottles made in Palestine.

Dizengoff set up the glassworks at Tantura, but neither he nor anyone else took into account the nearby Kabara marshes. Malaria decimated the workers. Malaria made Zina Dizengoff give birth to a stillborn child, Dizengoff's only offspring.

The glassworks moved. In 1901, Dizengoff quarreled openly with Baron Rothschild, who had his own ideas about how to build a national home for the Jews. In an open letter to a Zionist weekly, Dizengoff said the Baron was self-seeking. "You can build a synagogue to your taste," he wrote, "and invite anyone you like. But the humblest of your guests will be right in barring you from entering your synagogue with your head uncovered."

The letter lost him his job. He went to Jaffa in 1905, the head of a settlement group called Geula, for whom he had raised money to start settlements in Palestine. Out of Geula came the Ahuzat Bayit, and out of the Bayit, Tel Aviv.

By 1920 there was nothing left of the Russian revolutionary. By 1920 the former anarchist was arguing as a hard-headed realistic mayor that it was futile to insist that the Jewish plantation owners hire only Jewish labor. "Where," he asked, "would towns like Petah Tikvah find the car drivers, the ditch diggers, and the watchmen, if the plantations had to switch over suddenly?" But in 1920, Dizengoff was not only the mayor of Tel Aviv, with visions that the city would grow to 100,000 someday; he was also a successful shipping magnate and an inveterate optimist. At the ceremonies which announced the work on Tel Aviv's harbor, Dizengoff threw the first symbolic stone into the water where the docks were to stand. "Now that Tel Aviv is a great world port . . ." he began his speech.

Before his death in 1936, Dizengoff and his town clerk paid a New Zealand pilot one half a Palestine pound for a five-minute ride over Tel Aviv in a three-seater airplane.

Dizengoff was spellbound. When they landed, he asked the town clerk, "Will I see it like that from up above?" It was the only time he ever mentioned the hereafter, the one kind of future for which his common sense and vitality could do little to prepare him.

Not far from the Tel Aviv Museum, across Allenby Street at 22 Rehov Bialik, is Bet Bialik, formerly the home of Chaim Nachman Bialik, Israel's national poet. Bialik was the first Hebrew poet to gain a worldwide reputation. It was he who said that the Jews would become a nation on the day a Jewish cop arrested a Jewish whore who was sentenced by a Jewish judge.

Bialik was born in Radi, a small Russian town in the Ukraine, in 1873. By the time he was thirty, he was an established poet living and writing in Odessa.

In 1903, Russian Cossacks massacred the Jews in the city of Kishinev. The Zionists commissioned Bialik to go to Kishinev and bring back a report. Instead of a report, Bialik wrote a bitter poem, "In the City of Slaughter." The response of Russian Jews was overwhelming, as intense as the response of the American abolitionists to Harriet Beecher Stowe's *Uncle Tom's Cabin*.

Bialik inspired Jews in the Pales of Settlement to set up not only defense organizations but Zionist organizations to help settlers move to Palestine.

Bialik settled in Tel Aviv in 1924. His poem "Strength to the Hands Who Toil for the Homeland" is the Jewish workers' hymn, as well known as the "Hatikvah," the Israeli national anthem. Bialik died suddenly after a minor operation in Vienna in 1934. His wife donated their home, as spacious and as comfortable as Dizengoff's, to the city for a national museum and library. It has been preserved much as Bialik left it, his desk and its cluttered papers undisturbed and intact, books marching up the stairs, easy chairs facing for casual conversation. Among the many curios in this pocket museum is a clock, the gift of a Jewish watchmaker in Paris who toiled over it for ten years. On the hour, its chimes ring out the strains of the "Hatikvah."

The razzle-dazzle show is at Bet Haganah, at Sderot 23 Rothschild. This museum displays the weaponry, uniforms, and early photographs of the Haganah. It is housed in what was formerly the home of Eliyahu Golomb, the Haganah's founder. *Haganah* means "defense" in Hebrew, and Golomb, who immigrated to

Palestine in 1909, formed this underground army from various groups which belonged to the Histadrut Defense Committee.

The anti-Jewish riots of 1920–21, 1929, and 1936–39 called the Haganah into existence. It trained its members in the use of small arms fighting and in small independent units. The Haganah differed from Arab organizations in that it insisted on a high standard of discipline, that it was remarkably mobile for a force without regular transport, and that its members learned from the British how to fight at night.

There is no museum in Tel Aviv which re-creates the accomplishment of Eliezer Ben-Yehuda, the Jewish scholar from Lithuania whose life work was the revival of Hebrew. Perhaps Ben-Yehuda doesn't need a pocket museum. All of Hebrew-speaking Israel is Bet Ben-Yehuda.

As a matter of curious fact, the only biography of Eliezer Ben-Yehuda is by the American writer, Robert St. John (Doubleday Anchor Books, 1958). But anyone who comes to Tel Aviv must cross Ben-Yehuda Street, which slices through the heart of the city. The pedestrian ought to know that early in his life Ben-Yehuda saw that if Jews from all over the world were to collect in the Jewish state they would need the unifying force of a common language. So after he left Russia in 1881, he spent the next forty years fitting the language of the Bible, Talmudic prayer, and homiletics into practical everyday use. Palestinian Jews worried how the Ben-Yehudas could raise a child whose baby talk was Hebrew. Ben-Yehuda refused to speak to anyone but in Hebrew. By the time of his death in 1922, Hebrew, a "dead" language, was the universal language among the Palestinian Jews. Ben-Yehuda brought this about by the publication of a Hebrew dictionary he had spent thirty years compiling. It was no mere list of Hebrew words and definitions. Each Hebrew word was translated into German, French, and English. He included Arabic and Syrian references and Greek and Latin precedents. There are twenty columns of type defining the Hebrew word *kee* ("because"). The dictionary is one of the first multilingual dictionaries published, and it is a source book as well.

The revival of the Hebrew language is a cultural miracle. The first question Éamon De Valéra, the President of the Irish Free State, asked Ben-Gurion when they met was, "How did you do it with Hebrew? We could not succeed with Gaelic and we are patriotic as you."

The answer to De Valéra's question is that Gaelic had to compete with William Butler Yeats, John Millington Synge, and James Joyce. Hebrew was the language of the book of whom the Jews are the people.

The romantic profession

I LOOKED forward to a luncheon conversation with several Israeli writers. Since the Six-Day War, the work of Israeli writers has attracted a larger and larger foreign audience. This seemed a conversational gambit.

In my time I have interviewed several American writers and enjoyed the company of many more. American writers never talk about their work. They talk about taxes and world affairs or taxes and World War II, and now they talk about taxes and Vietnam. If you ask an American writer what values he hopes to achieve, he will stare at you as though you had asked him did he or did he not love his wife. Only one American ever gave me an answer to this question, and all he said was, "You must be one of those madmen from the little magazines." Writers, I suppose, are like baseball players: if you cannot write or play baseball naturally, you cannot do it at all; there is no need for nomenclature.

Whatever made me think Israeli writers were any different? I sat with three of the most prestigious in the lobby of the Hotel Sheraton and listened to them discuss taxes and the Arabs. It's all right to be poor or rich in Israel, they agreed. If you're poor, the government will give you an apartment, train you in a skill, and find a job where you can fit in easily. If you're rich, they will give you all the tax breaks you need, because the government needs your capital for investment. It is just terrible to be a middle-class writer. The government wants all your money.

There isn't that much money for the government to claim. A successful Israeli poet can expect to sell 5,000 copies of his book, which would be a fabulous success for an American poet.

No Drinking Fountains in Tel Aviv Parks   135
But if the Israeli poet sold 10,000 copies, he still couldn't pay the airline fare to New York City.

The writers voicing these complaints were Dosh, the famous cartoonist, who looks like a New England farmer, with crooked teeth and weatherbeaten face; Ephraim Kishon, the playwright, journalist, and Israel's foremost humorist, whose play *Goliath* opened off-Broadway to good notices in January, 1970; and Yoram Matmor, another playwright, famous for his wit, whose novel *Who? Me??* was published in America by Simon and Schuster.

The true difference between these three and any three American writers is that the Americans will drink more at lunch. These writers didn't drink at all. The supreme privilege of writing for a living is that luncheon always signals a mid-week Sabbath, as it were, with the rest of the afternoon off because talking is so fatiguing.

Israel is a small nation, these writers complained. Consequently, the fellows in the Internal Revenue Service know everybody.

As a professional reporter, I have found I must work hard to get a writer off the subject of taxes, lest he sink into profound melancholy and deprive literature of his genius.

I asked these gentlemen about American writers.

What they admired about American writers, the three men agreed, was their utter professionalism. An Israeli with a manuscript submits it to a publisher who chooses or does not choose to publish. That is the beginning and the end of editing. Only one house in Israel employs editors who go over the manuscript.

They admired American and English publishers, who are businesslike and submit royalty statements to authors. Getting money out of an Israeli publisher is a matter of convincing him you really need cash this week.

Writing is not the romantic profession in Israel, they said. This is not due to any failure of personality within the writers themselves, who, as you can see, are jolly chaps. The romantic professional is the journalist.

The reason for this is that the men who created Israel were first and foremost journalists. Theodor Herzl came upon the conception of the Jewish state as a columnist for an Austrian newspaper reporting about the Dreyfus Affair; David Ben-Gurion, the first Prime Minister, edited a labor paper in his youth; Vladimir Jabotinsky was also a journalist. There are more streets and houses in Israel named after journalists than there are after generals.

The day to day agitation by journalists in England, Poland, America, Palestine, and Russia was what convinced the world that Israel was a possibility. Tommy Lapid's little boy brags that his father is a journalist for *Ma'ariv*, and never mentions that his father's play was one of the greatest successes ever staged by the Kameri, the best repertory theater of Israel.

Lunching here at the Sheraton, the sun splashing across the damask tablecloth, I was quite impressed with these three fellows. I came to the conclusion I was in the presence of really good writers. I came to this conclusion possibly because I didn't get to talk half as much as I usually do. Maybe because I had to do the drinking for all of us.

Please is *bavakasha*

THE TWO Hebrew words you need to get around in Israel are *ba-vak-a-sha* which is "please" and *to-da-ra-bah* which is "thank you." You need not memorize them now, for they will be the first two words you learn upon arrival.

Every conversational exchange in Israel, whether it is paying a cab driver or discussing an itinerary with Mr. Landor at the Government Press Office, is preceded by *bavakasha* and terminated with *todarabah*, and sometimes in reverse. You can pay your cab driver with *todarabah*, and as he makes change he will say *bavakasha*, as though you were both schoolboys parsing a sentence to find the predicate.

"Please" and "thank you" do not indicate the formal society. Indeed, the opposite is true in Israel. The only man in the country who would dare wear a jacket and necktie in the summer is Abba Eban, the Foreign Minister.

No, the Israelis are informal. They repeat "please" and "thank you" because, though they all suspect there are class distinctions, they want to pretend such distinctions do not exist.

The officers and men in the Army address each other by their first names. There is no need for spit and polish, of course, when not far to the soldier's rear is his own home. And almost every Israeli officer was at one time an enlisted man.

In the composing room of *Ma'ariv*, the publisher addresses his typesetter by first name and the typesetter addresses the boss similarly. The request for locked trays or dummy layouts is included within the parenthesis of *bavakasha* and *todarabah*.

Behind the politeness, the informality of dress, the camaraderie of officers and men is the deep-rooted Socialist ethic. All work is honorable. Work confers dignity upon the worker. Money in Israel doesn't make that much difference. The average Israeli family spends 1,000 pounds a month, which means the average Israeli family makes 1,600 pounds. Out of $110 a week, the taxpayer takes home $80. More money means a car but not a larger house. Most of the apartments and villas are built to the same scale. More money means a vacation in Greece but not finery, because no one wants to compete with the elegant Abba Eban. One month out of the year, the wage earner is in the Army reserves, for which he receives the better part of his salary through a special arrangement between his employer and the state.

But everyone in Israel, salaried or self-employed, executive or laborer, receives complete medical security, from eyeglasses to heart surgery, and not only for himself but for his family, for as little as $5 a month. The average Israeli can hardly afford an auto, but for another $2 a month he can guarantee some of the costs of a college education for his children.

The Socialist ethic insures an absolute and universal equality. And the ethic makes a profound political impression.

The extreme conservative in Israel corresponds to the American who voted for Hubert Humphrey. The Israeli in the political center would vote for Lindsay as mayor on the Liberal Party line. On the far left there are only Socialists—not Social Democrats, not labor leaders (for everyone in Israel is involved in labor), not Communists (for there are few among the Jews here) —but pure-bred Socialists who would think Norman Thomas knew what he was talking about. But the same Socialists

staunchly believe in capital investment, which goes to show that
the Israelis are a versatile people.

Economists call it natural increase

"ISRAEL," SAYS an American who has settled here, "has
done a lot to encourage the birthrate."
Later, I began to wonder: How do governments encourage
"natural increase"?
An American gets a $600-a-year tax exemption for every child
to whose support he substantially contributes. This $600 exemp-
tion is hardly a bonus. Six hundred dollars doesn't go a long way
when it is split up among doctors and dentists, supermarkets, and
shoe stores. An Israeli receives a similar exemption. The money
goes no further. I seriously doubt that either the Israeli or the
American has children in order to claim the exemption.
The Israeli government meets the hospital expenses of birth
and also pays a small bonus to parents who have a fourth child,
but I have not met any middle-class Israeli who have four children. Three children is the maximum, and old-timers say that in
the '30's middle-class parents raised only one child.
The Knesset has often argued about a law which would pay
a bonus for every child. I rather suspect this is one of those bills
to be argued about, not passed. Anyway, to argue that a government encourages a growing birthrate by tax exemptions or small
bonuses is like insisting the government encourages old age by
social security.
A government can boost the birthrate by providing housing
for family units, but neither Americans nor Israelis get an extra
room by virtue of a third or fourth child. Israeli middle-class
housing is cramped by American standards, and I have heard
Israelis complain that much of the new government-sponsored
housing goes to the new immigrants.
A system of free schools certainly should encourage parents;
free schooling equips a child with the skills necessary to make his
or her way in the world. But this is too simple. The American
birthrate has started to decline not because of the pill but be-

cause of the realization of the heavy cost of higher education. Putting four kids through college in middle-class America costs a family upwards of $20,000. A university education is as expensive in Israel, and there are no Merit Scholarships.

The highest birthrate in the world, according to United Nations statistics, occurs among the Arabs who are Israeli citizens. A great majority of the Israeli Arabs live in Arab villages. They are primitive people. Among primitive people there is always a high incidence of birth and an equally high incidence of infant mortality. The Israeli Arabs were suddenly absorbed by a highly industrialized, highly scientific, twentieth-century society, with all of the attendant health facilities of such societies. Arab birthrates did not diminish, but infant mortality did.

People in love do more for the birthrate than all the governments put together.

Deborah

THE DEBORAH HOTEL—pronounced D'vorah—is on the corner of Gordon and Ben-Yehuda streets. It is a modern building, fifteen stories high. It caters to the ultra-Orthodox tourist. There are more yarmulkas on guests in the Deborah than there are in the whole neighborhood.

On Friday afternoon, the girl on the switchboard not only goes home, she throws a white muslin sheet over the switchboard. Over the Sabbath, the desk at the Deborah looks like an early American living room where all the furniture was always covered. Even the tourist brochures disappear until Sunday morning. The management screws a plate over every elevator button, both those in the halls and those in the car. The elevator works automatically, stopping at every odd-numbered floor for five minutes over the next twenty-four hours. There are two signs by the staircase. One reads NO SMOKING, and the other reads POSITIVELY NO SMOKING ON THE SABBATH.

On the street level of the Deborah is the Gordon Cinema; on the lobby level is a dairy restaurant; on the mezzanine, the hotel restaurant; and above that is a synagogue. There is a synagogue in the Hilton Hotel, but the rabbi there wears a yarmulka of white silk; the rabbi at the Deborah means business—his yarmulka is as black as his beard.

No guest can check out on Saturday because it is against Orthodox law to handle money on the Sabbath.

The kitchen prepares the food for the Sabbath before dusk on Friday. No one cooks on the Sabbath. Breakfast is fruits, bread, and hard-boiled eggs; luncheon, cold meats and salads; dinner, cold borscht and gefilte fish. Which led Moshe Barzilai to remark that while the ultra-Orthodox Jew loves fried or scrambled eggs on Sunday, he always manages to forget someone has to transport those eggs on Saturday.

Tel Avivians call the Deborah the "Jewish hotel."

Man does not live by chicken soup alone

ONCE YOU say the food is substantial, you have said it all for the Israeli cuisine. If you like the Israeli breakfast as your main meal, which derives from the kibbutz and consists of all the citrus you can drink, olives, cheeses, tomatoes, peppers, fish, and eggs, you are in business.

Otherwise, the food is simply terrible.

All meat is kosher slaughtered, bloody cuts which are, to say the least, unfamiliar. Personally, I have seen better meat on dying cows than I saw in any Israeli steak house. Meat in America is aged, "marbled" as the butchers call it. An abattoir looks neater than the meat counter at the Super Sol. The clever Israeli housewife buys her meat two weeks in advance and lets the cuts marbelize in the refrigerator.

In addition, meat is dear because it is all imported and kosher slaughtering and its supervision incur extra costs. A pot roast which would feed my son, his wife, and their little boy for two meals costs $8.

Chicken is cheap. Along Ben-Yehuda Street a shopper can purchase a four-pound roasted chicken for $2. Turkey is also a staple of the Israeli diet. The Israeli butcher calls turkey "schnitzel" and sells it in white meat slices, again already roasted and breaded. It passes for veal.

Fish is cheap. And eggs. And an avocado as big as a man's head costs 25¢. The Miron cheese is superb and the bread and the rolls are freshly baked. How did we Americans ever become addicted to bread with additives which comes wrapped in wax paper? An egg and tomato sandwich from an open-air stand costs 12¢ and is an *hors d'oeuvre* of which no one need be ashamed. But there is no pastrami in Israel. There isn't a bagel the length and breadth of the land. The blintzes are crepes suzette. I truly doubt if the Israelis have heard of matzoh ball soup.

On the package of one of the few frozen foods is the warning, "Open within twenty-four hours."

The country is poor, admittedly. But what really devastates the cuisine are the kosher laws. It is against the law to sell ham in Tel Aviv, although the clever housewife again manages. There are small under-the-counter butcher shops. Not only must a chef subtract ham and pork and shrimp and clams from his repertoire, but he cannot mix milk and meat. Beef stroganoff at the Hilton or the Sheraton or the Dan or the King David Hotel is Argentine stew meat disguised by a garlic gravy laden with spices. As I say, it is substantial, but it isn't beef stroganoff. Take away cream sauces from the chef and his ingenuity cannot meet this challenge. Nor should it.

Teddy Kollek remarked that as the mayor of Jerusalem he found Jews crafty, devious, unreasonable, and sometimes corrupt, but never boring. Teddy made that statement because he wasn't thinking about the food in Jerusalem.

Israel is the only civilized country in the world which has yet to produce an internationally famous dish. Even the Swiss have their fondue.

Arbah Arnon *

ARBAH ARNON is 4 Arnon Street in Tel Aviv, the address of a dun-colored concrete apartment house in a neighborhood

* This is by Richard.

one block from the Mediterranean. Our furnished apartment consisted of three small dark rooms on the ground floor—living room, kitchen, and bedroom, and a hall connecting them wide enough to accommodate a dining table. The apartment also had three terraces: one off the bedroom, one off the kitchen, and one off the living room which faced the street. The women hung their wash on clotheslines which crisscrossed these terraces, and every morning Arnon Street echoed with thumping housewives beating rugs hung from the terrace railings. We had no oven in the kitchen, only a small gas range which made cooking difficult, but the bathroom had a tub set on legs and a sunken shower stall whose faucet did not work.

After almost fifteen hours on an El Al flight and three days in the Sheraton Hotel, the apartment house looked like the western prairies to my son, John Goldhurst, twenty-two months old. At the Sheraton, he would point to the jet flying above, then to the luggage, then run to the door saying, "Home." He was happy to settle for Arbah Arnon, with its adventurous terraces, its front yard filled with cactus, and its lobby checkered in marble tile.

Our rent was 900 pounds a month, over $260, expensive by American standards, extravagant by Israeli. We had a couch, two chairs, two tables, and a rug in the front room, ill-matched cutlery and china in the kitchen, and a bed and one reading lamp in the back.

The advantage of Arnon Street outweighed the expense. We were in the middle of Tel Aviv, a taxi stand two blocks away, the florist shop, the Super Sol, the embassy library all within walking distance. And we had a telephone, the only one in the apartment building.

With the kid cavorting around the lobby all day, we met the neighbors. There were Mr. and Mrs. Izzy Merlin. He was a retired photographer. They invited us for tea and television. We had called our apartment "the tenement," but their apartment was stunning, one room larger than ours, with louvered screening around the living-room terrace. Oriental rugs covered the terrazzo tile, a photographic mural decorated one wall, and we sat on expensive, upholstered furniture. On the second floor was Mrs. Mickey Grietzer, the pert pretty mother of four-month-old Donna and five-year-old Elan. One Sabbath, as she and my wife,

Doris, chatted in the lobby, her apartment door blew shut, putting Mickey on the outside without a key and the baby, who was hungry, on the inside. Elan led me through the streets to the restaurant his father owned, and we secured his key, raced back, and all hands were safe. Below us in the basement, beside the air raid shelter, was the studio of Hugo Fisher, a commercial artist. Hugo invited Doris and me and John downstairs one noon to sample his martinis, which he boasted were the best in Israel. A martini to an Israeli expert is a splash of Martini and Rossi Sweet Vermouth.

To the left of Arbah Arnon was a small park and playground. One exit let upon Gordon Street and the other upon Hayarkon, right above the beach.

Beside this park was Israel Shragar's grocery. Its high shelves were filled with canned goods which rusted quickly because the store was so near the sea. In the back of the store was a large refrigerator-counter, behind which Israel dispensed milk, cheese, rolls, yogurt, butter, and herring. There was also a shelf on which two huge jars yawned, filled with penny candy. It was the kind of neighborhood store where customers settled accounts with Israel once a month. He didn't need a cash register.

With the other neighbors, many of the women still in bathrobes, slippers, and hair curlers, I used to make an appearance every morning for the rolls, two bottles of milk, grapefruit juice for Doris, apple juice for John, and three liters of Israeli beer for me. I am sure I was the only customer who bought beer regularly and, when the case was emptied, I asked Israel why he didn't order more.

"I did," he said.

"Why don't you tell them you need it right away for a thirsty American?"

"Because beer in Israel is a monopoly. You don't tell monopolies anything."

Israel was a burly man, quite handsome, perhaps twenty-six years old. He had broken his back in the Army and he told me, "If you are a perfect physical specimen, the Army gives you a rating of 95. If you have an ulcer, say, you're 85. Deaf, you'd be 70. My rating is 45. You know the auxiliary police, the old men who open ladies' handbags in search for bombs in the movies? I don't even belong with them."

He didn't appear handicapped when he dragged eight cases of milk into his store each morning or when he unloaded cartons of canned goods from a waiting delivery truck. He spoke four languages: Hebrew, English, Arabic, and German—for the neighborhood was German. I had to consult him often about what directions the post office was giving me when the mailman left notices in my box.

Shoshanna was his wife. Israel called her Shoshi. She was petite, with big brown buttons for eyes and beautiful black hair in high curls. Just before Thanksgiving, the Shragars had a baby boy named Itzhak and Israel invited us to the bris.

I asked Tommy Lapid about an appropriate gift and he said, "You go into a baby store and ask for a bris present. They have them already wrapped. Bris presents are big business in Israel."

Itzhak's circumcision took place in the lobby of the Metropolitan Hotel, three blocks south of the American Embassy. In the rear of the lobby were several tables laden with cold cuts, bread, fish, brandy, soft drinks, cakes, and cookies. The front was jammed with relatives, many of them, like us, accompanied by a small child, all of whom kept performing their toiletries on the gravel outside.

In an anteroom behind the lobby, Shoshi tended Itzhak. Her eyes were damp with tears of concern. She told Doris the mohel would give Itzhak a baby bottle filled with wine, which would get the baby drunk so it wouldn't hurt so much.

The mohel, who performs the ritual, was an hour late. The *mispochah* in the lobby was rapidly becoming the *gantza mispochah*. At last the mohel arrived, shrugging at his tardiness, telling the impatient father, "I'm a busy, busy man." He clothed Israel in a gold-tasseled shawl, produced a silken pillow for Itzhak, and made himself resplendent in a white silken robe and blue felt yarmulka.

Itzhak entered in the arms of his mother, who was now unabashedly crying as she passed the baby over. The *mispochah* formed a thick semicircle to watch the ceremony. As the mohel began his circumcision, Itzhak abandoned the bottle of wine and quite naturally started to cry also. Israel, the father, started sobbing. Out of total sympathy, John Goldhurst began to cry and so did Doris, which I believe was the tip-off * she wasn't Jewish.

When Shoshi thanked us the next day for the baby's jumper, Israel asked, "Your wife, Doris, she isn't Jewish?"

"No, she's not," I said.

"Then your son isn't Jewish," said Shoshi.

Israel put his big hand gently over her mouth and said, "Women have an opinion about everything."

"Being Jewish works differently in America," I explained. "My mother is Irish, but no one has ever called me McGoldhurst."

Shoshi removed Israel's hand and dogmatically said, "You're not Jewish either."

Israel put his hand back and said patiently, "He's a cash customer, Shoshi. He'll tell you what he is." I gathered he also meant one more word and it is five of the best, right across the choppers.

The question, "Are you Jewish?" implies one complete set of attitudes in America and a completely different set of attitudes in Israel. As my grandfather once put it, *gurnisht helfen.*

Since Israel had not one but two cases of beer in the store the next morning, he must have imagined I took offense, which I did not. Since we had arrived in Tel Aviv various Israelis had undertaken to tell us what I was, what Doris was, what John was, and what the book should be about and demanded, "Why isn't that baby down at the beach?"

"Because he eats the sand."

"That makes no difference. He's too pale. Take him to the beach at once."

Walking along Arnon Street, away from the park, led me to Rehov Keren Kayemet. Ten blocks over was the Tel Aviv Zoo. Modest though it is, it is very well planned.

John Goldhurst could traverse the entire diamond of the zoo in an hour and a half. It is a much more interesting zoo than the Biblical Zoo in Jerusalem, whose cages supposedly contain every animal mentioned in the Bible.

Two blocks past the Tel Aviv Zoo was the skyscraper of the

* I can't help myself.

municipality—Town Hall—fronted by a broad four-block-long plaza. In the center of this plaza, one lone tree struggled for life in a big square sandbox. Fourth graders chased soccer balls. Three-year-olds pedaled tricycles. Infants dozed in perambulators. As many fathers as mothers took their children out for a romp, and all of them talked easily to strangers. I told them about America and they told me about their neighborhood or their job. The one subject never discussed was the war along the Canal or on the Jordan. Except once. An Israeli father and I were comparing notes about the physical accomplishments of our sons and I said John had learned how to make a fist.

"Mine will learn," said the man. "He'll wear a uniform, too."

On the way back to Arbah Arnon, John, in his stroller, stopped at all the water gauges. These gauges are set close to the ground in front of the apartment houses. They consist of two dials, the interior one always spinning. The most interesting water gauges in Israel are the double pride of gauges in front of the Basel Hotel on Hayarkon, although the gauges in front of its neighbor, the Ami, around the corner, are not to be passed up either.

Part V

Old Guard and New Force

A morning with the war horse

BEN-GURION does not indulge a dialogue as much as he conducts a history lesson.

Some Israelis confided that Ben-Gurion's time had passed. I insisted I wanted to talk to him anyway. He was, after all, Israel's first Prime Minister and, at eighty-four, just retired from the Knesset where he was one of four members of the State List Party.

David Ben-Gurion is more than an old war horse. He is the only Israeli of Biblical proportions. He fills these proportions because he represents both a political and a moral force. He helped create Israel in the way King Arthur helped create England or George Washington the United States; and he is part of this land and of these people in the way the prophets were part of the land and of the people.

Most of the time Ben-Gurion, a widower, lives in Sde Boker in the middle of the Negev. His home there is a rude affair, a corrugated tin roof covering a small wooden bungalow. An old lock secures a sun-beaten door which is guarded by an Israeli corporal. Ben-Gurion also has a house in Tel Aviv, a villa on Keren Kayemet Street. A sentry shack protects a soldier and a policeman from the light drizzle. Ben-Gurion thinks the soldiers are unnecessary and has recommended their commanders relieve them of this duty—to no avail.

The Tel Aviv villa is spacious. Bookshelves line the walls

of three large rooms on the second floor where the ex-Prime Minister does his work. There are editions in Hebrew, Russian, English, and the complete Greek edition of *Platonis Opera*. Once Ben-Gurion greeted the Prime Minister of Greece in classical Greek—to the Prime Minister's absolute confusion. The white tiled floors are covered by Persian rugs, and Ben-Gurion sits behind a large desk piled on three fronts with newspapers, clippings, magazines, and manuscripts.

He is even smaller than I expected—he had changed in the eight years since I had seen him at a press conference the night before the Eichmann trial opened—a bantamweight, really. And age has snow-whited the tufts of hair around his ears. He met us—I was with Richard—dressed in matching vest and trousers, a big necktie, and—his one concession to comfort—old slippers.

We asked him why he had chosen to live in Sde Boker? On what new projects had he embarked? What were Israel's problems? And what did he think of the recent elections?

He settled behind his desk and began to talk. He said, "I will discuss the election with the Israelis but not with you."

He moved to Sde Boker because it was a kibbutz and because it was a kibbutz in the Negev. Usually he insists his interviewers come there so that they pass through the Negev. The Negev is Israel's future. Even after the acquisitions of the Six-Day War, the Negev is a large portion of Israeli territory. It is the most underpopulated area in the country and, with the exceptions of the Sinai and Saudi Arabia, the most underpopulated area in the Middle East.

Land, he said, is almost as important to Israel as people. Sixty years ago, for a man to make a living in Israel he needed 250 *dunam*. Today a rich Jew owns at best 25 *dunam*, because this small land has been made to yield its total capacity.

With water, the Negev will become industrialized. Then Israel will find its markets in Africa and Asia, to both of which the Negev is nearer than to Europe. The Negev means independence. A country achieves economic independence only by vast and ever-continuing exports.

Sde Boker was a new kibbutz. That was why he went there. The goal of the kibbutz is to become a self-contained community with its own farmlands, industry, and specialized schools. Ben-

Gurion has not outlived his usefulness, nor has the kibbutz outlived its. When he joined Sde Boker, it had 18 members. Today
it has 90. Young men, it is true, leave the kibbutz for the ad-
venture and opportunity offered in the cities, but it is also true
that more young men join than leave.

Lastly, he confessed, he went to the Negev because he dislikes
the confusion and anonymity of the big city. When the Turks
expelled him from Palestine during World War I, he went to
New York City, because he had the name of a valuable Zionist
contact there. For one full year, he searched for that man. He
went over the membership lists of every Zionist organization,
the rolls of the Jewish brotherhoods, and the membership of
every shule and temple on the Lower East Side. This potentially
helpful Zionist had vanished from the face of the earth. Then
one night, ascending the stairs to his tenement apartment, he
met the man he wanted on one of the landings. They had lived
in the same building for the last year, passing each other in the
halls, trying to meet each other by looking into registers.

The projects which engaged him these days weren't the
projects he had anticipated would claim his attention when he
left the Prime Ministry. He had planned to write a comprehensive history of Israel. Modern Israeli history begins, he said, in
1870, and it begins with the founding of Mikve Israel, an agricultural school near Jaffa. The Turks gave the Jews the land and
the building on a 99-year lease. "The lease, by the way, is up
this year," he said, his eyes twinkling, "but there are no Turks
to give it back to."

He discovered this history was an enormous project, claim-
ing too much of his time. It would take him years to complete.
He gave it up. Instead, he wrote a history of the state of Israel
which, he said, is now in the process of being translated into
English. He is midway into his autobiography, which describes
his years in Israel. When he finishes that he will undertake his
autobiography of his youth in Russia.

There were many painful decisions he had to make as Prime
Minister. And some less painful but more personal. "Twice I
had to punish my own son. The first time I was asked to approve
a list of young men recommended for commissions in the Army.
My son's name was on it. I felt if the Prime Minister made his

son an officer, he would be accused of favoritism. So I took his name off. Another time I was asked to approve his appointment to an important administrative post. Again I thought the Prime Minister cannot show favoritism. But my son became an officer anyway and he has always held a steady job."

As to the problems of Israel, the first is and always has been security.

"We have had trouble with the Egyptians since the time of the Exodus."

He told us when he was a young man, newly settled in the Galilee, three Zionists from Jaffa came to visit him. On the way, Bedouin marauders attacked them. In defending themselves, these Jews killed one of the Bedouins. Everyone in the settlement knew that the Bedouins would kill a Jew in revenge. And they did.

In World War I, he went on, it would have been quite possible for the Arabs to have massacred every Jew in Palestine. The Turks didn't care and would gladly have given their permission. What saved the Palestinian Jews was Germany, which at the time was seeking the sympathy of worldwide Jewry. They interceded with the Turks. German influence prevailed. The massacre did not happen.

"Israel's security has always depended upon unlikely allies," he said.

"When the United Nations voted for partition," he continued, "the first chief of state to recognize us was Harry Truman. But the American State Department begged me and the Cabinet not to declare the state. The Americans thought we couldn't last two weeks. But we did declare the state and the Americans placed an arms embargo on the entire Middle East. It is impossible to beat anybody without weapons, not even Arabs, and we wouldn't have lasted but for the Russians. The Russians have been dreaming about Constantinople for centuries. They were anxious to get the British out of the Middle East. They arranged to sell us arms through Czechoslovakia. Now they are dreaming of Constantinople again and they are selling arms to the Egyptians."

He paused. He studied his clenched hands, then put them

behind his head, leaned back, and said, "I thought absorption would be a crucial problem. I don't think so now."

Absorption is the integration of Oriental Jews into the economic and cultural life of European Israel. The government managed to build the housing for these immigrants and full employment eased the color problem. "The European and the Oriental Jews have two things in common," said Ben-Gurion. "They have the same God and the animosity of the world in general."

What Ben-Gurion wants now for Israel is aliyah, immigration. Israel needs all the immigrants she can get. Independence and the state are made by population, not by treaties. "When I say I want more Jews for Israel, I mean I want American Jews. Israel needs an American aliyah." He also wants Russian Jews, but Moscow says no.

As an officer in Zionist organizations over the years, Ben-Gurion always argued that the approach to the Americans should be primarily for people and secondarily for money. His colleagues disagreed, arguing Israel needed first things first.

"I told them America was settled by Europeans, not by European money but by European peoples. I lost the argument but I was right."

Israel has had a widespread East European aliyah, a widespread Oriental and North African aliyah. It will have a widespread aliyah of the English-speaking Jews.

Since this is a golden age for the English-speaking Jew in Britain and the United States, I asked, what made Ben-Gurion feel they would give up Senate, Congressional, and Parliamentary offices, their roles in the arts, in teaching, their seats on the stock exchange?

They will come, the ex-Prime Minister replied positively. There will be an American aliyah to Israel even if there is no widespread anti-Semitism in the United States. The Americans will come because Israel knows what to do with Americans, it can provide places where Americans will realize goals and aims they think important and places where they can realize goals and aims Jews think important. "They will come," he said, "and they will not all be young."

In the nineteenth century, the French Rothschild gave

millions upon millions to encourage the growth of Jewish industries, farms, and utilities in Palestine. In the twentieth, British intellectuals and statesmen, like Lord Balfour, thought they were fulfilling a Biblical obligation by supporting the Zionist cause.

John Adams, the second President of the United States, wrote a Jewish officer that he expected Palestine one day to be both home and state for all the Jews in the world.

I suspect Ben-Gurion has a special affinity for John Adams. Adams was an intellectual, a Bostonian who turned some agrarian mutiny into a mercantile revolution, as Ben-Gurion is an intellectual, a Zionist who melded the refugees from one hundred pogroms into a unified people. Moreover, another Adams, John Quincy, was the only President to return to the House of Representatives after his term of office was over, as Ben-Gurion returned to the Knesset.

Our interview was clearly drawing to a close. Ben-Gurion began reminiscing about other Americans he had known. Roosevelt, he said, was a great friend of the Jews but he could not believe Jews would emigrate to the Middle East after the war. He told Ben-Gurion somehow Germany would want to make a home for displaced European Jewry.

"I told Roosevelt he would have to drive the Jews to Germany with bayonets."

Wryly, he recalled his first meeting John Kennedy, at the time Kennedy had announced his candidacy for the Democratic nomination. "I didn't take the man seriously," Ben-Gurion confessed, "and yet Kennedy became the first American President to sell arms to Israel. His assassination was tragic, not only because it took his life, but because it helped seal the great American mistake of the twentieth century. That mistake was for you to try to isolate China. Had Kennedy lived to succeed himself, I believe he would have moved to correct that mistake."

It was noon. The light rain had stopped. The two sentries were walking around the garden.

"Do you have children?" Ben-Gurion asked my son.

"A boy of two," said Richard.

"Leave him here," said Ben-Gurion. "We'll call him a sabra. I promise."

Win one for the Gipper

ONE OF the reasons why Golda Meir is Prime Minister is
that she is given to homilies, a skill noticeably lacking in most
Israelis. Golda is perfectly capable of telling newspapermen,
"We Jews have learned to hate the Arabs because they made
our boys killers," a sentiment which will come as news to the
grandfathers of these boys, who learned night fighting with Orde
Wingate thirty-five years ago, blew up the King David Hotel,
and helped Yitzhak Sadeh form the Palmach.

Similarly, one of the reasons why Abba Eban is Foreign
Minister is that he can be, on occasion, circumlocutious, another
skill which astounds the Israelis.

Anyone who talks with Israelis will find them shamefully and
painfully direct.

Last fall, the Israeli soccer team beat Australia 1 to 0 in
Ramat Gan. Both teams were trying to qualify as one of 16 to
be invited to the world championship matches scheduled for
Mexico in the summer of 1970. Israel's victory forced a playoff
in Sydney. Israel fought off the Aussies' desperate rally to save
a 1 to 1 tie.

Israel had qualified. The country was jubilant. It was the first
time its national soccer team had won such an honor.

Deputy Premier and Education Minister Yigal Allon wired
the soccer players that his ministry would extend every possible
assistance to help the team prepare for its contests in the World
Cup Games. He promised that nonroutine preparations would
include intensive training, morale boosting, and practice games.
He concluded that all of Israel wished the team well "even
though we know you haven't got a chance to bring home the
Cup."

It is not the kind of pep talk Knute Rockne used to give the
boys in the dressing room. Everyone remembers how the Fighting Irish of Notre Dame trailed Army badly at halftime. Rockne
told the boys he was still proud of them. Before he sent them
back to the field for another mauling, he wanted to tell them a
story about George Gipp, a gentleman, a fine Catholic, and the
greatest football player he had ever coached. George Gipp

caught pneumonia playing in his last game for Notre Dame against Southern Cal and died.

"I was at his bedside the night he passed away," said Rockne. "His last words were, 'Rock, someday when the going's tough, when things look black and Notre Dame doesn't have a chance, ask the boys to go out and win one for the Gipper.'"

I recall the scene as though it were yesterday. Pat O'Brien played Knute Rockne and Ronald Reagan played George Gipp and Notre Dame tore out of the dressing room and chewed Army alive. There are lieutenant generals today who still shudder, remembering that second half.

Israel! Listen to Golda Meir. Listen to Abba Eban!

Go out and win one for Yitzhak Sadeh!

The overcrowded Knesset

THE ISRAELI constituency is represented by 12 political parties. In the order in which the voters returned them, these parties are:

Alignment (the coalition of the Labor-Mapam parties)
Gahal (the loyal opposition)
National Religious Party (11 men in yarmulkas, one lady in a hat)
State List (Ben-Gurion's party)
Independent Liberals (non-Socialist, liberal do-gooders)
Free Center (extreme right wingers; no influence)
Rakah (pro-Soviet Arab Communists)
Arab Lists (*hamoolahs*, huge tribelike Arab families whose head represents them in Parliament)
Agudat Yisrael (extreme right wing of the Othodox Jews)
Polei Aguda (also an Orthodox party with social overtones)
Ha'olam Hazeh (mavericks)
Maki (Jewish Communist party which rejects Moscow's anti-Israel line; slightly respectable)

The Knesset holds 120 members. Each party offers the electorate a list of 120 candidates. If the party wins 51 percent of the vote, it seats its first 61 members on the list. If it wins 10 percent of the vote, it seats its first 12 candidates. If a man does

not mind languishing on a list, it is not hard at all to get into
Israeli politics. Tommy Lapid was number 36 on a list which
elected 4 members. This was an upset election. His party was
hoping for 3. Tommy was the second youngest member on the
list. Had he waited a few years he would be in the Knesset today.
But journalism was more exciting in a country where mothers
brag about "my son, the writer."

The '69 election was low-keyed. The reason? Television had
come to Israel. Television has enlivened American politics.
Everyone in America owns a TV set, and therefore politics becomes an immediate concern to the folks out in viewerland
during October and November. Before television came to Israel,
candidates toured every city, village, and kibbutz, entertaining,
haranguing the constituency at open-air rallies. But now television has led the candidates to concentrate on the larger cities
for public appearance. Since everyone in Israel does not have a
TV set, the election became remote.

The Israeli electoral system has its advantages and disadvantages. No party in Israel promised to retrieve the two Israelis
that the Syrians had kidnapped from the hijacked TWA plane.
A desperate candidate can often offer irresponsible promises in
America, but it is too risky for a party in Israel. Levi Eshkol
once complained during his term in office, "What has happened
to politics? Can't a man make promises anymore?"

One of the disadvantages is that the crucial electioneering
goes on within the party, which leaves the voters no real power
in determining who will preside over the country.

An Israeli MK earns 17,000 pounds a year, a little less than
$5,000, and enjoys a small expense account if he lives outside
Jerusalem. The bus drivers of the Egged cooperative make more
money than Cabinet ministers, because the bus drivers own their
buses and get overtime. The members of government do not.

Politically, the extremist parties don't have a chance, neither
the Arab Communists on the left nor the Merkaz Hofshee (Free
Center) on the right. The extremists make fiery speeches from
time to time, but most of the Knesset members hear them out
as a necessary nuisance.

The Alignment, the party of Golda Meir, Abba Eban, Moshe
Dayan, and Yigal Allon, is the party of the left, and the Gahal—

the fusion of Herut and the right wing of the Liberal Party—is the moderate wing of the nationalists. The Gahal contains the men who gained fame during the British mandate as the Irgun, the terrorist underground. Menachem Begin, the one-time leader who blew up the King David Hotel, has mellowed in his late years. He has become a soft-spoken democrat. Israel cannot afford the luxury of a partisan foreign policy. The Arab pressure makes all policy bipartisan, because foreign and domestic policy are one and the same.

Geographically, Israel is part of the Middle East, but politically she is light-years away from that area where democracy is nothing but mockery. The Arabs always have a chronic shortage of colonels; every colonel who succeeds in a coup immediately dispatches his predecessor. The Syrians are down to captains.

I do not mean to insist the Israelis have solved the art of the politically possible. I imagine there are Cabinet ministers who sit at their desk and cry over the intransigence of their colleagues. Nor are Israelis always happy with their representatives or the Cabinet. There are Israelis as unhappy over some Cabinet appointments as Democrats at a clambake who have to listen to Spiro T. Agnew. Well, not that unhappy. As unhappy as college-educated Republicans at a clambake who have to listen to Spiro T. Agnew.

Though Israelis think their government is a good one, one of the best in years, they still voice these complaints. The Tel Aviv lawyer complains the Knesset is overcrowded with kibbutzniks. They hold seats out of all proportion to their number.

Some complain that the Knesset is overcrowded with Arabs. Not only are the Arabs Communists, they are also Arabs.

The young complain that the Knesset is overcrowded with the old, who are still reciting deeds of their derring-do in the War of Independence and remembering old feuds, irrelevant to these times.

Women complain that the Knesset is overcrowded with men.

Men complain that the Knesset is overcrowded with women.

There are Knesset members who spent four years complaining the Knesset was overcrowded with the New Force Party, there being just one member of the New Force Party in the whole of it.

I can do without the falls

SHE HAS a deep convincing voice which 40 cigarettes a day often makes husky.

She is seventy-three, the toughest grandma in the business.

Ben-Gurion once said of her, "Golda is the only man in my Cabinet."

She is called the best-dressed woman of the nineteenth century.

She still combs her hair like a Ukrainian peasant girl.

Golda Meir was born in Kiev, the capital of the Ukraine, in the midst of anti-Semites and Jews. To understand the Israeli Prime Minister, it is important to remember that anti-Semites and Jews formed her first ideas—not Jews and Christians, but Jews and anti-Semites, because there are few non-Jews in the Ukraine who are not anti-Semites. The prejudice she encountered as a girl explains her basic mistrust of the non-Jewish world. Hitler's holocaust convinced her there were two types of people in the world: Jews and those who put Jews into gas chambers.

The rest of the world stood by. The Jews, she thought, could only rely upon themselves. The Jews, she now insists, should only rely upon themselves. This insistence lets her work easily in tandem with hard-liner Moshe Dayan.

She and Moshe Dayan once traveled in disguise into Jordan to conduct secret talks with King Abdullah in 1950. Abdullah became convinced after the Arab defeat in 1948 that only a peace treaty with Israel would settle burning problems in the Middle East. He feared his fellow Arab rulers and therefore began secret negotiations with Israel. For these talks, the Israelis dispatched Golda Meir, a middle-aged woman of proven political ability, and Moshe Dayan, a young colonel on his way to becoming a legend. It was easier to disguise Golda—she entered Jordan dressed as a man—than it was to disguise Dayan, whose eye patch was difficult to conceal and was recognizable even then. He managed with sunglasses and a British pith helmet.

Abdullah, an Arab sheik with little respect for women, took offense at the presence of Golda Meir; he suspected a deliberate slight. As their talks progressed, however, he came to respect her and they got on very well.

Unfortunately, rumors of the talks seeped out. An Arab nationalist assassinated Abdullah as he left the Al Aksa Mosque one Friday, accompanied by his young grandson, now King Hussein.

The talks must have convinced Golda and Dayan that a *rapprochement* was a lively possibility, because the idea of an alliance with Jordan among Israeli government officials is still discussed. The assassination convinced Hussein, however, that any *rapprochement* with Israel was the quickest way out of this world. Adamantly, he refuses to negotiate. Though Jordan is the weakest, the poorest, the most vulnerable of the Arab nations, and though it has been punished the hardest, Hussein still casts his lot with the United Arab Republic.

Golda Meir was the compromise choice as Prime Minister when Levi Eshkol died in office in 1969.

The Labor Party had two logical choices as Eshkol's successor, both of them present members of the government: Yigal Allon and Moshe Dayan. There is a photograph from the 1930's which shows General Yitzhak Sadeh with his arms around smiling Lieutenants Allon and Dayan. The chances are they haven't smiled at each other since.

In 1969, Allon owned the party apparatus and Dayan owned the people. Most of us know what the people count for in a political decision, but in this instance Dayan owned *all* the people, which would have meant a desperate extra-party fight.

Fearing a split within its ranks, the Labor Party put up Golda Meir. The party leaders knew she was sick, but they hoped she would hold out until the general elections. In this instance, the Jews rather resemble the Catholic College of Cardinals who couldn't decide on Pius's successor; therefore they elected an interregnum pope, hoping to give the contending factions a six-month breathing space. The Catholics chose Giuseppe Cardinal Roncalli, Pope John, who gave Catholics a whole new church. Golda Meir, too, threw away her crutches on nomination and declared, "I am Caesar."

The challenge transformed her. She became vigorous, strong, energetic, a consummate politician, dominating the men, leaving no doubt as to who was boss. Only she can make peace between contending and sometimes bitter Cabinet members.

Her reception in the United States was more enthusiastic than any ever received by Ben-Gurion or Dayan. She handled herself so impressively that President Richard Nixon remarked he was glad she was on his side.

The surprising toughness, however, is not a newly developed characteristic. The toughness is surprising only because she is a woman. Israel sent Golda as Foreign Minister to the independence celebration of the new African nation, Zambia, in 1963. The neighboring Southern Rhodesian government invited all the plenipotentiaries to cross over the border for a view of the Victoria Falls, the highest in the world.

These guests, black and white, accepted the invitation. As they approached the border checkpoint, the Southern Rhodesian police asked them to show their passports in two different lines: one line for whites and one line for blacks.

No sooner had the police made these arrangements, than Golda Meir said quite loudly, "No thank you, I can do without the falls," and turned and left. Every ambassador and dignitary turned and followed her, an exodus she had not anticipated. Golda Meir was so excited by the incident that on the way back to the Zambian capital she fainted, the only womanly privilege she has ever allowed herself.

Her presence in the Israeli political scene irritates the Arabs. Allah deals out punishment to them from the hands of a woman, a Jewish grandmother.

The Israelis have no complexes about having a woman as Prime Minister. There is a Biblical tradition for women leaders which dates from the days of the Prophetess Deborah; and the Jewish mother, as everybody should know by now, plays as prominent a role in Jewish family life as the father.

Golda Meir has little time now for family life. She has a daughter, Sara, who lives on a kibbutz and is married to a Yemenite Jew—Israeli ideals in practice; and a son, Menahem, a gifted cello player who has studied with Casals in Puerto Rico. Both Sara and Menahem have children, and what spare time Golda manages is reserved for home life with these grandchildren.

When not dining out, the Prime Minister still cooks for herself. She is an exquisite chef with Jewish dishes. Better put, she

can do with food what Jewish women are supposed to do. The
government official to whom Golda serves her goldene zup
(a golden chicken soup) knows he is in good standing. She insists
her gefilte fish is better.

She still betrays a fondness for Milwaukee, where she was
raised. She entertained a young American Jew who presented
himself to her office with the explanation, "My parents are from
Milwaukee and they told me when they went to the theater
Golda Meir used to baby-sit. I wanted to thank her for her
kindnesses."

Golda emigrated to Palestine at the age of twenty-three, a
young schoolteacher whose late husband (his name was Myerson) followed her only halfheartedly. Their family life was unhappy and ended in separation. She never discusses personal
history.

For many years she was Foreign Secretary, before becoming
general secretary of the Labor Party. She served as Minister of
Labor and general secretary of the Histadrut, a particularly
meaningful post to her because she is deeply committed to the
Socialist tradition.

Twenty years ago, she used to prophesy that Israel would
become a Socialist state "in our generation." Such prophecies
escape her less and less. She has apparently decided that only a
mild social democracy coupled with private enterprise can create
the economy which will one day make Israel financially independent of foreign aid, including the millions of dollars contributed annually by American Jews. Idealism, she says, will not
induce a large American aliyah; realism will. Somehow Israel
will have to promise Americans they can make a living in the
country.

She can be petty and vengeful; she can be unforgiving; she has
a long memory; she is often Victorian. As Foreign Secretary, she
demoted two promising career diplomats because she knew these
men kept mistresses. And it was not the security of the state
which moved her, either. She moralizes and she likes to teach
and preach, although, in her favor, she is adept and forceful at
both.

With the exception of a carefully chosen few, she mistrusts
journalists and entertains a low opinion of the press generally.

She condescends to newspapermen's questions and gets away with it because she is always able to speak with total conviction even about unconvincing matters. When a reporter asked her if it was more difficult for a woman to be a Prime Minister than a man, she answered, "I don't know. I never was Prime Minister as a man."

She rises early. She works hard. She is in her office by 8 A.M. She spends the day receiving people: members of the government, foreign dignitaries (inevitably Jewish leaders from all over the world), delegations from the kibbutzim and border settlements, trade unionists, and party leaders. She travels constantly, actively participates in conferences, makes three to five speeches a week, and dictates all her official letters. She virtually never answers her private correspondence.

Recently, she confided in Rafael Bashan, an Israeli journalist, that when she went to New York on a mission in 1948, before the state was proclaimed, the immigration officials asked if she had any relatives in the United States.

"I told them yes, I had a sister, but I couldn't tell them her address. They became suspicious. How could a woman have a sister and not know where the sister lives? But how could I explain that I didn't know her address because I never answered her letters? I knew she lived in Bridgeport, Connecticut, and finally one of the officers looked up her name in the telephone book and let me in."

Living in Palestine in the 1920's made her frugal out of necessity; by now, frugality is ingrained. She can agonize over the memory that forty years ago she bought a red blouse in a Tel Aviv gift shop she couldn't really afford. She is sorry she couldn't spend as much time with her children as a good Jewish mother should. But, on the other hand, she doesn't think they suffered by her absence or their poverty.

"When Sara was nine, I had to stop her music lessons because I couldn't pay for them. Sara never complained." Golda loves music, though she has little time for concerts. The last concert she attended was an evening of Yiddish folk songs given by the famous singer Nehama Lifeschitz, who emigrated from the Soviet Union to Israel in 1969. Her favorite composers are

Haydn, Beethoven, Brahms, and Schubert. "I am *alt modish* [old-fashioned]," she declared.

She is *alt modish* about current fashions, too. "A miniskirt on a young woman may look pretty, but when I see a miniskirt on a fat woman, with legs like trunks, I am dumbfounded. Just because a young man in Paris decided this was fashionable? Really! And why do some women think dyed hair is more beautiful than gray?"

The Prime Minister wears only simple dresses which, like the old Model-T Ford, come in a variety of colors—all black. She carries a big handbag stuffed with cigarettes. She smokes Chesterfields, a luxury in Israel, the only one she permits herself. And she looks forward to the day when she can spend more time in her kitchen, the shrine of the Jewish grandmother.

The green line

THE GREEN LINE, according to the Israelis, is the line demarcated by the United Nations' cease-fire order in 1948. The Israelis say they call it the green line because on their side, from the Mediterranean to this line, the land is green; beyond, the land is desert.

Traditionally, in every war room on every map in every modern country, the green line is the front line, behind which is all yours, in front of which is all his.

Maybe the green line in the Tel Aviv war room is red.

Whether the green line is a garden or whether the green line runs from the Golan Heights to the middle of the Suez Canal is unimportant at the moment. What is important is that Arabs are crossing the green line to work on Israeli road gangs, in construction, and in the factories.

Minister of Labor Yosef Almogi authorized the passage of 20,000 Arabs over the green line because the labor shortage in Israel is acute. He was hard-pressed by some Israelis to defend this policy, not so much because the Israelis were afraid of terrorists entering the country, but because they were afraid Arabs would take away jobs from deserving fellow Jews.

The more things change, the more they remain the same.

Minister Almogi argued that the Israeli economy desperately needs manpower. There are no unemployed Jews in Israel.

Also, Israel must do something with these Arabs who have to make a living. Relief is costly and a negative solution. Giving them a job seems the most beneficial of all programs.

Since 1967, Arabs who have crossed the green line have widened 300 miles of old road, built 100 miles of new road, and asphalted another 120 miles of dirt roads.

Industry on the kibbutz is profitable and successful, but it is year-round. To gather the harvest, the kibbutz authorities have often depended upon Arab workers.

Worrying about an Arab stealing a Jew's job only seems new. It is one of the oldest problems in this country.

The basic worry is that if all the Arabs inside the green line were counted in the Israeli census, they would number 1,250,000 —one third of the population.

Twenty thousand Arabs who want to cross the green line is one of the reasons Israel's neighbors do not want peace.

The Israelis are speeding toward the twenty-first century with some of the worries of the twentieth still attending them; the Arabs are still wondering what the nineteenth century did to them.

Musical chairs

THE COALITION of the Labor and Mapam parties won 56 seats in the 1969 election, not an absolute majority. To form a government, Golda Meir had to include members of some minority parties in her Cabinet.

Golda Meir's new Cabinet, therefore, consisted of 24 portfolios (a portfolio being the attaché case in which a Cabinet member transports his peanut butter and jelly sandwich to the Knesset). Twenty-four portfolios, more than ever before, presented the Knesset sergeant at arms with an emergency few offered to help him solve.

The Cabinet table in the plenum of the Knesset was originally planned to accommodate 20 ministers, each minister equipped with a luxurious swivel chair.

On the eve of the Six-Day War, Levi Eshkol enlarged the Cabinet by 3: Menachem Begin and Joseph Sapir as Ministers Without Portfolio, and Moshe Dayan as Minister of Defense. Workmen dismantled the swivel chairs. It was hardly likely that Moshe Dayan would tolerate a straight-backed chair while all about him swiveled at their leisure. Comfortable bentwood chairs ringed the Cabinet table.

Had the coalition won 51 percent of the vote, the swivel chairs would have come back. Golda would have needed only 20 ministers.

Alas.

Mrs. Meir had to create new posts to give members of the National Religious Party and the Independent Liberal Party something to do.

Not only was the plenum crowded, but there was not enough room at the table for 24 ministers. The immediate problem was not acute, because Minister Without Portfolio Yisrael Galili was recovering from an auto accident and Foreign Minister Abba Eban and Minister of Labor Yosef Almogi were both abroad.

A similar problem surfaced in the Knesset Chamber. The coalition had necessarily to alter the seating arrangements. It brought Gahal, with its 26 seats, from the center bloc over to the Speaker's right and pushed several of the other parties into the back, far from the Speaker's dais.

Although the changes had been approved by a special seating committee, the opposition protested that it was deliberately removed from the TV cameras. It appealed for redress to the Speaker, Mr. Reuven Barkatt, who left for Europe immediately.

The Free Center pointed out that the Communists had not been moved, while Ha'olam Hazeh had moved only a fraction. Free Center said it would sit where it always sat, which induced Aguda and Independent Liberals to make similar complaints. They, too, appealed to the Speaker.

Acting Speaker Yitzhak Navon ruled the situation was frozen until Mr. Barkatt returned from abroad.

Which proves my father was right: we Jews are like everybody else only more so.

Go get 'em, Jews

BEFORE CHRISTMAS, 1969, United States Secretary of State William Rogers delivered a statement defining the Nixon administration's Middle East policy.

The statement did not make American Jews happy.

It infuriated the Russians; the Kremlin, in fact, immediately withdrew its earlier, more moderate proposals for a Middle East settlement.

The Arabs did not have time to study the American policy because they were busy stalking out of their own summit meeting at Rabat.

The statement, to say the least, annoyed the Israeli Cabinet, which convened in an emergency session until midnight.

Other Israelis were more casual. An informed consular official told me Secretary Rogers had not laid an egg. His policy statement was designed to get Martha Mitchell, the wife of the Attorney General, off the front pages and get Golda Meir on. Mrs. Mitchell, remember, had spent the fall threatening several Senators with dire punishment if they did not vote to confirm Clement Haynsworth as a Supreme Court Justice. Mrs. Meir, of course, could be depended on to describe "worsening ties" and "deteriorating relationships," which were living literature compared to Mrs. Mitchell's pique.

"You see," said the official, "we are quite aware of what is going on."

When I told another Israeli that life would have been simpler if Moses had turned left instead of right, because then the Jews would have had the oil and the Arabs would have had the sand, he told me to stop worrying. He was quite sure Alaska would prove the biggest gusher in all history. That tundra, he went on, is over a lake of oil. When it comes in, the American oil interests are going to reevaluate their relationships with the Arabs. The Arabs will cease being suppliers and become, instead, competitors, and the American oil interests will say, "Go get 'em, Jews."

There is an area of the collective Israeli consciousness which is never leavened by disappointment.

Desperado

RUTH BONDI, whose book *The Israelis* is required reading
for newly posted American embassy personnel, told me at tea
that Uri Avneri was a dangerous man. Her husband, popular
columnist Rafael Bashan, agreed.

Tommy Lapid said, "Yes, he's dangerous. The idea of an
autonomous Palestinian state for the Arabs is a twisted idea and
a twisted idea is a dangerous idea. But he is important in the
sense his ideas are important and never boring."

Professor Shimon Shamir of Hebrew and Tel Aviv universities,
who doesn't think an autonomous Palestinian state is dangerous,
said, nevertheless, "Avneri is dangerous. He is trying to dilute the
Jewish religion."

Uri Avneri is the Hugh Hefner of the Middle East. He is the
publisher of the magazine *Ha'olam Hazeh* (*New Force*). As many
bared breasts prettily decorate Avneri's magazine as decorate
Playboy, some of the Israeli breasts even prettier, if, indeed, such
a phenomenon is possible. But there is this difference between
them: where Hugh Hefner publishes so that he may philosophize
about a life style in which a playmate becomes soft tonight and
off your hands tomorrow, to use the description of sociology
professors, Avneri publishes to urge peace with the Arabs, a
separation of church and state, a larger Israeli Supreme Court,
and a written constitution.

Hefner has become a multimillionaire while Avneri went into
politics.

Avneri is one of the founders and political leaders of Ha'olam
Hazeh, the New Force Party, named after his magazine.

I met the desperado one November evening at the Knesset in
Jerusalem. It is as hard to get in the Knesset when it is in session
as it is to get into Fort Knox. To top it off, I had forgotten my
passport, so if Avneri did not acknowledge our appointment,
I was going to spend a long time explaining my presence to the
Knesset guards. For the next half hour, I studied the colossal
menorah which stands in front of the Knesset, a gift from the
British Parliament. At last I was directed to the members' dining
room in one of the subterranean floors of the Knesset.

Avneri is a trim, handsome man with a graying Vandyke. A Berliner, he came to Israel as a little boy in 1933. After the War of Independence, he and several of the soldiers he fought with started their magazine. There was no way he thought he could succeed politically in Israel except with a journal. The last successful political party formed in the country was formed by Jabotinsky in 1924. Petitions were futile. At that, it took him almost twenty years before the New Force built a constituency numerous enough to publish its first lists a few weeks before the elections in 1965. Avneri was the only member to win a seat.

In the 1969 elections, the New Force doubled its representation. The assistant editor, Shalom Cohen, also won. The Knesset still rides herd over them, but a desperate Lone Member now has a Tonto.

I think he was suspicious of me at first, but when I told him Ruth Bondi thought he was dangerous, I tapped a wellspring of vanity.

The Six-Day War was one of the most logical in history, he said. It was fought by two peoples who wanted the same thing. Jews and Arabs cannot live together, but each wants the same land. In 1967, the Jews won the war in one of the quickest and most decisive military victories ever scored by one nation over its enemies. Three years later, however, the Israeli military budget is three times as large as it was before the war.

The way to resolve this impasse between Jew and Arab is to create two separate states on the same land. One state is Israel, the Jewish; one Palestine, the Arab.

In March, 1968, Mr. Avneri proposed a 10-point Plan to the Knesset:

1: *THE COUNTRY*
The country as a whole is the homeland of two nations— the Hebrew nation and the Palestinian nation.

2: *THE UNITY OF THE COUNTRY*
The unity of the country, which is spiritually, politically, economically and strategically imperative for all its inhabitants, can be achieved only through an agreement between the two peoples living in it, each of which has a right to national independence.

3: *TWO STATES*
The national integrity of the country's two peoples shall be assured by the existence of two states, the State of Israel and the State of Palestine, linked by political, economic and strategic ties.

4: *THE STATE OF PALESTINE*
Israel shall encourage the establishment of an Arab State of Palestine on the West Bank and in the Gaza strip, provided this state enters, upon its inception, into a political and defence pact with Israel.

5: *BOUNDARIES*
The internal boundaries between the two states shall be based upon frontiers existing prior to the 5th of June 1967. Possible alterations of these demarcation lines can be effected by the mutual consent of both states.

6: *JERUSALEM*
The united city of Jerusalem shall be the capital city of both the State of Israel and the State of Palestine, as well as the seat of their joint institutions.

7: *EXTERNAL AFFINITIES*
The ties between the two states of the country shall contradict neither the particular association between Israel and the Jewish world nor that between Palestine and the Arab world.

8: *TRANS-JORDAN*
The people of Trans-Jordan shall be invited to join the Israeli-Palestinian Pact, either by merger of Trans-Jordan with the State of Palestine or by co-option of Trans-Jordan, as a third state, in the Pact.

9: *SOVEREIGNTY*
Each state of the country shall have full sovereignty regarding any matter not explicitly included in the Pact between them.

10: *THE ISRAELI-PALESTINIAN PACT*
  (a) POLITICAL AGREEMENTS: neither state participating in the Pact shall be permitted to enter into any political arrangement directed against the sister state. Neither state shall enter into any treaty with a foreign country without the prior consent of its sister state.
  (b) ECONOMIC UNION: there shall be no economic barriers within the country other than those established by mutual consent.

(c) SECURITY ARRANGEMENTS: no foreign military forces shall be permitted entry into the country, and effective military guarantees shall be established to prevent armed threats to the country as a whole or to either of its member states. Such guarantees might include demilitarized zones and/or military bases of each state within the territory of its sister state and/or the establishment of a federal army, as prescribed by the Pact.

(d) FREEDOM OF MOVEMENT: there shall be no limitations whatsoever affecting the free movement throughout the whole country of citizens of either state.

(e) BAR TO SETTLEMENT: the settlement of Palestinians in Israel or of Israelis in Palestine shall be allowed only by the mutual consent of the two states.

(f) REFUGEE SETTLEMENT: all Palestinians, whether refugees or emigrants, shall be invited to return to the country. The settling of refugees shall be carried out under the joint responsibility of Israel and Palestine.

(g) IMMIGRATION: each state shall have full sovereignty over all matters concerning immigration into its territory.

(h) OFFICIAL LANGUAGES: Hebrew and Arabic shall be the official languages in both states.

(i) FEDERATION: The Israeli-Palestinian Pact shall serve as a first step towards the establishment of a full federation of the two member states.

(j) ANNULMENT OF THE PACT: The annulment of the Pact, or any part thereof, shall be effected only upon the mutual consent of both states. Any arbitrary annulment of the Pact by one party shall confer upon the other party freedom of action in ensuring the vital interests of its existence and security.

(k) INTEGRATION INTO THE REGION: one fundamental aim of the Israeli-Palestinian Pact shall be to effect the eventual integration of the whole country, with both its states, into an overall regional framework based upon a just peace, political cooperation, a common economic market and collective security provisions, leading towards the establishment of a regional confederation.

The Knesset turned it down, 99 to 1.

In May, 1969, Avneri proposed a resolution in favor of the Four-Power Initiative: In part, it read:

> The absence of any political initiative by the Israeli govern-ment, the frustration of the feelings and aims of the Palestinian nation, and the prolonged military occupation of the Arab ter-ritories of Palestine without any proposed solution have worsened the security situation, increased the loss of life, and have created the possibility of a new war with the very real danger of hostile military intervention by a great power.
>
> In view of this deteriorating situation for which the Israeli government, because of its tragic lack of policy, bears great re-sponsibility, the Great Powers have taken the initiative for creating a settlement between Israel and the neighboring coun-tries. The New Force Party views positively any peace initiative from any source, including a peace initiative by the Great Powers, United States, Russia, France, and Britain, which honors Israel's right to sovereignty, security, and peace.
>
> It is understood that a Great Power settlement according to the principles of the November 22, 1967, Security Council Reso-lution cannot take the place of a real peace—this can result only from a solution of the basic problems reached by way of a direct dialogue between Israel and the Palestinian nation. But such a settlement can arrest the steady deterioration of the situation, solve the most urgent topical problems, and give the peoples of the Middle East the time needed to reach a more meaningful solution to the Arab-Israeli conflict.
>
> Our party calls upon the Israeli government to forgo object-ing in advance to the 4-Power initiative. Rather, we urge the government to adopt a positive attitude toward this initiative and to cooperate with it in order to ensure that the settlement achieved will satisfy Israeli interests according to the following principles:
>
> (a) safe and recognized borders, without annexation of ter-ritory.
>
> (b) recognition of the sovereignty and territorial integrity of Israel, termination of the state of belligerency, de jure and de facto, and liquidation of the Arab boycott.
>
> (c) the unity of Jerusalem—according an appropriate status for the Arab population of the city.
>
> (d) de-militarization of evacuated Arab territories.

(e) freedom of navigation through the Suez Canal and the
Straits of Tiran.

At the same time, the Party urges the government to secure
the participation of the Palestinian nation in all negotiations and
in the settlement.

This proposal was also defeated by the Knesset, this time by
85 to 2.

When I pointed out to Mr. Avneri that he was losing by some
lopsided scores, he said the Israel population had been brain-
washed by the government. The government had *a priori* insisted that no peace was possible and that, therefore, annexation
was the next logical step. Ever since 1967, the country has been
drifting without charting a direction. Alone among industrial
states, Israel is the only one which has never produced a five- or
a ten-year plan for economic development.

I think Mr. Avneri is right when he discusses the political and
economic drift of the state, but there is no military drift. Israeli
air power overcame Egyptian artillery along the Suez in the fall
of 1969 and in the early months of 1970; Israeli air power kept
attacking Egyptian war potential deep inside the country. Egypt
is the only enemy who counts, and the Israelis are close to convincing Egypt that any attack past the Canal is suicidal.

What really should worry the Israeli constituency, Avneri said,
is not the damage terrorist organizations effect, but the counter-
terrorism they inspire.

The New Force Party has engendered bitter feelings among
many Israelis and suffered ridicule from others. Its support is,
according to Avneri, sabra support with relatively more votes
from the Army and students than from the civilian populace.

Professor Dr. H. Shaked, an expert on Arab affairs, told me the
Palestinian state is essentially a Jewish invention, devised by
Ben-Gurion and the Zionists in the 1930's to create an Israel to
which the German Jews could immigrate. No Arab leader has
ever mentioned such an alternative, no Arab organization has
ever endorsed its existence, no Arab economist has ever suggested a Palestinian state would be viable. Some of Avneri's sym-
pathizers admit the Palestinian state he would like to create

would be an Israeli satellite, which is surely contrary to the exercise.

But another expert on Arab affairs said Avneri had his lights. At the end of the Six-Day War, it may not have been possible to bring the Palestinian state into existence, but it was possible to have opened a dialogue about its possibility. The government proved sticky about Jerusalem. Hardly anyone outside the Arab countries ever recommended giving back the Old City, with its shrines, to the Arabs, but Israel could have given back the northern suburbs, which are all Arab, it could have given back Hussein's unfinished castle and perhaps even the brand-new Intercontinental Hotel the Jordanians had just finished financing. This expert was Professor Shimon Shamir, who complained Avneri was dangerous because he was diluting the Jewish religion, a subject to which Mr. Avneri and I next turned.

"American Jews," said Avneri, "are absolutely uncritical about Israel. They worry about the plight of the Jews in Russia. They worry about the plight of the Jews in France. They worry about the plight of the Jews everywhere except the plight of the Jews in Israel. American Jews tolerate conditions in Israel which would drive them to the barricades at home."

I interrupted to wonder just what rights American Jews had in the internal policies of Israel and Mr. Avneri quieted my objection with the statement, "American Jews have paid for Israel. They built it. Why shouldn't they have a voice in the country's religious policies?"

Many Israelis admit Mr. Avneri has a point. Last summer, when a convention of Jewish Reform rabbis wanted to hold services by the Wailing Wall in which men and women would stand together, Orthodox rabbis threatened a fistfight to keep them separate. In the end, responsible officials prevailed upon the Reform rabbis to visit the wall individually. A similar incident in America would quite simply have brought one million Jews to the steps of the Lincoln Memorial for a march on the Capitol.

Avneri asked, "If Israel says it is the home of worldwide Jewry, what does that mean? Whoever heard of a Jewish country where a Reform rabbi cannot go to the Wailing Wall with his wife?"

This situation obtains because Israel has no written constitution. Its Supreme Court, therefore, cannot rule on what constitutes rights but rather on what is equitable. A ruling by the Israeli Supreme Court, which numbers nine men, can be overturned by a majority vote of the Knesset.

Every four years, Avneri said, the political parties promise the electorate they will draft a constitution. But they simply never have the time to get around to it. Without a constitution, the Knesset remains all-powerful. "But then," he sighed, "how can you write a constitution which says it is illegal for a Jew to marry a Christian? A constitution has to be a sensible document and a sensible constitution would insist on a separation of church and state."

Church and state are not separate in Israel.

I put the question directly to Avneri. "Why is there no separation? Why is there no constitution?"

"It is a simple answer," said Avneri. "Ben-Gurion had to devise a coalition with a minority party in order to form his first government. He chose the National Religious Party rather than make compromises with the right or the far left. And the National Religious Party has found that religion is a pork barrel. Who appoints the rabbis? The National Religious Party. Whom do they appoint? Only the Orthodox."

Thus the maverick. But then, what civilized society ever existed without someone to give voice to its internal tensions and contradictions? Israel would be dangerous if there were no Uri Avneri. Tommy Lapid and Ruth Bondi and Rafael Bashan and the professors and some members of the Knesset—no more than 200 people all told—can decide tomorrow what Israel will do with the conquered territories, if they choose. They may well decide upon annexation, but they will certainly have given the matter thought because of the Uri Avneris.

Uri Avneri is the Socratic gadfly of Israel politics. The next day he asked the Prime Minister why she was the only head of government in the world to send Nixon a telegram congratulating him on his speech detailing his plans for Vietnam.

The Prime Minister replied that when Mr. Avneri's declamations were as thoroughly studied as Mr. Nixon's—why she would send him a telegram, too.

Part VI

*Thou Art a Stiff-necked People,
Saith the Lord (Exodus: Ch. XXXIII)*

Comfortable partners

THE SIGN for "plus" is ⊥, not +, because + is a Christian symbol. In taking the oath before a court, an Israeli raises one finger, because there is only one God. Two fingers could mean Father and Son, and three fingers the Trinity.

Israeli jurisprudence yields some of the most advanced and some of the most antiquated laws in the civilized world. There are some laws which were obsolete 3,000 years ago when they were first passed and other laws which socially conscious countries dare not yet implement: a month's severance pay, for instance, for every year of employment, whether severance is for an executive, an unskilled factory worker, or a domestic servant. In America, this severance plan is a unique arrangement between the publishers and the Newspaper Guild. In Israel, it is the law.

Jurisprudence suffers in Israel because there are a dozen political parties, too many for any one party to enjoy an absolute majority in the Knesset. Government always proceeds by a coalition. Neither the left nor the right can summon enough members for a working majority. One minority is always in demand. That minority is the representatives of the religious voters. They are a small minority, barely 15 percent, always ready to join a coalition. They are comfortable partners because they do not have specific foreign or domestic policies or theories about the balance of payments, for that matter. They care only about religious issues. They make few demands. But the demands are still encompassing. They are:

(1) The government coalition (which often extends into municipalities) will keep the Sabbath by force of law. Consequently, there is no public transportation on the Sabbath except for cabs, there are no public services except for the telephone and radio, and there are no financial transactions of a public nature;

(2) The government will finance the cost of religious schools;

(3) The rabbinical courts will have jurisdiction on all matters of personal status.

Personal status most importantly includes marriage and divorce. The rabbinical court determines who may and who may not marry and who may and who may not be divorced (although civil courts determine child support). As a result, there is no civil marriage in Israel. The khadis marry Arabs, the ministers or priests marry Christians, and the Orthodox rabbis marry Jews. There is no intermarriage, because Orthodox rabbis will not marry a Jew and a non-Jew. There is no legal way for two people of different faiths to marry in Israel.

The rabbinical court takes its precedents from ancient Talmudic law, the law of a patriarchal society. All of the legal advantages belong to the man. Adultery on the husband's part is not sufficient reason for divorce; adultery on the wife's part is. A woman is not even an acceptable witness.

Talmudic law prescribes that a widow marry her husband's younger brother if he is still a bachelor. If he chooses not to marry her, he may give her a waiver. If she doesn't have the waiver, she is committed to a lifetime of widowhood, because no rabbi will marry a widow without one. There have been cases where the court ruled that the husband did indeed have a younger brother who thirty years ago chose to remain in Russia. Nevertheless it was the duty of the widow to prove either that the younger brother was married or had died or to secure the waiver.

Cohen in Hebrew means "priest." In Biblical times, the Cohanim constituted the priestly caste. They are forbidden to marry a divorced woman. Rabbis have steadfastly refused to marry any Cohen, Cogan, Kahn, Kahane, or Kaner to a divorcee.

These are not dead letters of the law. Israelis devise ingenious ways to circumvent them.

Keeping the Sabbath is hard on the government-owned airline, El Al. Keeping the Sabbath means putting all the planes in hangars. El Al schedules no flights on Saturdays. But then, this introduces a problem in training new jet pilots. Six days of the week the jets are in service. The only day they are available for training purposes is Saturday.

If you listen hard on the Sabbath you will hear jet airplanes circling the cities. Allegedly, the authorities at El Al discovered a Talmudic injunction which permits a Jew to work on Saturday if he is going to save a life on Sunday. One can only say this is a remarkable textual interpretation. Imagine, one of the prophets anticipated the Boeing 707.

Jewish dietary laws prohibit the eating of shellfish—lobsters, shrimp, clams, etc. Israel has a large fishing industry. When shrimp swim into the nets, the fishermen have been constrained to throw this catch away.

But shrimp, after all, is a valuable seafood. It may not sustain life, but it has sustained many a hungry guest at a cocktail party. Shrimp is a luxury. It commands a high price.

With a constantly expanding population, Israel is always in need of new industry. Someone in authority recently decided it was not the Jewish fisherman's fault if the shrimp swam into his net. Israel needs exports and there are dozens of countries whose population has never heard of the Jewish dietary laws. The government therefore is financing a cannery where these errant shrimp will be frozen and packaged. Lest anyone misunderstand, the government has promised to plaster the plant with signs reading FOR EXPORT ONLY and, if pressed, will also ring the plant with barbed wire in case a shrimp tries to get away.

Wanderers in the suburbs

TUVIA BEN CHORIN is the only rabbi in Israel who goes to war not as a chaplain but as a corporal in a tank regiment.

Though he is only one of five rabbis in the country with a college and graduate school degree, he is the only full-time rabbi whose salary the government refuses to pay. Even his congregation cannot support him.

Rabbi Ben Chorin is an anomaly. He is a Reform rabbi, a Jewish missionary in a land of Jews who supports his wife and two children on the salary paid him by the Central Conference of American Reform Rabbis.

Reform Judaism, the Judaism of many American and English Jews, is for the time being a losing proposition in Eretz Israel.

The rabbis who came in the first four aliyahs were Orthodox rabbis who scrupulously kept to the letter of Talmudic law. They came from Poland, Russia, and Lithuania. They know little if anything about Reform Judaism, which started in Germany in the 1850's. By 1900, however, the Orthodox rabbis in Palestine knew that the Reform rabbis elsewhere were not Zionists. Reform Jews, in fact, were anti-Zionists. Some Reform Jews opposed the emergence of the state of Israel. Supporting Israel, they feared, would affect their loyalty to their adopted country in the West. English, American, and Western European Jews insisted that the universal expression of Judaism was monotheism, that Jews did not need a national movement.

It was not until the 1920's that Reform rabbis like Stephen S. Wise and Abba Hillel Silver and Conservative rabbis like Israel Goldstein began to transform American Jews into Zionists. Rabbi Wise argued that the Irish-Americans had Ireland, the Swedish-Americans Sweden, and the Italo-Americans Italy. Every American had a second homeland and the second homeland for the Jews was a future Israel. While these rabbis did in the end educate their congregations, they never inspired any large-scale American-Jewish immigration into Israel. There was money and sympathy from the Reform Jews but no Reform Jews.

Reform Judaism did not come to Israel until the Germans came in the 1930's, and then it did not take hold. Reform rabbis who fled Germany were forced into other professions as teachers, librarians, or lawyers, because their congregants couldn't support them.

The first Reform synagogue in the state of Israel, Har El, the Mount of God, was established in Jerusalem in 1957. Its founders were Professor Ever Ari, the then vice-president of Hebrew University, a botanist; Ben Or, director of the Israeli Ministry of Education; and Shalom Ben Chorin, a noted lay theologian, the author of *Conversations with Buber, Our Brother, Jesus,* and *The Answer of Jonah.*

Har El's first cantor was Tuvia Ben Chorin.

On the evening before the tanks moved into the Sinai in 1956, Tuvia asked the regimental sergeant in charge of religious affairs if the men could hold a service. The sergeant replied the men could not leave their tanks. Without ten men, a minyan, there can be no Orthodox service.

On his own initiative, Corporal Ben Chorin went from tank to tank and led the men inside in prayer. That more than anything else determined him upon the career of a Reform rabbi.

After being graduated from Hebrew University, Ben Chorin studied for ordination at the Hebrew Theological Seminary in Cincinnati, a more intensive preparation than that undertaken by an Orthodox rabbi who is ordained through studies at a yeshiva, not all of which subscribe to a system of accreditation.

Israel's second Reform temple was founded in 1962 by a small group of mostly working-class families in Ramat Gan, a suburb of Tel Aviv. Its first services were conducted in the home of Yehuda Wholl, the composer. The next year the congregation officially established itself as Temple Emet V'anava, Truth and Humility.

As it attracted more congregants, Emet V'anava found Yehuda Wholl's living room too small. Truth and Humility began its wanderings through the suburb for another home.

For a while, Friday night services took place in the home of a Ramat Gan municipal employee. Nearby lived an Orthodox rabbi, who shortly presented himself before the mayor of Ramat Gan with a complaint. The mayor publicly promised that by Passover he would cleanse Ramat Gan of this "reform *chometz*" (unleavened bread). The mayor promptly called the employee into his office and offered him some fatherly advice, namely, cease these meetings or lose your job.

The congregation went back to its wanderings. But in 1964, with the help of Rabbi J. Kaufman of New York, Mr. Gerald Newman donated $10,000 to Emet V'anava, with which the members bought a large flat. They hired a contractor to make renovations. They asked Tuvia Ben Chorin to become their full-time rabbi.

The neighbors sued, charging Emet V'anava was a public nuisance. The temple would depreciate property values if it persevered in its renovations. A court issued an injunction against these plans.

The congregation counter-sued. After protracted proceedings, the High Court ruled in favor of Emet V'anava. The court instructed the Minister of the Interior to license the congregation. But the court couldn't rule against the neighbors. When Emet V'anava held Friday night service, the children on the block conspiratorially made concerted noise, tenants poured water on the worshipers as they entered the apartment house, lawn mowers chattered in the garden, and trucks and cars honked their horns on the street.

What diminished neighborhood resistance was the fact that Tuvia Ben Chorin is a sabra, and there is a point beyond which even the most intransigent of the pious will not challenge national identity. A sabra enjoys certain advantages over neighbors who are not.

Rabbi Ben Chorin is a muscular five feet seven with a large, sensitive clean-shaven face and a shy, almost diffident manner. He is meticulous in dress. His library in his apartment on Aranha Street resembles that of any American counterpart, except the rabbi works without an air conditioner (but so do Orthodox rabbis in Israel). A secretary typed away furiously at correspondence and attractive Mrs. Ben Chorin, the daughter of a conservative rabbi in Philadelphia, served nescafe. On the rabbi's desk were the typical pictures of his two sons, his wife, and one of himself—in his tanker's uniform standing on the treads with his hand on the cockpit, not looking at all diffident. Tropical foliage grew high in the yard, surrounding a stone terrace.

"Why would a smart Jewish boy like yourself want this kind of *tsouris?*" I asked.

He smiled at the question. I guessed it had been asked many times before. Without a Reform movement, he began, there are the alternatives of Zion without God or a ghetto from the Middle Ages. Orthodoxy does not allow twentieth-century expression.

Prayer books still describe animal and human sacrifice. Israeli women drive jeeps in the Army but are segregated in the shules. Without a Reform movement, Israel will perpetuate archaic laws and customs in which no one believes and which are only unwillingly observed.

"Our submarine the *Dakar* disappeared in the Mediterranean," said Rabbi Ben Chorin. "It went down with all hands. Under Orthodox law, these crewmen are not dead, not until some trace of them is found. Their wives could not remarry or collect insurance or make application to educate their children. An excruciating situation for these poor people, which the chief rabbis did nothing to resolve. It was resolved by the Army rabbi Colonel Shlomo Goren,* who invented fictitious evidence and ruled the men had perished."

The rabbi is counseling a Rumanian Jewess who married a Christian in Bucharest before emigrating. She wants a divorce. She wants to remarry and she does not want to split a small inheritance from her father with her Rumanian husband. No rabbi in Israel will divorce her because she is not married to a Jew. If she returns to Bucharest for her divorce, the Rumanians will not let her out.

True love, which conquers time, space, and the neuroses, always finds a way. The way was recently provided by a lawyer named Ben Manashe, who won an argument before the High Court that marriages and divorces legally sanctioned in other countries are legal in Israel. Israelis who run afoul of Orthodox requirements go to Cyprus to get married in front of a magistrate; Israeli grooms included one of the members of the Supreme Court.

"It has proved a bonanza for the Cypriots," said the rabbi. "Once the Cypriots charged ten pounds for a foreigner to get married. Now they charge several hundred."

The prospects for Reform Judaism, if it has any prospects, advance slowly. Outside of Jerusalem, the Reform movement has enlisted no intellectuals, writers, journalists, or government officials. Nor have we, confessed Ben Chorin, convinced the average Israeli that the country has a religious problem.

* Now General Goren.

This is because the synagogue has lost its attraction for the non-Orthodox. Eighty-five percent of the Israelis do not attend temple services. Perhaps they feel living in Israel is living in a shule, but it is demonstrably certain that more Israelis attend a performance of Bach's *St. Matthew's Passion* than attend a service in the course of a whole year. More Israelis have seen soccer games than have seen the inside of Rachel's Tomb.

"But it is by no means hopeless," said my friend. Now he sounded like the tank corporal. "In the United States I saw television, waited with the crowd for motorcades, went to hear the evangelist Billy Graham. Mass communications are one way of awakening the religious consciousness, unconventional methods another. The Reform movement will have to use them. Israelis are complacent. They live here, speak Hebrew, defend their country. They ask, what more does anyone want? The Jews in the Diaspora are also complacent. They give their money, they identify with us politically and morally, and the Reform movement has even scheduled its world conference for Jerusalem. They ask, what more does anyone want?"

"Specifically, Rabbi Ben Chorin," I asked, "what more could Reform Jews do for Israel?"

"What an easy question," said the rabbi. "If we had an aliyah of one million Reform Jews from America, we would be on easy street."

The other side of the coin

TOMMY LAPID said, "I am introducing you to Nephtali Krause to prove that some of my best friends are Jews."

Nephtali smiled. He is a big man. I would hate to have to squeeze through a door with him at the same time. He is an Orthodox Hassidic Jew. He is a copy editor on *Ma'ariv* and a good friend and close neighbor of Tommy's. Nephtali shook hands and said, "I keep Lapid around to prove that some of *my* best friends are anti-Semites."

We met in the composing room of the newspaper, as the men were getting the first press run ready. Printers walked up with galleys for Tommy or Nephtali to okay, while we indulged our dialogue. Newspapermen develop an uncanny ability to tune out the clatter of linotype machines, the cal-umps of the presses, and the smack of guillotining paper cutters.

Nephtali wiped ink from his hands and said, "The law of the Orthodox is what kept us a people in exile. The law kept us a people, and because we are a people, now we have a state. Israel's future is with Orthodoxy. Even your Reform Rabbi Abba Hillel Silver said so. Orthodox law is more than civil law, more than politics. Orthodox law is the prophetic destiny of the Jewish people."

We talked over a counter which housed shelves of type already locked in their trays. Several times we had to move to let a compositor pull out set type.

"Supposing," said Tommy, "Israel had an aliyah of one million American Jews. What would happen to our prophetic destiny then?"

"Why would an American come here if he is not religious?" asked Nephtali. "To get shot up on the border?"

"I came to write a book," I said. "For the sake of argument let's suppose a million Americans immigrate next year."

Nephtali thought. "I'll tell you what," he said at last. "If one-*half* million Americans come, I will take off my yarmulka, I will shave my beard, and I will smoke cigarettes on the Sabbath."

Nephtali's head is so big and his hair so curly I had to crane to spy his yarmulka. It was a small one which he kept in place with a ladies' bobby pin.

"Ah," said Tommy, leaping with an argument as though it were a rapier, "you are a Zionist before you are Orthodox."

Nephtali lazily waved his big hands, shattering the slender sword. "Zionism is over," he said. "Zionism is the return of the Jews to the homeland. The homeland is ours. The American may well be a nice fellow and a kind Jew but he is not a Zionist."

"Let's skip the aliyah," I said. "Supposing the intellectuals here take up cudgels for the Reform movement? Supposing the writers and the editors and the poets and the teachers insist the Army commission Tuvia Ben Chorin?"

"It will never happen," Nephtali laughed. "The intellectuals like Lapid are too busy trying to convince me, the ultra-Orthodox, to go to Ben Chorin's temple to find the time to go themselves."

"Don't discount us," warned Tommy.

"You eat ham canapés," said Nephtali.

"But you have to admit," I said, "you're carrying an awful lot of old luggage you ought to discard."

"The kibbutz discarded the dray horse and the cart when they became outmoded," said Tommy.

"The 'Hatikva' is only fifty years old," said Nephtali, "and already it is outmoded. Yet everybody stands up and cries when we sing it. Our prayers have survived a long, long time, over two thousand years."

"No one demands the Orthodox get rid of all the prayers," I said. "We just say the prayer books need revision from time to time. The Protestants and the Catholics often revise their prayers."

Nephtali stared at me. "I am happy for the Protestants and the Catholics. I am all for their fooling around with their prayers. The Protestants and the Catholics sit around at night and talk about how crafty we Jews are and we Jews sit around and talk about how dumb they are."

"Dialectics," said Tommy. "Tell me, why should an Israeli who is married to a woman who is crazy or drunk need the approval of one hundred rabbis to get a divorce in the twentieth century?"

"There is no law in the world which doesn't penalize someone," said Nephtali. "Education penalizes the childless. The taxes for new roads penalize the man who flies."

I watched another editor come up beside me and correct copy on a nearby typewriter. Everyone knows Hebrew is read backwards, from right to left, but not everyone realizes that therefore the typewriter platen must also move backwards. But in Hebrew, Arabic numerals read as they do in English. Which means when the editor typed out 1969 he had to type 9691. A fascinating country. He didn't stop to think about it at all.

"If Orthodoxy is so good," I asked, "why haven't we had a prophet since Malachi?"

Nephtali held up his hand sternly to halt a copy boy running to him with corrections. "We Israelis do not resemble Isaiah.

I agree. Each age gets the prophets it deserves." He summoned the copy boy and made his corrections with a flourish.

TV or not TV: Friday night's question

ISRAELI TELEVISION is shamefully dull, as dull as anything on ABC, CBS, or NBC. I'll go further: Israeli television is as dull as anything aired over the BBC in London.

Prime Minister David Ben-Gurion used to admonish the constituency that Israel could not have television until it could afford excellent television.

The Six-Day War changed things. The Israelis acquired a hostile Arab population of 1,000,000 potential viewers with television sets tuned into Egyptian and Jordanian propaganda. Forthwith, the Israeli government instituted television on a crash program to lure the Arabs away from the lies they were hearing.

The Broadcasting Authority prevailed upon some successful journalists and radio producers to get television going. They were headed by an American-born professor of communications—Elihu Katz.

Argued the authority: "There is no trick in producing successful shows with proper equipment, good lighting, and expert cameramen. It is easy to amuse the public with competent actors and natural-born script writers. With enough studio space, an inventive director can televise anything. The trick, fellows, is to produce excellent television with none of these."

It is a trick none of these fellows has managed to pull out of the hat.

After ruining several promising careers, the government discovered the Arabs were still tuned in to Jordan and Egypt, Syrian and Lebanon, even to harmless Cypress. But there are only 5,000 sets in the Administered Territories.

What enlivened the dreary round of Arabic- and French-language programs on Israeli television was the ruling in the fall of 1969 by Justice Y. Berinson that it was a citizen's right to see television on Friday night, the Sabbath eve.

During the summer of 1969, the Broadcasting Authority, a government agency, had announced it would soon schedule programs seven evenings a week. Friday evening programs would bear the prominent legend, "Prepared on Weekdays." By saying nothing, the Cabinet gave its tacit permission for the change.

But after the election, Golda Meir's party was five seats short of a majority, which meant a coalition with the National Religious Party, to whose heart nothing is dearer than the purity of the Sabbath Eve. Accordingly, the Cabinet instructed the Broadcasting Authority to renege on its decision for Friday night television.

The Israelis were outraged. I use the word "outraged" advisedly. Remember that when NBC cut off the last few minutes of the New York Jets-Oakland Raiders football game to show *Heidi*, red-blooded American sports fans were so outraged they blew out the NBC switchboard with over a million angry telephone calls.

Artillery duels rage along the Canal, argued the Israelis. Terrorists invade the large cities. Jet aircraft strike daily. The country is at war in all but name. Is this the time for sectarian politics? Is this the time to deprive the constituency of *The Forsythe Saga?*

Mr. Adi Kaplan of Tel Aviv did not bother telephoning the authority. He took his citizen's case to the courts where High Court Justice Berinson ruled that the Cabinet had to show cause why it rescinded the order to broadcast on Friday evenings. In effect, this show cause "order" permitted the telecast that Friday of the serialization of John Galsworthy's *Forsythe Saga*, produced by the BBC and syndicated all over the world, including the Soviet Union. This drama was followed by the special weekly revue produced by impresario Giora Godik at the Alhambra Theater in Jaffa, which featured belly dancers, who, cute though they were, did little to cool tempers.

Needless to say, chief rabbis Untermann and Nissim made an early appearance at Golda Meir's office on Sunday morning. The entrance to the government building was black with beards and yarmulkas. The rabbis demanded an immediate end to the desecration of the Sabbath.

"Friday television," said Rabbi Untermann, "was a destructive act hitting at the very soul of Judaism."

Golda told them politely Friday television was a political matter.

"You call the Sabbath a party matter?" asked the incredulous Nissim.

Friday night television is still legal in Israel, and a study made by Beilenson Hospital near Tel Aviv proves that since the *Forsythe Saga* auto casualties dropped 80 percent during the Friday programming.

"All of which proves," said my friend Yorem Matmor, the writer, "that Cabinet ministers live remote from the people they govern. An Israeli pays 2,000 pounds for his television set, which is a lot of money. He wants full value for that purchase. He wants television seven, not six, nights a week. A Cabinet minister always has something to do on Friday nights and he cannot understand there are people who do not. Israel is studded with beautiful beaches. The government provides each Cabinet minister with a car, so he can enjoy the beaches any time he wants. But a workingman doesn't have a car. He can enjoy the beaches only on his day off, which is Saturday when there is no public transportation."

For further details, tune in next week, same time, same station.

Heat wave

THE *Sabra Core,* a 10,000-ton refrigerated ship, docked in Haifa carrying 3,600 tons of frozen meat from South America. The captain planned to unload his cargo over the next three days and steam for Australia. But the *Sabra Core* ran into unexpected difficulties.

Though it was December, Israel was suffering an unusual heat wave. Temperatures often reached the low 80's. According to Health Ministry regulations, frozen foods could only be unloaded at night once the temperature reached 68°, because Israel has no refrigerated trucks.

Each extra day in port cost the captain of the *Sabra Core*

$3,000, an expense he bore with fortitude. On Friday afternoon, he learned the port was legally closed that evening and that there was no Saturday night shift.

He plunged down the gangplank and stalked over to the Port Authority. He told the harbor master in no uncertain terms that he had some complaints. It was not his fault Israel did not have refrigerated trucks. They had refrigerated trucks in South America. He failed to see why he and the *Sabra Core* should be penalized for Israel's lack. It was not his fault the government prohibited daytime unloading. They loaded round the clock in South America. Six thousand dollars was a high price for him to pay because the Jews wanted to close down the port on Friday and Saturday. They loaded on Friday and Saturday in South America.

"Wait a minute," asked the harbor master. "You mean you loaded meat on Saturday?"

"They load seven days a week in South America," said the captain, trying to make his point, like a man refusing the blindfold after he has dug his grave.

Up until then, the captain only thought he had trouble. He didn't know what real trouble was until the Haifa rabbinate pointed out to him he had contracted to deliver *kosher* meat. Meat loaded on the Sabbath is not *kashrut*. Perhaps the meat was not kosher.

He waited until Sunday to get rid of the last of the meat, then quickly got up steam for Australia.

Have we already too many nice people?

WHEN ISRAELI naval officer Benjamin Shalit sought to list his children on the Population Register as Jewish, the clerk refused. Lieutenant Commander Shalit is married to the former Anne Geddes, who is of French-Scotch descent. The religious law, the Halakah, defines a Jew as one born of a Jewish mother or a mother who has converted.

When the commander registered his son, Oren, the clerk filled out: *Nationality*—blank; *Religion*—blank. When Shalit registered his daughter, Galya, a different clerk filled out: *Nationality*—father—Jewish, mother—foreigner; *Religion*—none.

Shalit asked the High Court to instruct the Interior Ministry's clerk to register his children as Jewish. By a vote of 5 to 4, the court ruled that a parent could register his child as Jewish by nationality rather than by religion. In simpler terms, the court ruled that a Jew could decide his children are Jewish even if by Talmudic law they are not.

"The Court may have scored a dubious point for civil liberties, but it has put us in danger of losing the whole contest for Jewish continuity," said one rabbi; another said that "the decision can create chaos not only in Israel but the world over." These sentiments came from American rabbis. You can imagine what an Orthodox rabbi in Jerusalem had to say. The most moderate sentiment voiced by the Orthodox was that of the National Religious Party, which threatened to leave the coalition unless the Cabinet reversed the decision.

Which the Cabinet did, within the week. On January 29, 1970, the Cabinet recommended that the Knesset change the Population Registration Law. Only Jews who met the criteria of Halakah could register as Jews (although it did not reverse the law of the case regarding the Shalit children).

I have no intention of rehashing the question of "Who is a Jew?" The question seems only to bother Jews. No anti-Semite ever needed a who's who. Hitler said a Jew was anyone who had a Jewish grandparent and the Germans proved you could tell a Jew by looking at him. Jean-Paul Sartre said it better than anyone else, "A Jew is a man whom other men call a Jew."

It is the Cabinet's business to determine who is and who is not an Israeli. I cannot help feeling the Cabinet is presumptuous in determining who is and who is not a Jew. By what virtue does an Israeli minister determine for 5,500,000 Americans, 3,000,000 Russians, and 1,000,000 Europeans what they are?

The Cabinet and the Knesset have been led to this determination because now two kindergarten kids are walking to their classroom with a card which says "Jewish" on it. Is the toughened Israeli constituency worried it will be inundated by other kindergartners? Does our race or our nation or our people or whatever we want to call it already have too many nice people to let in any more?

I have chosen to point up this issue in Israel not for purposes of criticism but for purposes of prophecy. This issue of Orthodoxy is close to the surface in Israel and it has a short fuse. Were it not for the Arab menace, it would have blown up long ago. Despite the Arabs, it will blow up soon, though I seriously doubt the issue of Orthodox intransigence will rend the country. I incline to think the Israelis will temper the ridiculously stringent and often ineffectual laws of Orthodoxy to facilitate their basic impulse, which is to get along with one another. Getting along with one another, as Samuel Butler once remarked, is the obvious purpose of society.

Part **VII**

Way Down upon the Sunny Negev

The high cost of water

THE IDEA of ridding sea water of its salt is as old as the first drought. No one, however, got around to the chemistry of desalinization until the twentieth century. Scientists and the public have since discovered that even where water is plentiful, still it is costly, and where it is scarce, the cost of water is almost prohibitive.

Water has always been expensive. For centuries, the expense was measured by time and effort, not by money. Men dug wells and installed pumps or built cisterns to trap rainwater, or they carried water from running streams. Time was what everybody had. The Romans invented viaducts to supply the cities with water from the hills, but slave labor kept down the costs.

The mechanical twentieth century demands that time and effort be translated into dollars and cents. One of the facts of this translation is that to supply barren areas with water is so expensive that the supply must be subsidized by the government or the place abandoned.

The Israeli government provides water for the Negev from three sources: it pumps fresh water to the desert from its reservoir, the Sea of Galilee, through underground conduits nine feet in diameter; it can provide water for the southern area from the Red Sea; and it can distill the brackish water which gushes from wells sunk deep beneath the rock shelf of the desert.

These last two, sea water and brackish water, must be desalinated.

The Israelis started desalinating sea water first. Some years ago, a Russian scientist named Alexander Zarchin circulated to all the ministries, newspaper offices, and university science departments the announcement that he had invented a method of desalinating sea water which would insure Israel's survival. No one listened. Except Ben-Gurion. Israel built a desalinating plant in Eilat.

Zarchin's process, which was in operation for several years, consisted of freezing sea water and brushing the salt away from the blocks. It needs a massive flow of electricity which must subsequently be consumed to make the expense of generating it feasible. The desalinated water must be piped to those who will pay for it, also expensive. Complicating the process is the fact that the operation is continual. No one wants to pay for water when it rains and no one needs electricity at noon or midnight. Nor did Zarchin help matters when he sued the government for his patents. The plant at Eilat, nevertheless, provides water for kibbutzim in the south and for industries in the area.

No responsible scientist is optimistic about the prospects of irrigating the Negev with desalinated sea water, certainly not Joel Schecter, the director of the Negev Arid Zone Institute in Beersheba. If there were a cheap method of generating power—perhaps. But nuclear power has proved even more expensive than electricity, said Schecter. Instead, the Arid Zone Institute has concentrated on other processes to desalinate brackish water.

The water under the Negev seeps there from the rain which falls on the Judean hills around Jerusalem. This seepage takes forty years. The water does not seep to the Sinai because the rock drains flow into the gulf.

There are probably one hundred Arid Zone Institutes throughout the world. This network of geologists, chemists, and engineers produces a voluminous literature every year treating on every conceivable aspect of the desert: heat, soil, temperature, plant life—and water. The largest Arid Zone Institute is in India, at Jodhpur. The one at Beersheba is not much bigger than an American junior college, precisely the atmosphere in which these Israeli scientists live. Despite the cool corridors and the shrub-

bery, one feels the desert. The ground is yellow, the sun sometimes merciless, no one moves without a hat, and the beverages
offered guests are cold apple juice, Tempo, or lemonade, not
tea or coffee.

Brackish water is desalinated by two processes. One is reverse
osmosis which uses waterpower instead of electricity, and the
other is electrodialysis, a relatively new invention. Both filter
the salt by flooding the water through huge membranes.

The desalinization of brackish water was first developed by
South African diamond miners. While the Israelis have added
many innovations, their scientists have not succeeded in reducing
the cost of the physical plant. The lifetime of the desalinating
membrane is fifteen years, which means those who want the
water must amortize their costs in this short time. Industries or
kibbutzim in the Negev must realize high profits to afford a
desalinating plant. There are dozens of desalinating plants in
the Arab countries, where profits are not as closely figured because of the oil royalties.

Yothvath is the first kibbutz in the Negev to build a desalinating plant strictly for irrigation. Desalination was a paying proposition for this kibbutz because it could ship melons, strawberries,
lettuce, and beans to Europe by air during the five winter months
and earn the profits luxuries like desalination command.

Haim Cohen, a chemist from Massachusetts who looks like
Lou Gehrig, said all brackish water does not need desalinating;
the purer the water, however, the more improved the crop.

Cohen told us about a Negev kibbutz which saved up for ten
years to afford a desalinating plant. He went down to supervise
the installation of the membranes, which look like gigantic lungs.
Cohen brought along his dog. Nothing amused the kibbutzniks
more than Rover's howling when he couldn't bring himself to
lap up their brackish water. It was Rover's turn to laugh when
the plant was operational. To a man, the kibbutzniks complained
the water had no taste, no taste at all.

The scientists at the Arid Zone Institute have also issued one
of the definitive reports on the effect of heat on humans, animals,
and plant life; it has initiated a landmark program in solar en-
ergy research; and on its faculty are the world experts in hydro-
ponics, the science of determining the practical use of soilless

cultures. They grow vegetables out of salt water rather than salty earth. Water is life in Israel and the Negev Arid Zone Institute is there to preserve as much moisture as possible.

In a simple but far-reaching experiment, it has determined what constitutes effective water discipline for armies. On several occasions, scientists sent three different battalions of paratroopers on a forced march through the desert to the shore of the Red Sea. The first battalion marched on a canteen of water a day; the second, with as much water as each man wanted; and the third was provided not only with water but coffee, tea, soft drinks, and light alcoholic beverages. Without exception, the second battalion made the best time and its members were invariably in better health. Moreover, the experiment proved that man can't get used to drinking less; those who had their water rationed for a longer time succumbed first when cut off from all water.

Desalinization is always a topical subject in Israel. There are more geologists per square foot in the Negev looking for water than any place else in the world. One of the ironies that befell one of these geologists was striking oil instead of water.

Many of the desalinating experiments are financed by the United States through AID programs, State, Agriculture, and Interior departments, and Rockefeller grants. Year by year since the Vietnam War these monies have decreased, not only for the Negev Institute but for Arid Zone Institutes in Jodhpur, Algiers, and elsewhere.

In the fall of 1969, the United States decided not to go ahead with financing a $40-million desalinating plant in the Negev, which would have provided American scientists with a pilot project and Israel with 120 million milligrams of water every year.

Well, it's back to the drawing board for the Jews, who are coming to realize that their real answer may be in the recycling of water. Otherwise, the American decision not to proceed inspired two reactions: realists sought to find a suitable financial substitute through higher water rates or through suspending other projects; pragmatists sent an urgent message to the Jewish lobby in Washington to reclaim as best they could the water appropriation.

Oil town

THE BIBLICAL homeland of the Jews stretched from Dan to Beersheba. Beersheba means "the well of the pledge" and it takes its name from the oath Abraham and Abimelech swore when they promised not to fight each other over the one well in the desert.

Beersheba is still the gateway to this desert, the Negev, whose name signifies simply "the south" and where nothing grows naturally except a thin green moss over the rocks. But in this 4,000 square miles of sun-scorched rock and earth, 31 kibbutzim force lettuce and fruits, mine phosphate, nitrate, and potassium, and pump oil from 28 wells.

Nowadays the "green line" goes as far as Beersheba, but before the Israelis proclaimed the state, Beersheba was complely ringed by desert.

In 1970, Beersheba has far from a Biblical appearance.

It has a population of 85,000—75,000 of whom are Oriental Jews, new immigrants who work in the factories and cement plants. Beersheba resembles nothing so much as an American oil town where lucky wildcatters have brought in gushers. The rough workers have money in their pockets and restlessly they patrol the streets for excitement. An Army Signal Corps detachment camps just outside the city limits, so Beersheba is filled with soldiers at night.

It is the kind of town where the stores will sell ten times as many Beatle records as they sell books, if they sell any books at all.

Beersheba has one main street, Keren Kayemet Leisrael, but everyone calls it the *Champs Élysées*. Vendors wheel pushcarts filled with nuts and figs. Steaks simmer on the grills of the open-air Yemenite restaurants. There are three movie houses along the street and young hookers offer themselves to the knots of men waiting to buy tickets. The stores are filled with mannequins clothed in flimsy summer dresses.

All night long trucks from the mills lumber to the highway leading to Tel Aviv. In the north end is a huge unfinished building—like a bombed-out cathedral. It was to have been a synagogue, but the rabbinate discovered it was too close to a movie house, so work on it was halted.

In the center of town is the Bedouin market, where the tourists can barter with the Arabs on Thursday mornings. In preparing his book on Israel, *The Prophet Motive*, George Mikes, the English writer, was particularly amused by the handsome moustachioed Bedouin who charged the ladies from American Hadassah and ORT chapters a pound each to gather around him and his camel for a snapshot.

A fellow with such a distinctive profession, thought Mikes, was certainly worth an interview. He got a scoop.

There had always been a Bedouin in Beersheba with his camel whom Jewish tourists sought out, to lend a touch of exotic romance to their visit. But some years ago, the tribe voted to move on and, Bedouins being Bedouins, the poser was constrained to abandon his lucrative profession and move with them.

His successor, Mikes found, was not a Bedouin at all. In fact, the Bedouin was a Jew, a Hungarian musician who found himself down on his luck in Beersheba about the time the Hadassies were looking for an Arab to pose with them.

The Hungarian rented a camel on tick and outfitted himself in robe, sandals, and burnoose. Shortly, he found himself gainfully employed.

He confessed to Mikes he preferred early Mozart to late and boasted that both his sons were university graduates. With one exception, the Negev had made him happy.

"What is that exception?" asked Mikes.

"This bloody fool camel still frightens me out of my wits," said the Hungarian.

Moving south

AT DIMONA, to the east, the road to the Dead Sea starts its steep, curving descent toward Sodom, 1,500 feet below sea level, the lowest inhabited spot in the world. It is a dangerous road, winding past huge orange cliffs and red arroyos. Except for these vivid colors, Matthew Arnold would have recognized

the place as one of the "drear and lonely shingles of the world."
Anyone who grew up in this desert would be at home on the
moon.

Along the precipitous way are two monuments dedicated to
the engineers and road builders who lost their lives before they
saw the Dead Sea. They were killed by Bedouins who murdered
workmen for their tools or watches. Later, I learned that a government agency has a list of every Bedouin who lives in the
Negev.

Halfway from Dimona, the road divides. To the right, it leads
200 miles to Eilat, Israel's southernmost city, to the left to the
Dead Sea and then north toward Jericho. One stares in amazement at the two soldiers standing at this deserted crossroads
hitchhiking to Kibbutz Ein Gedi. They must have beautiful
girls at Ein Gedi.

This is where Sodom is, the city on which the Lord rained
brimstone and fire out of heaven. Ahead is the Dead Sea itself,
48 miles long, 11 miles wide, 1,319 feet deep, where no fish
has ever swum because the salt kills all organic life. The shore is
white-crusted with crystallized salt, like foam flecking the lips
of the beer drinker. The smell from the sea is noxious. We have
penetrated a cloud of sulphur.

Two hotels flank a mosque-like restaurant and pier. Signs
in the bathhouse caution swimmers not to admit salt into eyes
or ears or mouth, to shower immediately after leaving the water.

At least once a month, a virile American tourist cannonballs
off the end of the pier, hitting the water as though landing on a
sheet of soft lead. It puts an immediate end to his sightseeing
for the next day or so.

Thirty percent of the sea is salt, and its buoyancy makes the
bather into a rubber ball bouncing in a bathtub. The water
is warm. No one ventures more than 15 feet off the shore to the
warning hawse.

The spa and the two hotels are filled with elderly Israelis who
come to the Dead Sea for the salubrious effect of the salt. A
banker in Jerusalem told me the lowest interest rates for any
enterprise in Israel are extended for tourist facilities by the Dead
Sea. Scientifically, he explained, the beneficial effects of the

Dead Sea may or may not be real, but Israelis with bad backs think they are. At these hotels, the philanderer can encounter any number of old ladies he wants.

Stretching across the southern end of the Dead Sea, like a huge finger across the brine, is the first dike, three more smaller dikes to its south. From the beds the dikes create, the workers mine the potash, which is then transported to Ashdod. The night before, the potash works had been shelled by two automatic bazookas which the Arabs set in the hills on the Jordanian side.

On the northern shore of the Dead Sea are the old British potash works. British soldiers then accompanied every truck which wound upland. When the mandate ended, the plant became the property of the Jordanians, who let it fall into disrepair.

A middle-aged lady sat in profound shock at one of the tables on the terrace of the restaurant. She had lost her car key while bathing. Richard offered to jump the wires for her. She nodded no, she said it was a brand-new car.

"This isn't something we can leave to Golda," I said.

She was going to call her son-in-law who lived in Haifa, ask him to go to the garage, have another key made, then take the bus to Sodom, and perhaps hitch a ride from there.

"He must love your daughter very much," said Richard gravely.

The mystery of the shields at Arad

ARAD IS A brand-new town, not yet seven years old, built all at once on one of the plateaus above the Dead Sea. The day after the contractors left, 5,000 immigrants moved in. The air is dry but the winds constantly whip small clouds of dust across the landscape.

The government has financed two knitting mills in Arad, started an auto assembly plant, and constructed two motels for the tourists who come to visit nearby Masada or take a dip in the Dead Sea.

It is made of cement with wide, black asphalt streets, some lonely eucalyptus trees set in the stone sidewalks, two school buildings, and about ten blocks of low-rise three-story apartment houses.

Mysteriously, the bottom half of each apartment house window is fronted by a gaily colored plastic shield.

I thought at first these shields were installed to protect the window from the blazing sun. But they are set too low to serve this purpose. Awnings would do as well. Besides, I saw no such shields in Beersheba or Dimona, also Negev towns where the sun is as punishing. Why should I see them in Arad?

Nor did these shields rail narrow terraces.

Decoration?

Perhaps.

I went to the corner of one of the apartment houses and examined the building in profile. It was immediately clear what practical function these shields served. They hid the housewife's wash from the purview of the world.

There are few washer-dryers in Israel. With a population of 2,500,000, there isn't much of a domestic market, and Israel could hardly compete with America and Britain in the world market. The result is that housewives are forever hanging out the laundry. Apartment house terraces are crisscrossed with clotheslines as no-man's-land is with barbed wire.

Personally, I am 100 percent in favor of laundry. I agree with the poet Richard Wilbur who proclaimed, in "Things of This World," there should be nothing on earth but laundry. Here in Arad, however, a hometown boy came up with the architectural answer for the scrubbing housewife's worry. Now the neighbors can peep all they want.

Jenny

JENNY MERIOZ is slender, pretty, and vivacious. She has black hair, green eyes, and red freckles which never popped until she came to Arad. She teaches music in one of the town's two schools.

Jenny was born in Brazil, the daughter of an Orthodox Jew in Rio. She never felt at ease as an observant Jew. When she was eighteen, she won a contest in reading Hebrew. First prize was a trip to Israel, where she decided to stay. A few years ago she settled in Arad because her oldest son was an asthmatic, bedridden most of the time. The dry, hot air of Arad relieved him.

Her husband, Leiada, manages an art gallery in Jerusalem at 1 Jews' Street.

She got her part-time teaching job by attending an Israeli normal school. This year she starts at Hebrew University for her BA, which will enable her to work in the high school.

Jenny is proud of Arad, the only town in the Negev with a Scotch family named Campbell. Arad, she boasted, has only two "social" families, an Israeli euphemism for welfare cases.

"Why are they 'social' cases?" I asked.

"The husbands drink," she said, lowering her voice.

Now why would a couple of men who have escaped from a *dorf* like Paris or Budapest to this healthy desert town with two knitting mills nearby want to drink? I asked myself.

Hammada, Rimf, and Manna

GEOGRAPHERS AND geologists believe the Negev is a small continuation of the Sinai. Once the Suez Canal was secured, Israeli scientists and research teams moved in. At first they concentrated on the area known as Ras-Muhammed, in the south, where they could plainly observe the geological effects of the Afro-Syrian break which separated the continents (in Africa, the break is covered by jungle).

Ja'acov Ben-Tor, a geologist from Hebrew University, insists the break strengthens the theory that the continents are moving and floating, not fixed. Every ten years, Jordan and Saudi Arabia drift one millimeter farther away from Israel.

Other Israeli geologists concentrated on minerals. The Sinai produces manganese, clay, and coal. But three Polish advisers, trapped by the Six-Day War, told the Israelis the Russian mining machinery was useless. Tests also convinced the Israelis the coal in Mrera is uneconomical to mine. Nor is it profitable to ship the manganese across the desert to Ashdod. Israeli phosphates are much better than the Sinai's, and Israel already has enough of these.

What's in the Sinai is oil. The Sinai is what geologists call a "mirror" of Libya. As the wheat grown by the kibbutzim pays for the occupation of the Golan Heights, a lease to an oil company pays for the occupation of the Sinai.

Geologists from Hebrew University have discovered three new minerals in the Sinai mountains. No one has determined yet to what use these new minerals can be put, if any. It is one thing politically to lease oil rights to foreigners who will stay in the Sinai whether the Egyptians come back or the Israelis stay; it is another to start the expensive process of extracting a lode when the site may be quickly abandoned.

Zoologists have found flamingos near the Canal.

The big news from the Sinai comes from the botanists, one of whom, Avinoam Danin, thinks he has found the Biblical manna on which the Jews subsisted while they wandered forty years in the desert, making their way from Egyptian bondage to the Promised Land.

Once it was thought that the lichen which grows on Sinai plants was the proverbial manna. But Danin says that in all his trips through the desert he has yet to find sweet lichen.

Earlier, another Jewish botanist, named Bodenheimer, identified the real plants in the Sinai with the plants in the Bible. He suspected manna was the sweet excretion of aphids which live on tamarisk. The Bedouins made a habit of collecting this honey-like substance.

Danin, who is preparing his doctorate, went into the Sinai to map the flora. He has served in the Army as a "weed man," one who teaches soldiers how to subsist in the desert on edible plants, insects, and animals. He is devoted to "natural soups" and he discovered plants with a much sweeter excretion than the tamarisk; the caper bush, for example, was sweeter and more plentiful and so was the acacia, on which the goats of the Sinai survive.

But the most common plant in the Sinai is the hammada bush which grows in relative abundance. Its sweet excretion, the result of insect feeding, bubbles at the head of its blossom, called "the gall nut," in early summer. Danin found that the Bedouins continually tap this excretion, calling it "Rimf," and feed it to their children as a candy.

Danin is convinced that the hammada bush produced the manna Moses ate when he led the Children from bondage. Summer is the crucial period for survival in the Sinai. The Sinai will provide some kind of food in all other months, but it is barren from May until October, except for the hammada.

No one believed Wolff in the beginning when he insisted the ambrosia which made Zeus and Hera heady was milk, but even the heavy drinkers came around eventually. If I had to take my chances for forty years in the desert, I would make for the hammada bush.

Gaza

THERE ARE check points which warn the visitor he is approaching the border. Kibbutz Yad Mordechai, named after one of the leaders of the Warsaw Ghetto Uprising, is the last Israeli station. Passing it, the visitor can see the Gaza Strip ahead, and he must roll up his car windows lest some Arab's aim with a grenade be true. What truly marks the beginning of the Gaza Strip is a monumental pile of rusting beer cans, the legacy of the United Nations force which kept peace here until May, 1967. The United Nations left quickly. The soldiers did not have time to bury the cans before Israeli tanks swept through.

The Gaza Strip, a finger which points toward Tel Aviv, extends from the northeastern tip of the Sinai for 31 miles along the Mediterranean coast. It is 4 miles wide. In this area live 500,000 angry and embittered Arabs, 360,000 of them Arab refugees living in squalid camps. The Egyptians maintained a curfew for almost two decades which the Israelis abolished, but that is the only way in which their lot has improved.

Near the border is the city of Gaza, where Samson pulled down the Philistine temple on his tormentors. Probably the city takes its name from this event. *Az* in Hebrew means "strong" and *Azza* is the Hebrew name for what was once an Egyptian Army staging area. Gaza was also famous for the invention of a light cloth—gauze. Many men have died here. The British lost 10,000 men taking Gaza from the Germans and the Turks in World War I, and in 1956 and 1967 Jews and Arabs died fighting in and around it.

The Jews took it on the second day of the war. In the center of Gaza is a pockmarked pedestal lacking its statue. The statue was of Nasser and the first Israeli tank streaking through the street for the Sinai pulled it down.

Opposite the statueless pedestal is a post office, its roof ringed by sandbags. An Israeli major pointed to it and said, "Those sandbags were there when I came through in 1956. They were there in 1948. The British put them up there long before. Nothing changes in this town, nothing."

He was not accurate. The traffic signals and the sidewalk railings are Israeli. And there is a branch of the ubiquitous Bank Leumi Le-Israel. I had seen such branches in Hebron and other towns in the Administered Territories and I had innocently supposed these banks were for the convenience of the tourists and the soldiers. But the soldiers make $10 a month and those opening bank accounts are few and far between. The tourists who come through here, adventurous as they may be, come through at a fast gallop. Some Israelis venture here, but only on official business. The banks, someone told me, are set up to lose money.

Interest rates are ferociously high in Israel; and in some instances, debtors pay interest rates daily. The banks can afford branch offices, so they have become the new missionaries—they and traffic control experts.

Part *VIII*
Out of the Hills, the Miracles

Keeping tabs on the neighbors

"WHAT NEW miracles shall we see come from those hills of Judea," telegraphed an exultant Josephus Daniels, Woodrow Wilson's Secretary of the Navy and an early Christian Zionist. Daniels was addressing himself to Arthur Lord Balfour, who had written his famous letter, the Balfour Declaration, in which he said His Majesty's government looked with favor upon the establishment of a Jewish national home in Palestine. Balfour's letter was addressed to Lord Rothschild for reasons still vague— except that if you wanted to communicate with Jews in those days, you preferred to get in touch with a Rothschild.

Twenty-one years later, when Chaim Weizmann became its first President, he remarked that Israel was the only country in the world where miracles became a part of state planning.

Now with the jumbo jets making their runs, the miracles are there for all to see, right over the horizon. Before these miracles became too commonplace, I signed a contract with my publisher, solemnly promising to describe each and every one of them so the folks would have no trouble admiring them when they got off the plane.

But there is a higher price on miracles than a first-class round-trip ticket.

At Kfar Habad, I saw a vocational school where Yemenite and Moroccan Jewish boys learned printing, ironworking, and auto mechanics. I remarked that, in my time, I have seen more

vocational schools around Lynn, Massachusetts, than there are
in all of Israel.

"But the miracle," exclaimed my hosts, "is that these are
Jews!"

"The miracle," I said, "is that Avis and Hertz are still in
business since, for all their schooling, the Israeli mechanics have
yet to learn how to file points or charge batteries."

"The Army," said my hosts, "the Israeli Army is a miracle."

But the generals shook their heads and said their victories
are hardly miraculous. They knew what they could do and how
long it would take. If the Egyptians won, that would be a miracle.

Nor did the chemical plant outside of Tel Aviv seem miraculous to anyone who has seen the chemical complex around
Baton Rouge. Nor is the cuisine at the Hilton miraculous, to
say the least.

"A miracle," I said, "is *sui generis,* one of a kind."

They conferred. They said, "This is an interesting country.
Why not perambulate around until we come up with something
sui generis."

It was on my own, then, that I came across the Afro-Asian
Institute, a graduate school for foreign students who come from
countries as diverse as Burma and Zanzibar. Since the institute
is over ten years old, both Israeli and American newsmen have
ceased describing its activities for the United Jewish Appeal,
ever hungry for newer and bigger miracles.

Akiva Egers, the principal of the institute, looks like a typical
Israeli. He has the heft, the big shoulders, and the ham hands of
a farmer. Indeed, he still lives on a kibbutz outside Tel Aviv.
He wears a white sports shirt, its collar neatly overlaying the
lapels of a decidedly unstylish sports jacket. His office on tree-
lined Nehardea Street in Tel Aviv is modest, and his desk is
stacked with reports, correspondence, and pamphlets. There the
typical ends.

"Our students are not typical," he said. "They are Africans,
Asians, and South Americans. They are officials of their governments, union leaders, university teachers, and frequently corporation executives. They are older. They stay here only four or
five months. We do not offer them set courses of instruction;
instead they and their governments advise us what courses they

want. And the first thing we do after they register is disillusion them. They come to Israel with the idea that once they are graduated, they can go home and develop their countries right away. We prove to them techniques cannot be transferred and that independence does not come from assimilation with others."

"What do you teach them beside Hebrew?" I asked.

"We don't teach them Hebrew. Why should we? So they can read the Bible? They can read it in Swahili. We conduct our courses in French one half of the year and English the other. We don't even stress lectures. Lectures are for the Middle Ages. We have a laboratory and the laboratory is Israel."

Shambayela Karawe is six foot four, which probably makes him one of the tallest men in Tel Aviv. Dr. Karawe is from the Cameroons, a country whose name means "shrimp," he told me with a smile. Before coming to Israel, Dr. Karawe had graduated from the Sorbonne and attended Lumumba University in Moscow.

"It was an unhappy eighteen months in Russia," he said. "It took me a long time to learn the language. While the Russians called me 'comrade,' they didn't want their sister to marry one. The Jews don't want their sister to marry one, either," he went on, "but I came to Israel with my wife."

What absorbs him about Israel is that it is still a developing country. He has studied the kibbutz, the communal farm, and the *moshav*, the cooperative village. The Jews who first came to Israel in the 1880's knew little about agriculture and less about industry, crafts, building, and transports. They had no expertise in the professions needed to bring about development. Of necessity, they had to work together to wrest their living from the land. They developed their country cooperatively. The cooperative structures not only helped them survive, but it helped the Israelis train the manpower to extend development.

"My people live in rural areas," said Dr. Karawe. "The only thing they own is the soil beneath their feet. We cannot start by building cities. We have to start with rural projects."

An economist by training, Dr. Karawe is a trade unionist by profession. He is an officer of the Socialist Party. I asked him what he had learned in Israel that he couldn't have learned from Henry George or Bellamy, and he replied, "I have learned that higher wages are not enough. I have learned that education is more important than higher wages, that the health and hygienic conditions are more important, that applied science and technology are more important."

Opel Quizmine is as short as Dr. Karawe is tall. A mathematics teacher, Quizmine was born on a kraal in Tanzania. He has served as an adviser to the Ministry of Finance. This summer he will set up a school system in one of the mountain areas. In Israel, he is studying computer technology and has become thoroughly familiar with the computer at Tel Aviv University. He told me he knew the computer could guide man to and from the moon as well as forecast economic cycles. What he didn't know was that with it an unsophisticated secretary could not only pay everybody in the university in twenty minutes but also schedule all the classes and assign the students to them.

He took me in. I was in the simple-minded process of congratulating Israel on its beneficence in revealing the practical applications of the computer to an African, when I discovered that Quizmine had been chief of the Computer Reading Room at the United Nations. His work at the University of Tel Aviv is of a sophisticated nature.

I suppose he teased because he knew he was never going to have a computer of his own, which made more poignant Akiva Egers' parting remarks. He said, "The tragedy of this world is not that there is a lack of capital, it is that there is a surplus which cannot find its way into the qualified hands which can guarantee proper investment, management, production, and a fair return."

The Histadrut, the general organization of all labor in Israel, sponsors the Afro-Asian Institute.

What in the world does it want with it? The grim truth of the matter is that Africa is a failure, a failure in democracy and a failure economically.

Awakening nationalism in Africa has secured the political independence of a score of new countries, many of which have large Moslem majorities. Moslem friends may one day prove advantageous to Israel (though on the very day I visited the institute many of the African nations sided with the Arabs in

the United Nations over the question of the refugees in Gaza
and on the West Bank of the Jordan).

Another reason for the institute is that most Israelis are aware
that their country is a bridge between three great continents:
Europe, Africa, and Asia. Israel wants economic independence,
but she cannot fully compete in the industrial European market.
She can export her climate to Europe, sending oranges to London in December and avocados to Paris in January, and even
bathing suits to California, but she cannot depend upon Europe
as a customer for medium or heavy goods. Israel's industrial
neighbors will be Africa and Asia, and both sides could benefit
from closer relations and mutual understanding. The distance
between the United States and Afro-Asia is vast, so vast there
is little likelihood either Africa or Asia can truly benefit from
our know-how and experience, while Israel's development is
close enough in material terms and in time to become comprehensive to Asians and Africans.

We think because our democratic way of life works for us, it
must work for everyone, which is not so; and we think money
will do everything, which is not so either. We have never complained about the skyscrapers we built in Africa which are always
empty or about the roads we built in Asia which go no place.
Neither money nor ideals develop a country; skills and labor do.

And there is a third reason for the existence of the Afro-Asian
Institute. That reason is altruism. Israeli aid missions are usually
the most effective in Africa, because Israelis understand the
difficulties and obstacles of industrial development, because the
influence of the kibbutz gives the Israelis a social approach of
equality without paternalism, and because Jewish sympathy
does the rest.

Slavery was a gigantic hemorrhage for Africa. Two hundred
million Africans died during the century of the slave hunts.
Theodor Herzl, who created the Jewish state when he convened
the First Zionist Council, confided in his diaries that once he
had solved the Jewish problem, then he could devote all his
energies to the more serious problem of liberating the black man.

One has the feeling that the Afro-Asian Institute has always
been implicit in the Israeli moral and political scheme of things.

When we talk about miracles we are talking about making the implicit the emergent—which only demands work, imagination, and heart.

The Kremlin

ISRAEL HAS been described as a small country within a big labor union. That labor union is the Histadrut. Headquarters is a large building in Tel Aviv which resembles one of our mammoth public schools. Union members call this building "the Kremlin."

What differentiates the Kremlin from any other union headquarters in the world is that on every available square foot of wall space is a painting, a watercolor, a woodcut, or an etching. Portraits, landscapes, abstract expressionism, and nonobjective canvases decorate the offices of the union leaders. The Histadrut is Israel's biggest patron of the arts because most of the artists belong to it.

The Jews who founded the Histadrut in 1920 were more interested in their missionary zeal than in higher wages. They wanted to build a labor society. They succeeded—perhaps too well. The Histadrut owns hundreds of industries which it has been trying to give back to the workers. More often than not, the workers don't want the business. The Histadrut is the biggest industrial employer. In fact, the Histadrut owns a newspaper whose employees went on strike to win higher wages. They won the strike, from themselves.

For many years this powerful organization ran tranquilly. The men who governed the country were also the leaders of the labor union. As long as capitalists didn't raise prices, they didn't raise wages, except when the index of living rose.

But that day is past. Strikes do not by any means plague Israel, but the country knows them. Israelis said the same thing when their postmen went on strike that Americans did: the ordinary citizen bemoaned the fact that the soldiers wouldn't get mail from their girls and the ordinary economist said the pay hike would contribute to the inflationary spiral.

The postmen asked, "Why are only the workers supposed to show discipline?"

Flusser

To CALL David Flusser of Hebrew University portly is inaccurate but flattering, because sitting can make him huff and puff. To say he is an impatient man is to be obvious. To say he knows what he is talking about is a vast understatement, because Flusser, professor of Comparative Religions at Hebrew University, is one of the world authorities on the meaning and interpretation of the Dead Sea Scrolls.

Briefly, the Dead Sea Scrolls are the recently discovered writings of the Essenes, a Jewish sect which flourished in communal settlements near the Dead Sea around the time of Christ. When the Romans conquered Judea, overcoming the last defenders at Masada in A.D. 73, these Essenes stored their holy writings in hermetically sealed clay jars and hid them in nearby caves. In 1947, a Bedouin shepherd in the Qumran Wadi, casually throwing stones to amuse himself, heard the unexpected clatter of shattered clay.

I have neither the wit nor the facility to describe the recent history of what these scrolls reveal; notably, Edmund Wilson, our premier critic, has done this in *The Dead Sea Scrolls* and *The Dead Sea Scrolls: 1947–1969* (Oxford University Press, 1956, 1969). Nor do I have the scholarship to estimate what the scrolls portend for theology, religion, and history. Doubleday Anchor Books in paperback editions has embarked upon the publication of each of these scrolls as it has been translated with detailed commentaries. But I will hazard that since the writings of the Essenes are undoubtedly one of the precursors of the writings of the New Testament, the clatter of clay shards on the dry cave floor has become a crescendo of historical, archeological, religious, and theological revision and speculation.

Professor Flusser has been at work on these scrolls since they were discovered. Over the years, Israel has acquired almost all of them, first through purchase and, in 1967, through capture. The scrolls the Israelis purchased they housed in the new Museum of the Book in Jerusalem. The scrolls they captured are housed in the Palestine Archeological Museum, which was built in the Old City with Rockefeller money in 1929. While the Jordanians owned the scrolls, they apportioned them for translation to foreign scholars, Hebraists from France, England, and America, not one of them, naturally, a Jew. When the Israelis took over the Palestine museum, they perpetuated the status quo to the exasperation of Professor Flusser. He became exasperated not because these men were Gentiles but because they were scholars and insisted on scholarly propriety.

Scholarly propriety insists that a second scholar will not look at a first scholar's scroll until the first scholar has published his translation. Not all the Christian scholars are as adept at Hebrew as the Jewish scholar who grew up reading and writing the language. This inutility slows down the translation of all the scrolls. Their significance has yet to be assessed in totality. Even when a scroll is published and available to everyone, additional time must be wasted for emendations and corrections.*

As Flusser was warming to his topic, we were interrupted by the arrival of an ex-Lebanese Jew who was beginning his studies for his doctorate. He had come to ask the professor if there was any chance for a seminar on the New Testament being offered in French.

Flusser struggled from his rocker, snorting like a hippo surfacing in the Ubangi River. "I can teach the New Testament in English," he stormed, speaking French. "I can teach it in German and in Hebrew. How can I teach it in French? To teach the New Testament demands I learn a nomenclature of thousands of definitive phrases, a whole vocabulary. Go into that room until I am finished," he commanded.

The student disappeared. The squall had subsided. We were back on the subject of the Dead Sea Scrolls.

"Of course there will be revisions," said Flusser. "There will be more Christian revisions than Jewish revisions, because by

---

* Israeli archeologists demand as strict a propriety. Each has his empire. When an archeologist at Hebrew University goes off to Oxford or Harvard for a sabbatical year, often the dig is closed until he returns.

the time of the Essenes, the Jews had the Old Testament and the Christians had yet to write the New."

"What will the nature of the revisions be?" I asked.

"Hah!" he suddenly shouted, stamping his feet. The buffalo had returned. "I am glad you asked me. I cannot venture this to a class filled with nuns, priests, ministers, and young girls from I-o-wa. The scrolls will reopen the dialogue between Jews and Christians, because everything cruel and harsh in Christianity comes from the Essenes. The Essenes said they were the Children of Light and they hated the Children of Darkness. They invented Divine Election, which has played a crucial and thoroughly difficult role in Christianity. How can you reconcile the Doctrine of Divine Election with the Doctrine of Original Sin?"

We proceeded.*

The dialogue about religious differences between Christian and Jew suffers, Flusser argued, because the disputants polarize their differences in order to clarify them. Polarization frequently leads to oversimplification and makes it easy to forget that Christianity emerged from Judaism. What the scrolls will do to bring Jew and Christian to a common ground is prove that Christianity did not proceed from Old Testament Judaism but from the Judaism of the intertestamental period for which the linguistic convenience is "the Judaism of the Second Commonwealth."

The God of the Old Testament was novel and unique not only because He insisted He was the only God but because He also insisted He was a just God. He brought to the world a novel social order which applied to all peoples. He promised to reward the just and to punish the sinners.

Yet Jews throughout Old Testament history saw just men suffer and saw sinners succeed. They wondered if that was what He meant, that He would compensate for good works? Sometimes it didn't seem that way. Questioning led to differences.

By the time of the intertestamental period there were three Jewish sects: there were the Pharisees, who believed in written

---

* In my writing I am indebted to one of Flusser's essays, "A New Sensitivity in Judaism and the Christian Message," which appeared in the *Harvard Theological Review*, 61 (1968).

law but also accommodated common law, which grew out of usage (Pharisaic Judaism is the Judaism which survived); there were the Sadducees, who denied resurrection and any oral traditions; and there were the Essenes, militant kibbutzniks living out in the desert hills.

The Pharisees resolved the question of the just and the unjust by charging their forebears had served God only through the dread of punishment and retribution. They had failed to love God unconditionally. There was a priority in the religious impulses. Love was supreme, for it made men righteous.

During the Second Commonwealth, this new Jewish sensitivity selected the commandment "Do not do unto others as you would not others do unto yourself" on which to base the foundation of Mosaic law. Hillel later summarized the Judaic ethic as "Whatever is hateful to you, do not do unto your fellow. This is the essence of the Torah, the rest is corollary."

The Pharisees had sustained the religious rationale by a complex understanding of human nature, a development which had profound effect on Jesus.

But so, too, it seems, did the teachings of the Essenes, who had a more radical concept of good and evil and the necessity for reward and punishment. They believed God had ordained both good and evil and had elected some men as the chosen sons of light to maintain a perpetual war with the accursed sons of darkness. It was the Essenes' duty to pursue evil with ever-continuing hatred. This theology, Flusser believes, is a reaction to the Pharisaic philosophy, which emphasized the solidarity of man in sin and virtue. At the end of time, the Essenes were sure God would reward the righteous and destroy the wicked. They hated evil and the sinner, but the Essenes were constrained to wait for vengeance until God decreed evil disappear.

Since they were forced into "peaceful coexistence" until the apocalypse, they developed an ethic to accommodate their long wait. They resolved not to return evil to any man but to pursue the sinner with good. The pursuing Essene found he did not have to love his neighbor, he could hate him with all his heart, as long as he wanted to overwhelm him with a human approach.

"According to the teachings of Jesus, however," says Flusser, "you have to love the sinners, while according to Judaism you have not to hate the wicked. It is important to note that the positive love even toward enemies is Jesus's personal message. We do not find this doctrine in the New Testament outside the words of Jesus himself. With the exception of Matthew and one verse in Luke, the word righteousness is not found in the Gospels. Christianity did not develop a specific Christian concept of social righteousness until it became a state religion."

As the Essenes were in reaction to the Pharisees, perhaps Jesus was in reaction to the Essenes. Their influence nevertheless came into the New Testament through the writings of St. Paul, who knew their teachings as he knew the metaphysics of the Greek Orphic mysteries.

The Essene doctrine was that you convert your enemies by hating them, which is hostility; it was St. Paul's doctrine that you convert your enemies by praying for them, which is philanthropy. It was Jesus's doctrine that you convert your enemies by loving them, which "surpasses Judaism, at least theoretically, in its approach of love for all men, but its only genuine answer to the powerful wicked forces of this world is martyrdom."

The telephone rang. Flusser excused himself and took the receiver in the hall. His conversation consisted of a series of "*Nein, Nein! NEIN!*" growing louder and louder and more and more agitated. He bit his thumb in Germanic anger when he hung up. It seems the editor of a Jewish encyclopedia wanted Flusser's article on Christianity within the week, which Flusser, biting his thumb again, proclaimed to the inhabitants of the apartment was impossible. "*Nein, Nein! NEIN!*" he yelled, while Mrs. Flusser calmly went about her cooking and ten-year-old Flusser, Jr., never turned from his playmate.

"It will never do," he said suddenly, "to let a Christian write this article for a Jewish encyclopedia. But first my Lebanese." He started to stomp toward the room where I can only presume the doctoral candidate sat cowering.

I thanked Flusser for the books, for the afternoon, and said I hoped I hadn't usurped too much of his time.

"Nothing better," said Flusser. As I left I heard him bellowing in French.

David Flusser is the second genius I have ever met (the first was Oscar Geiger who founded the Henry George School of Economics). I felt after my two hours with him as Edmund Wilson said he felt after he had completed his study of the Dead Sea Scrolls, "... to visit modern Israel and to see what is going on there now is to feel oneself partly released from the narrow constrictions of today's and yesterday's newspaper and to find oneself thus rising above the years, with their catastrophes and their comings and goings, in touch with one of the greatest forces for the tenacity and authority of our race."

To the heights

"To THE heights" is a free translation of "El Al," the name of the government-owned airline.

In the beginning, the Knesset, which was meeting in an abandoned movie house, complained bitterly about the cost of financing an airline. "It's like putting a top hat on a naked man," shouted one opponent. But Ben-Gurion had his way.

Fortunately.

For three times El Al has proved integral to Israel's security, providing the country with its only link to the outside world. The first time was in 1948, then again in 1956, and lastly in 1967. When war starts in the Middle East, other airlines cancel flights until the shooting stops. El Al flies without interruption.

The airline has become an intricate part of the Israeli economy. Tourism and the export of citrus vie annually as the number one industry. The majority of the visitors, who spend millions of dollars, come by El Al. Most of these tourists come from the United States or South Africa. So in addition to providing security for the state, El Al is a money-maker, turning, if not a substantial, still a constant profit every year.

Under President Mordechai Ben-Ari, a hard-driving Hungarian, it operates ten airplanes as of this writing—which makes its schedules brilliant exercises in financial logistics—and is sixteenth in volume of business as recorded by the International Air Transport Association, which has 106 members. El Al has never lost a passenger through accident and has the best safety record in the world.

It is true that Arab terrorists have claimed the lives of a student pilot and four Israelis (and have claimed the lives of other nationals on other airlines). Terrorists have hijacked an El Al plane to Algeria, killed a passenger in Athens, tried to machine-gun an El Al flight in Zurich, and attacked the terminal in Munich and again in Athens.

When Arab terrorists threw a grenade into the El Al waiting room in Athens, which killed a seven-year-old Greek boy, Al Fatah spokesmen asked, "How much longer must innocent Greek children die because of Israeli intransigence?"

These terrorist attacks have increased El Al's passenger and freight loads. After British ground crews and pilots threatened a Middle East boycott because of sabotage to a Swissair flight, El Al had a ten percent increase in business. The Jews are afraid to fly into Lod on another airline lest they be thought cowards. This kind of thinking makes it possible for El Al to dispense with in-flight movies or champagne parties.

The longest scheduled nonstop flight in the world is between New York and Tel Aviv (a Pan Am flight from New York into South America is longer in hours, but not in miles).

Because it is the only kosher airline, El Al pays more for food than any other company. This is not because kosher cuisine is more expensive, it is because kosher airline catering is not a competitive business. El Al cost accountants have discovered kosher catering is a seller's market. These same cost accountants know the day El Al abandons its kosher cuisine, the government will fall.

No El Al official will talk about the two men who ride shotgun on every flight, one in first class, one in coach. But an American movie company has already acquired the rights to film the adventures of Yuri Rahamin, the shotgun rider who beat off the terrorists in Zurich and was acquitted by a Swiss court in a trial at Winterthur.

El Al pilots are the best-salaried men in Israel. There are seven hundred applicants for forty places as El Al stewardesses, who are required to be pretty and speak fluent English as well as Hebrew.

The kibbutz in Rehovot

THE MOST important kibbutz in Israel is the Weizmann Institute of Science, named after Chaim Weizmann, the Manchester chemist whose inventions and arguments persuaded the British to publish the Balfour Declaration in 1917.

The Weizmann, as its kibbutzniks call it, is fifteen miles south of Tel Aviv in Rehovot, a small town with spacious, shaded streets and neat sidewalk coffee cafés. Weizmann founded the institute in 1934, called it then the Sieff Institute, and housed it in a single stone building. The Sieff Institute was intended as a haven for Jewish scientists escaping Hitler and, in fact, Albert Einstein was asked to serve as its first president. He refused and the great majority of Jewish scientists did not immigrate to Rehovot; they immigrated to the United States or to Britain or were murdered. By the time the Sieff became the Weizmann in 1944, in honor of its founder's seventieth birthday, its faculty was largely homegrown.

There was no strategic reason for locating the institute in Rehovot. The town was only sand and citrus when the cornerstone was laid, and Weizmann himself called Rehovot "the boondocks." Weizmann and his benefactor, Lord Sieff, had hoped to establish the institute in Jerusalem as part of the Hebrew University, but one of those political wrangles which often transpire between men of destiny and university administrators became irreconcilable. Now, across the street and a block up from the Weizmann Institute is the campus of the School of Agriculture of the Hebrew University—which proves that if you wait long enough, the mountain indeed will come to the prophet.

The Weizmann occupies a 250-acre compound with 17 modern laboratory buildings. Touring it, no one doubts that Meyer Weisgal, the Broadway producer who succeeded Weizmann, was one of the all-time champs in the race for the philanthropic dollar.

Meyer Weisgal is one of the most colorful and striking figures in Jewish life. A passionate Zionist since his youth, he soon came under the influence of Chaim Weizmann. This affected his whole life and he became Weizmann's closest associate. Without his boundless dynamism and his ability to charm, the Weizmann Institute, one of the jewels of modern Israel, could never have been established.

He served as the president since its inception and in 1969 he was succeeded by Professor Albert Sabin. One of the buildings is a graduate school where 400 students, foreign and Israeli, work for their PhD's. Along the center walk is the villa of Isaac Wolfson, the British philanthropist. Israelis call all separate housing units, whether bungalows or two-story affairs, villas. They will have to coin another word for Wolfson's splendid home.

At the end of this ellipse is Yad Weizmann, where Weizmann and his wife, Vera, are entombed. The Israelis are devoted to yads. They never tire of showing the visitor Yad Herzl or Yad Rothschild or Yad Weizmann or any of the others. Paraphrasing Spiro Agnew, however, I believe if you have seen one yad you have seen them all: black marble tombs set in circular parks.

Calling the Weizmann a kibbutz is a conceit and, like most conceits, stretches a point. Yet it is true that over the years, and perhaps unconsciously, the Weizmann has had to incorporate many of the modes, values, and conveniences of the kibbutz. There is a compelling reason why.

There are two auto assembly plants in Israel, which would both lose money but for government subsidies. There are some dozen textile factories, most of which lose more money. There is even the gigantic potash works on the Dead Sea, which loses a great deal of money. The one Israeli invention which turned a profit from the beginning was the kibbutz.* The kibbutz succeeded because it served a function, it served that function efficiently, and its members found expression in service. Could the Weizmann say the same?

Indeed, many Israelis asked if a developing country at perpetual war with hostile neighbors, contending constantly with the elements, could afford an expensive scientific establishment devoted to pure research. The answer was, probably not.

The Weizmann found it could serve a function by becoming

* Tommy Lapid says the kibbutz is not a profitable investment money-wise, only otherwise. Okay, Tommy, have it your way.

the catalyst to exploit one of Israeli's great natural resources. That resource is brains, especially scientific brains.

A scientist can assemble a truck no better than an illiterate nor can he sell more potash than a Cabinet minister. But he can turn a profit with a science-based industry.

IBM is a science-based industry, so is Xerox, so are the gauges manufactured by Perkin-Elmer up in Connecticut, whose stock we all wished we'd bought. The components of a Xerox copier constitute only a fraction of what the consumer pays for. Competition is never going to reduce the price of a computer, because no one is ever going to mass produce computers. The consumer pays for the convenience these inventions provide.

Scientists at the Weizmann began to apply their research so that the country could turn an honest dollar out of its abundance of brains. There are economists who doubt that science-based industries will ever make a dent in Israel's chronic deficit in its balance of payments, but there are Israelis willing to try simply because they have no other choice. Two of these are Mrs. Ora Kedem, a research chemist who has been a member of the Weizmann faculty for many years, and Chaim Elata, a young engineer who is one of the founding partners of Hydronautics-Israel, a firm which manufactures the membranes for desalinating brackish water.

Mrs. Kedem is a graceful, gray-haired lady with a lively sense of humor. She complained in mock exasperation that every time a journalist showed up at the Weizmann to discover the facts about desalinization, Nehemiah Meyers, the public relations director, steered them straight to her office.

"There's a joke in our country," she said, "about the tourist who asks if there is any night life in Jerusalem and gets the answer, 'There used to be but she moved to Tel Aviv.' Last year I worked in the Negev Arid Zone Institute and I went to Nehemiah Meyers and told him, 'From now on, tell them she moved to Beersheba.'"

As a chemist, Mrs. Kedem concentrates on human cells, which, she explained, are membranes. One of the functions of membranes is to filter salt and water. She discovered that certain chemical arrangements filter salt from water and water from

salt more effectively than other arrangements. She won a prize
for this discovery.

Chaim Eleta, a young physicist just returned from MIT, found
that these novel chemical arrangements had commercial possibilities. He and his partner put up the brains and the Rehovot
Municipality and the Israeli Tourist Office put up the money.
The desalinating membrane is essentially a filter and Hydronautics-Israel manufactures these filters on a modular system,
so that a customer can desalinate hundreds or thousands of
gallons of water.

One of their first customers was the proprietor of a tourist
hotel on the Dead Sea, who had the choice of paying to pipe
water for his guests from the Sea of Galilee or sinking a well,
tapping brackish water, and installing his own desalinating plant.
The second was cheaper. Hydronautics-Israel has sold many
membranes since and has branched out into the manufacture
of other scientific instruments.

Thus some of the energies of the Weizmann, whose first
business venture came in World War II when it undertook
research into the manufacture of pharmaceutical supplies for
the Allied war effort in the Middle East. Now the Weizmann
sponsors the Science Based Industries Development Corporation, Ltd., which serves industries that manufacture nuclear
research instruments, small, low-cost computers, "Fragiligraphs,"
which measure the osmotic fragility of blood cells, and sophisticated spectrometers. Weizmann scientists have also developed
new wheat and barley strains that grow in sand; a magnetic
catheter which can travel through blood vessels; and a process
of determining the sex of the fetus within the embryo. And
it is one of the world's leading producers of heavy oxygen, supply-
ing radioactive isotopes for tracer work to laboratories throughout
the world.

This is not to insist the Weizmann is all business. The Weizmann faculty does not expect that every experiment will revo-
lutionize either Israeli finance or science. Many scientists are
still devoted to pure research. This devotion over the years has
changed the Weizmann.

There are qualitative differences in the careers of a scientist
who worked at the institute in its early days and one who works

there now. Consider Chaim Weizmann and Professor Ernest Winocur, who presently occupies the Everett M. Dirksen Chair in Cancer Research.

As a scientist, Weizmann started his first research into dyestuff chemistry. Before he was thirty he had taken out patents and initiated the present scientific study of borate compounds.

Weizmann's reputation is based on his discovery of acetones which made smokeless gunpowder possible for the Allies in World War I. The acetones, which Weizmann turned over to the British government, gained him entree into the drawing rooms of the influential and the offices of those who made foreign policy. The result, of course, was the Balfour Declaration, and to this very day no one really knows whether by "Jewish home" Sir Arthur meant refuge or state.

Another by-product of Weizmann's research was butyl alcohol, which has widespread use throughout the automobile and lacquer industries.

In Rehovot, one of the ways Weizmann cooled off against Hebrew University was to concentrate upon a local problem— how to make shale oil into a cheap and available fuel. He was inspired by the industry of a nonscientific neighbor, one Katzman, who had set up a crude apparatus in his Rehovot backyard to experiment with Judean shale. But the townsfolk were without mercy. They won an injunction against Katzman, charging that every time he stoked his furnace with shale oil, the whole neighborhood was enveloped by a gas.

Weizmann took the experiment indoors and succeeded where Katzman had failed. But Weizmann also discovered that shale oil is expensive to mine and Judean shale is too poor in quality to become a substitute for kerosene.

Weizmann's scientific method was trial and error. He had found that accidental observation led to significant discoveries. That day is gone and Weizmann probably knew it was going, which is why he, an eminently practical chemist, wanted an institute devoted to pure research.

Professor Winocur has spent his entire scientific life concentrating on viruses. He is a slight man with a bushy dark beard, so soft spoken one often has to lean forward to catch his remarks.

He is engaged in the tedious and desperate undertaking of discovering why viruses make some cells cancerous.

Winocur served in the Royal Air Force and then immigrated to Israel, where he worked on a kibbutz and educated himself. He was an agronomist but turned to biology after he had succeeded in isolating some viruses which afflict plants.

"How much more interesting it would be," he said to himself, "to isolate viruses which afflict human beings." Since then, his career has been spent in the identification of the environmental agents which cause cancer in healthy cells.

The effort, he explained, is not to find out what happens—we all know what happens; the effort is to see it happen and trace why it happens and out of every experiment to learn a little bit more. Setting up these experiments can take months and years of preparation.

Nor can these experiments be conducted in solitary study. Winocur explained that for every experiment he was dependent upon the electron microscope. "Were I to attempt to use the electron microscope myself, it would take up all my skills and time. Instead, I have to depend upon another scientist whose field of study is electromicroscopy, one of the many scientists upon whom a researcher has to depend."

When I told him I intended to compare the Weizmann Institute to a kibbutz, he told me it was a capital idea. "There is not much room on the kibbutz for the loner and there is less and less room for the loner in science. Little by little compartmentalization at the Weizmann is breaking down. Dividing us into chemists and biologists and physicists often gets in our way more than it helps. A chemist cannot content himself with test tubes these days but must understand the biologist's slides, and a doctor needs the mathematician to outline the formulas of his discoveries. No one communicates as easily as a family, and that is what the kibbutz is and what the Weizmann probably will become."

If anything dismayed him about the Weizmann, it was that there is only one in Israel. "I could not work any place else in this country," he said. "I am not a doctor, so I could not use the research facilities at Hadassah in Jerusalem or the Tel Aviv

Medical School. No Israeli industry can afford a research staff. We offer students courses which lead to a research degree, then tell them there is no place for them to work. We may at that have to go out like the early kibbutzniks and establish more institutes."

Part *IX*
Citizens, Refugees, and Terrorists

My door is always open

THE MAYOR of Nazareth has an easier time of it, say, than
the mayor of Trenton, New Jersey. The job is easier because
the mayor of Nazareth does not have to worry about the cops,
who are controlled by the Ministry of Police, a national agency;
nor does the mayor of Nazareth have to worry about the schools,
which are financed by the Ministry of Education, and the
churches; nor does he have to worry about unemployment, of
which Nazareth has none. What makes his job truly a political
plum is that in Israel it is illegal for an employer to differentiate
between the salaries paid to Arabs and the salaries paid to Jews.

Nazareth has a population of 35,000 Arabs, both Moslem and
Christian, and a tourist population of 50,000. Its mayor is Mr.
Mousa Kteily, a portly fifty-year-old Arab of Greek Orthodox
faith, who is finishing his first four-year term.

Nazareth, the largest Arab city in Israel, is built on one of the
mountainous slopes in the Galilee which falls precipitously to
the Jezreel Valley below. From the crest above, solemnly rising
in the distance, is Mount Tabor, where Deborah sent forth
Barach to defeat the Canaanites and where later Christ was
transfigured.

The mayor's office in the municipality building is off Rehov
Pope Paul VI, down which mules and bicyclists recklessly speed
and Mercedes Benzes as recklessly careen. The Mercedes came to
Israel after the Six-Day War, when the occupying forces found

235

many of them in deserted Jordanian franchises. Since their diesel
engines consume crude oil, they are an economical car to run
in a country where the tax on gasoline costs almost as much as
the gas.

The way to Mr. Kteily's office is up a steep flight of steps below
which blooms a semitropical garden. Mr. Kteily's office is as
big as that of the mayor of Trenton but more somber, for it is
finished in a varnished brown wooden dado. He sits at a polished
black desk flanked by portraits of Abba Eban and Golda Meir.
He delights in serving his guests Turkish coffee and explaining,
"My door is always open to those who knock."

The business of Nazareth, he explained, are its shrines. For
the last seven years, the Roman Catholic Franciscan Order has
kept thousands of Nazarenes busy constructing the magnificent
Church of the Annunciation, a great basilica, the most im-
pressive shrine in all the Holy Land. It is also the most expensive
shrine for the tourist, 6 pounds a head. I have no idea how
parishioners intent on a novena get by the Arab guides clustered
at the gates—I didn't, my son didn't, and his wife and Johnny
Goldhurst paid 6 pounds each, too.

The Church of the Annunciation is the fifth church erected
over the grotto where the Virgin Mary heard of her conception.
The Franciscans have preserved the earlier masonry. On the
same compound is the Church of Joseph, built over the shop
where Joseph cobbled.

"All is not contentment," said the mayor, tapping his fingers
together. "I have my worries. The Greek Orthodox Patriarch
complained the Catholics could have spent their money in doing
something for the citizens of Nazareth. Though I am Greek
Orthodox myself, I told the Patriarch there is not enough money
in the world to glorify the miracle of the Annunciation and
Conception. There are other Nazareths, I have been to one in
Texas, but this is the Nazareth where it happened."

Amen to that. It was obvious from his tone that indeed he
had had his troubles with the Patriarch.

Mousa Kteily spent twenty years as a Nazareth policeman
during the British mandate. In 1948, when the Israelis and Arabs
went to war, he immigrated to Lebanon but returned three
years later under the Israeli law for the reunification of families.

His family is an old one in Nazareth and he was a prosperous merchant and farmer until 1967, when he handily won election. He pointed to a corner of the office and said, "I slept there many nights as a police officer. This office was a barracks."

Hizzoner is cosmopolitan. He speaks English, Hebrew, Arabic, and French. He has made a whirlwind tour of America at the behest of the United Jewish Appeal, stopping at fifteen cities in thirty-one days. He spoke at Little Rock and at Jacksonville on successive nights, which, as the vaudevillians used to say, was a long split week. In New York and Birmingham he told Christian and Jewish audiences about Nazareth, the Arabs of Israel, and the Arabs of the Administered Territories.

Mr. Kteily is a dead ringer for Mayor Frank Zullo of Norwalk; Zullo and Kteily look like a younger and darker Lee J. Cobb. I have, in my time, interviewed many mayors in the United States and in other parts of the world, and I always find a refreshing wholesomeness talking to those who are real town boosters.

On the balcony, before descending the steps to the flower-scented plaza, I listened as Mr. Kteily proclaimed the eternal glory of his hometown. Indeed he had something to boast about. Only in Nazareth did the angel Gabriel tell Mary she would bear the Son of God, and this charismatic event is not one Mayor Kteily intends to let the folks forget.

Rastum Bastuni doesn't live here anymore

RASTUM BASTUNI, a forty-six-year-old Arab, once a prominent politician, has left Israel for the United States.

An architect, graduated from the Technion in Haifa, Bastuni was elected to the Second Knesset, although his party, the Mapam, dropped him from its list later for siding with the minority on a now forgotten issue (Israeli politicians are as ruthless with Jews, too). Bastuni was later readmitted to Mapam and then again expelled from its Arab section for charging that the existence of the section itself was "racial degradation."

Bastuni worked for the Town Planning Department of the

Haifa municipality. He spoke a flawless, idiomatic Hebrew, as well as English and Arabic. He founded the movement called the Arab-Jewish Association for Arab Identity and argued in newspapers and journals that, while the Arabs in Israel must become an integral part of the state, they should preserve their national identity.

But Bastuni was bitterly disappointed by the government, which he charged not only disregarded his efforts but actually hindered them. If Israel has a clear-cut policy regarding Arab citizens, it has never informed these citizens as to what that policy is. One school of thought holds that Israel should give full backing to Arabs ready to identify with the state, another that Israel cannot expect such an identification from the Arabs and therefore the first policy is mistaken.

So Bastuni left. The problem of identity, though not central to Arab life in Israel, was too much for him to resolve.

Most of Israel's Arabs are more pragmatic. In many respects, they never had it so good. Fifteen years ago, the Arab village of Majd el-Krum in the upper Galilee was a congeries of small adobe huts housing 3,800 people. Today the adobes are gone, in their place the small Israeli villas equipped with solar water heaters on the roofs.

Arabs are free to come and go, to take any jobs they can get. By law, they cannot serve in the Army, but they can work in some of the defense industries. Eighty Arabs who own their own cars control Haifa's night taxi service. In Nazareth, the Arab guides hold a monopoly on guiding tourists through the shrines, and Arabs enjoy almost a near monopoly in the Old City of Jerusalem. As often as Jewish guides complain about this unfair business practice, the Arab guides wail about discrimination.

Nine thousand Arabs, for example, share Acre with 28,000 Jews. There are Arab town councillors, Arab municipality officials, Arab teachers, doctors, shopkeepers, lawyers, and property owners. Housewives shop in both Jewish and Arab stores looking for the lowest price. Jewish and Arab workers meet in the factories. Seventy Arab families in Acre have already moved into the new Wolfson Housing Project, living side by side with Jews.

At Haifa University, there are 300 Arab students and at the exclusive Technion 30. Probably 500 Arabs are enrolled in prestigious Hebrew University, one of whom, two years ago, placed a bomb in the cafeteria killing several students.

The terrorism, directed or inspired by Al Fatah, has intensified the problem of identity for those Arabs who do not wish to live pragmatically. Reporter Ya'acov Friedler, of the Jerusalem *Post*, discussed this problem with twenty-six-year-old Ahmed Rhousy, who holds a government job in Jerusalem. Ahmed Rhousy addressed himself to the dilemma which afflicts some of the young men of Israel's 320,000 Arabs, of which 56,000 are Christian (for whom the dilemma is much less acute because they have never been part of the Moslem mainstream):

"My problem is one of identity, of identification. Who am I? Am I an Israeli? Then, why am I not trusted all the way? Why do I have to hide behind the shutters in the evening, now that some Israeli Arabs have joined the terror? Why can't I look my Jewish neighbors in the face any more? Am I an Arab? But the Arabs across the border consider Moslems like me, serving in the Israel government post, a traitor.

"We are confused and riddled with complexes. Even more than is usual with a minority. I know that part of the reason is subjective, part of our Arab character, but that doesn't make it any easier for us.

"Older Arabs had it easier. They were used to living under a foreign regime, the Turks and then the British, and they made their peace with the situation. But we, the young people who were brought up and educated in the state of Israel, find it hard to accommodate ourselves. You taught us democracy, and independence, and self-fulfillment in school. But when we finished school we found that we could not practice these lofty principles.

"On the one hand you destroyed our traditional patriarchy. We do not wish to follow our father's orders blindly as he followed his father's. But we cannot be completely free like the sabras either. Many jobs are closed to us. We understand that they must be as long as the Arab states are at war with Israel. But nevertheless a graduate doesn't want to be a simple worker. I even know that some of us have got jobs we believe

Arabs can't get, but that's part of our complex. It doesn't matter
that no Arab has had the enterprise to start a plant that could
employ us. Every *protectsia*, favoritism, or unfairness against us,
is magnified in our minds, and we're immediately convinced that
it's only because we are Arabs."

This problem for the Arab intelligentsia became pronounced
after the Six-Day War. Israeli Arabs came into contact again
with 1,000,000 Arabs in the Administered Territories, who may
not have known freedom or enjoyed a high standard of living,
but for the past twenty years had known a national identity. It
was they who influenced the Israeli Arab rather than the other
way around.

Thus Al Fatah has been able to recruit young Arabs in Majd
el-Krum, in Acre, and in other cities to join the terrorist movement.

Last November 23, for example, two young Arabs from Majd
el-Krum, Omar Hussein Mansour and Ahmed Mohammed
Bishar, drove into Haifa and planted bombs in two Jewish apartment houses. They drove back to Acre intending to plant two
more bombs. On their way, a police traffic car, wholly by chance,
swung in behind them.

Now if you are an Arab and you have planted two bombs
which will soon be detonated in Haifa and you have two more
bombs in your auto, behind which is a police car, you are in
BIG TROUBLE. One of these men started to dismantle these
explosives, when the car stopped short for a red light. The bombs
went off, hurling the two from the Vauxhall which exploded
in flames, as three absolutely amazed traffic cops sat in stunned
disbelief. The bombs in Haifa were defused fifteen minutes before
they would have blown up the houses.

As news of the incident spread, tension began to rise in the
Old City of Acre, the Arab section, and in the New City, the
Jewish section. The Arabs mistakenly heard that several Jews
had been killed by the explosion, and some of them began to
march through the streets singing. Many of the Jews in Acre
are Oriental Jews who were expelled from Arab countries in 1948
and who regard all Arabs with hostility. Hearing of the Arab
celebration, a large number of these Jews started toward the
Old City. The Acre police brought up reinforcements to keep

the two groups from each other. Three policemen and four civilians, all Jews, were injured before the fuzz quelled the riot.

Perhaps this near lynching convinced Bastuni that he had no future in Israel. At any rate, Rastum Bastuni doesn't live here anymore.

The "Canal of Fire"

Until the Israeli Air Force neutralized Egyptian artillery positions in the winter of 1970, the soldiers along the Suez called it "the Canal of Fire." Over 100 years ago the Arabs also called the Suez "the Canal of Fire," but these were the Arabs who dug the Canal, one of whom still survives.

Mordechai Gilat, a reported for *Ha'aretz*, the newspaper of the Mapam, went into the Sinai as soon as troops secured it and in El Arish he met Ali Hamden el-Halili, a legend to the townsfolk. El-Halili is one hundred twenty years old.

Gilat reports that el-Halili's home is a small dark room, the windows covered with shades, a small handwoven rug of cloth on the dirt floor. The furniture consists of two armchairs and a small footstool. The blue walls are vacant of decoration and the roof is corrugated tin with green paint peeling from it.

Ali Hamden el-Halili, a tall man but bent, squatted on the floor and commanded his son, Handi, only sixty-five, to bring the Israeli newspaperman something to drink. This aged Arab had a long brown face animated by green eyes. He told his story slowly.

"I was born in El Arish in 1849. I was the middle son of five. My father, Muhamed Ali, was a successful merchant, well known by the people, and rich. My mother, Habubbah, was beautiful and clever, very smart. She loved me more than the others. She gave me all her attention.

"When I was seven years old my father wanted to send me to the fields to make me a peasant. My mother objected. She shouted to my father that I was going to learn, that I was going to become a wise man. My father was laughing. Afterwards he was angry, then silent. Then he agreed. He sent me to school.

"I was Ali, the happiest of five children. I knew that only he who studies becomes the head of the family.

"My class was a tent in the middle of the desert, surrounded by date trees under whose shade we sat. My teacher sat in the middle of ten boys. We used dry sugarcanes as pens, which we sharpened with stones, then dipped into ink to write on a board.

"At the end of the day we erased the ink by scraping it with sand.

"I stayed in school for six years, then joined my brothers in the fields. After two years, my father lost his business. We were hungry. Therefore my father went to Egypt to find work. He got a job with the Suez Canal Company and because of his previous status was made foreman of six workers who did the digging.

"But this was not enough for my father. He wanted to make more money, as much as possible. One night he arrived at our home with camels and asked me to join him. He said, 'It's very nice there, it's nice work digging, and we are making progress.'

"I agreed. We rode the camels for a day and a night until we reached the village of Turna by the Canal. There were workers lined its whole length, little clusters of men with shovels. There were many foremen like my father, men who stood and shouted to others what to do.

"The labor was simple. Each foreman got a piece of land and he was told how deep he was to dig that week. There were two ways we used to move the sand—one was by little trolleys on rails and the other by camels. My father worked with camels. Easier and cheaper. We dug on both sides. Children took care of the camels. Most of the children were orphans.

"We started to work at the end of the night, very, very early, before the sun rose. It was hot then, the sand was heavy and a little bit wet on the bottom. The camels were difficult animals. They ran away and we brought them back and they ran away again. And we had to work fast, like horses, as the rising sun would drive us away.

"We dug as though there was gold at the bottom of the Canal. We were digging and digging and there was never an end. So much dirt, so much sand. Our faces were red from the sun like a watermelon, and our hands bled and our bodies were wet. We drank and drank and never had enough. Digging and drinking, digging and drinking, until we fell down.

"We took our strength from songs. We sang all kinds of work songs, shouting and singing not to feel how tired we are. Time passed slowly, very slowly, one day after the other, one week after the other, one month after the other. I became an old-timer at the work, but it didn't help my faith. The work was a nightmare. At nights I slept like a dog, dreaming about the work, about the sand and the camels and all the troubles my father brought upon me. I wanted to run away and walk until I reached my home, but I was afraid. I was young and weak and had no experience. So I stayed.

"I was the best worker. I wanted father to be *absuth* which means 'heavy,' then he would say, 'I am proud of you.' He was a difficult man, like a storm. He thought only about work, about sand, and money. And he was shouting and cursing. And then never did he say a word to me, only to work and to move the sand, the sand which was getting into my eyes. I couldn't look at him anymore. My father, the same father who one morning got a little ahead when a few people came from the company. They said nicely, 'You are progressing. You are doing very good.' They spoke to the workers and to father and they laughed among themselves and they said, 'If you keep on like this we will finish soon.' They promised that they would come again but they didn't.

"We continued to work, biting our lips in the sun, becoming weaker day by day. There were some who collapsed. One who worked next to me said, 'I can't see anymore,' and he fell down. Life is fate. We didn't know what to do with him. I was standing there and looking at him and thinking, 'What will happen to you?'

"My father came and said, 'The man is dead, dead. *Yallon.*' *Yallon* comes from *allah*; it means 'gone,' 'gone.' We put him into a grave. What a way to die.

"Then my father was summoned to El Arish, where he had been elected chief sheikh of the town. I followed him. I found my brothers still in the fields growing watermelons. And I stayed."

When he reached one hundred, Ali Hamden el-Halili saw no reason to continue working. He gave his lands to others, who pay him rents.

He is the only one of the brothers who still lives. The youngest died only three years ago. The oldest died many, many years ago, working on the Canal when he collapsed and was covered over by sand. A third brother was bitten by a snake in Jaffa and died when there was no doctor to attend him. A fourth was murdered by thieves.

"As for me," Ali went on, "I work in the garden, read the Koran, and listen to the radio. I can write in Arabic and I learned numbers from my sons."

Would he send his sons to dig the Canal? asked Gilat.

"My sons are the highest men," he said, closing his eyes. "They have learned in school. They won't make the mistakes I made. They are able to tell their sons, my grown-up grandchildren, about me, Ali Hamden el-Halili, who dug the Canal. Tomorrow morning I will get up, I will see if the sun is out and, if it is, I will dig a little trench to water my garden. I believe that man must want to work for as long as he is on the earth."

Free figs

ABDULLAH, THE Arab, is trying to take a nap. The nearby play of children disturbs him.

"Why are you wasting your time here," asks Abdullah, "when on the other side of town Mohammed Ali is handing out free figs?"

The children run to claim the fruit.

Abdullah goes back to his rest but rises with a start and asks himself, "Why am I wasting my time sleeping when Mohammed Ali is handing out free figs?"

This and many jokes like it make the rounds in Israel. I wondered whether the Israeli assessment of the Arab mentality and character was simply a self-determined brainwashing.

"No, it is not brainwashing. The joke has its truth," said bearded Dr. H. Shaked, a slight man, impeccably dressed, who speaks slowly and deliberately. Dr. Shaked is a specialist in Middle East Studies at Tel Aviv University and a director of the Reuven Shiloah Research Center in suburban Ramat Aviv.

The Reuven Shiloah Research Center is an institute devoted to the study of contemporary Middle Eastern and African affairs. It issues dozens of monographs, such as *Army Officers in Arab Politics and Society* and *Soviet Views on Arab Politics*. One of its most important activities is the publication annually of the *Middle East Record*, a fully documented survey of political developments in the Middle East arranged according to topics and chronological sequence. The *Middle East Record* is based upon a close study of over 200 Arab newspapers, periodicals, books, and official publications. The material for 1967 alone fills over 100 file drawers, and there were more newspapers still in bundles than the Salvation Army picks up in the suburbs on clean-up Saturday.

The *Middle East Record* is the most comprehensive publication in its field.

"It is the most comprehensive because," explained Dr. Shaked, "there are no secrets in the Arab world. Sooner or later everything finds its way into the press, together with contradictions. We determine what is actual, what has happened, by comparing how the contradictions vary from place to place and time to time. While the newspapers of the Arab world are controlled, you will find substantive policies discussed in a Cairo weekly you would never find in *Pravda*."

The Reuven Shiloah Research Center was founded in 1959 as a paragovernmental agency, but the Jews in the Middle East have maintained some sort of a center devoted to Arab studies since the first one was started in the late 1920's by one Reuven Shiloah. The Zionists in Palestine started an intensive study of Arab history, religion, and politics in the '20's, because they had the fact forced upon them that the Arabs were different than they were—not biologically different, not physically different, but different according to Western behavioral patterns. By Western standards Arab behavior was irrational and the Jews saw the importance of anticipating Arab responses.

Why are they different?

"First," said Dr. Shaked, "learning in the Arab world is by rote. Everything is memorized. On many occasions our own analytic learning leads Westerners into serious mistakes, but it does not on that account induce fatally bad habits. It is possible for an American and a Communist to enter into a dialogue and agree, say, that peace is desirable. Along the way it is even possible for them to cede one another's points. But this is impossible for the Arab. The history of the Arab world contains a self-destructive habit. The Arabs have always believed there is a secret about their enemy which once divined will result in Arab victory. But the Turks had soldiers, the British superb diplomacy, and the Israelis air power, all of which are patent strengths, not secret weaknesses."

Israeli specialists agree that rhetoric undoes the Arabs. Nasser, condemning the presence of United Nations troops, thought U Thant understood this was a nationwide prayer meeting, not a demand the troops be ordered out. By Arab standards, Nasser did not overplay his hand. Nasser, agree these specialists, perfectly represented and voiced the will of his constituency. Egyptian generals in the command tent on the eve of battle do not discuss flanking maneuvers or the problems of supply but prophesy the annihilation of the enemy and the shame that will attend his defeat.

"Rhetoric," went on Dr. Shaked, "has convinced the Arabs they are fighting a religious war, which they are not; they are fighting a national and political war. Their belief in their own rhetoric makes it hard for them to sit down and discuss peace, which is against Allah's will."

Dr. Shaked illustrated his point by tracing the history of Arab anti-Semitism. The Jews did not kill Mohammed, so in the beginning there was no Moslem antipathy toward Jews as such. The Jews were infidels. Under the Moors in Spain, in fact, the Jews enjoyed a golden age rivaled only by the golden age they enjoy in America and England today. The Arabs even displayed a fondness for the Jews when the muktars and the sheiks sold off their land to the Jewish Agency. By the time of the mandate, when the Arabs saw that the Jews intended to settle all of the land, they became bitter, like Esau, who sold his birthright to his brother, Jacob, for a bowl of porridge. They turned against the Jews. This hostility, however, was economic in its motivation. Even as this hostility grew more intense, it was not the Christian variety of anti-Semitism. The Arabs would have killed the Jews, but not because the Jews killed God.

"But now," said Shaked, "Arab printing presses turn out *The Protocols of Zion*, which are distributed free on every street corner in Cairo, Amman, and Damascus. The Arab has projected himself as the saviour of the world who will lay waste to the corrupting Semites. This rhetoric is not to the Arabs' interest. The world simply doesn't believe it needs Arabs if it wants to get rid of Jews."

Did he see any change?

Dr. Shaked pursed his lips. "In London," he said, "at a conference of Middle East specialists, I talked to an Arab who had just completed his doctorate. I argued that in 1948, Israel was hardly a state. It didn't have an Army, it didn't have an Air Force, it hardly had a government. What made Israel into a formidable Middle Eastern state were three wars with the Arab nations. Since war hasn't worked for the Arabs, I suggested they might try peace. It is possible Israel could rend itself in internal dissension, for there are many issues never raised because of our perpetual state of emergency. This Arab was a polite fellow. He thought about it. Then he said he didn't want to continue the discussion because he knew it was another Zionist trick. It was pure and simple projection. As long as the Arab projects he will run to the other side of town for nonexistent figs."

The camp in Bethlehem

THE ARAB refugee camp was on one of the Bethlehem Hills. Walls of dry masonry terraced the steep slope. These walls created a grid for the housing which consisted of small, hand-built huts of concrete walls with one small window and tin roofs. These rude dwellings often accommodated eight and sometimes eleven children. At the entrance to the camp was the village well, a concrete compound with five faucets at which Arab women filled ten-gallon pails they carried home on their heads.

The December day was bright. The paths were yellow and hard packed, for there had been no November rains. At one of the corners in the camp stood a moustachioed Arab vendor, hawking eggplants, carrots, lettuce, and tomatoes from a push-cart tilted against a fallen rock.

At the extreme end of the camp was a small factory, surrounded by barbed wire, which manufactured crates. Opposite the factory, outside the camp, was an enormous villa. It was three stories high, its porch of delicately inlaid marble. A dozen windows admitted the morning light. It was the home of the Arab mayor of Bethlehem.

By American standards, refugee camps aren't much. They are not much by Israeli standards, either. But the casual visitor would be hard pressed to describe the qualitative difference between the refugee camp in Bethlehem and the Arab village of Abu Ghosh, a few miles to the west of Jerusalem whose populace is Israeli citizens.

At the headquarters of the military government in Jerusalem, an Israeli major, responsible for the administration of these camps of West Bank refugees, removed his beret and put on a yarmulka, as we had tea.

"Let us agree," he said seriously, "that these refugees constitute a terrible waste of human potential, that their plight is pitiful, that they live barren lives. Israel is not going to solve the problem because of these moral considerations. The refugees are a political problem, part of a larger political situation. When that political situation is resolved, the refugee problem will be resolved, too."

So apparently the refugees will remain a static political problem for a variety of reasons, one of which is Israeli intransigence. Arab intransigence is another. Arab leaders have made political capital throughout the world on the fact of the refugees and still do.

The refugees themselves have not suggested a viable alternative to their condition. They have, on occasion, told the Israelis they want to return to the homes they abandoned twenty years ago, to which the Israelis have replied that it is an impracticable solution. The Israelis are not going to distribute 350,000 potential enemies around the countryside to homes which have been razed long ago for highways or new cities or industrial complexes.

For twenty years newsmen, journalists, and United Nations officials have traversed these dirt paths, taking pictures, interviewing the inhabitants. None of them have come up with any compelling solutions. For two and a half years, Israeli soldiers and social workers have patrolled the same streets without a new idea. For twenty years, the mayor of Bethlehem has arisen in the morning and the first thing that met his gaze was the refugee camp below his comfortable bedroom. If he had any ideas about relieving the plight of his fellow Arabs, he never made them known to King Hussein or to the military governor of Jerusalem.

The unique refugee

OF THE 17,000,000 refugees in the world, the 350,000 Arab refugees are unique. They are unique because most refugees sooner or later cease being refugees. Refugees become absorbed and integrated, assimilated, in the areas or countries to which they flee. The refugee problem in India in both numbers and duration is a greater problem than the refugee problem in the Middle East. Farmers have had to become laborers in India and lawyers have had to become clerks, but they do not remain refugees.

The Arab refugees are in their third generation. They remain unique because their problem was created in panic and perpetuated by propaganda.

After the United Nations voted on partition but before Israel declared statehood, many of the rich and upper-middle-class Arabs left Palestine. The merchant who lived in a castle in Acre moved to a castle in Amman and the doctor with a going practice in Haifa is treating patients in Cairo. They had various motives for leaving, chief of which were that the Jewish state, if successfully established, threatened their identity and the conviction that, in the coming war, the Arabs would win and they did not want to be caught in the middle.

Their departure left 1,000,000 other Arabs, workers, laborers, farmers, and small merchants without leadership. It is true that the Arab world does not have many leaders—there are many "notables" but few leaders—but had these rich and successful Arabs remained, their presence might have quelled the panic that overcame all the rest.

These unsophisticated, virtually primitive people thought the Jews would massacre them. And if the Jews didn't massacre them, certainly the victorious Arabs would. In 1948, six Arab armies moved against Israel—Egypt, Jordan, Syria, Lebanon, Iraq, and Saudi Arabia; there wasn't much likelihood an Arab who stayed in Palestine would escape vengeance. All they heard from the Arab nations was the exhortation to flee, to clear the roads for Arab tank and infantry columns. Arabs promised a quick victory and, once it was over, the refugees could return to Palestine and pick out the Jewish villa they wanted.

The Israelis, too, panicked. The mass exodus of over half the Palestinian Arab population made them fear the United Nations would revoke partition. They tried crash programs to calm the fears of these illiterate Arabs, to no avail.

It was apparently a lost cause and once it was a lost cause, the Israeli hard-liners took over. It was to Israel's advantage to clog the roads to the south and west with refugees impeding Arab military movements. Battalion commander Moshe Dayan toured the Arab town of Ramle with a loudspeaker telling residents this was their chance to get out, to get out while the getting was good. They left.

Even when the Jews stabilized their lines, keeping the Egyptians from Beersheba, clearing the upper Galilee, holding the Syrians at Degania, the exodus continued. Almost 300,000 Arab refugees made their way into Gaza and another 60,000 to the Jordanian West Bank. The rest fled north, many of them returning to Israel in 1952.

In May, 1950, the United Nations Relief and Work Agency (UNRWA) began providing assistance to these refugees in Gaza and the West Bank in the hopes of settling them in productive work. UNRWA provides refugees with rations, rudimentary schooling, and medical care. The agency has often claimed to care for over 1,000,000 refugees. The rolls of refugees are grossly exaggerated, because all refugees hold more than one ration card. There are some who hold as many as 500 cards, blackmarketing UNRWA food and clothing. They are, by UNRWA definition, "refugee capitalists."

In its annual report in 1951, UNRWA stated, "To increase or prevent decreases in the ration issue, the refugees eagerly report births, sometimes by passing a newborn baby from family to family, and reluctantly report deaths, resorting often to surreptitious burial to avoid giving up a ration card." In all its subsequent reports, UNRWA has never changed this paragraph.

The refugees in Gaza live in one of the world's pits of hopelessness. They cannot build a city out of sand, nor can they start a kibbutz in the desert. In all the refugee camps, all but the top-level administrators are themselves Arab refugees, incapable of organizing and directing efforts at self-help; more intent on the petty graft, they chisel here and there, jealous of the little empires they have constructed. The refugees on the West Bank have a better time of it. Many of them can find work in Jerusalem, for the Jews do not care whether they are UNRWA recipients or not.

What makes them truly unique is that, despite their realization that the world is concerned over them, they have been singularly unable to offer any program of their own toward resettlement.

They do not petition, nor do they agitate. Which led Professor Shimon Shamir, department head of the Reuven Shiloah Institute, to conduct an intensive research project among them to discover why. Shamir's report, *The Political Outlook of the Refugees*, has been published in Hebrew and will probably be issued in English by the Rand Corporation.

In this effort, Shamir was assisted by Arab students from the Hebrew University. Shamir discovered that indeed the refugees had tried agitation, but the Jordanians or the Egyptians shot the troublemakers. The refugees believe Israel is impregnable and that they have been used. They are as bitter about their Arab brothers as they are about the Jews, but they feel helpless before each. The young join the Al Fatah. They are not deluded into thinking they will bring down the Jewish state. It is just more rewarding to wear a uniform and carry grenades than to live stateless in the camps.

Israelis often shrug their shoulders on the subject of the Arab refugees. They will make the guess that the refugees will fare better under Israel in the next twenty years than they fared under the Arabs in the last twenty. The mechanics of how these people will fare better, however, is vague and ill-defined.

Many Israelis do not take kindly to criticism on this issue. Of all the criticism they receive from foreigners, they resent that from India and Britain the most. They argue that when India rids itself of the caste system and integrates the untouchables, they will consider the refugees; when India ends its war against Pakistan, they will consider their own motives in fighting the Arabs. And if India, which is quite free with its advice, antagonizes the Israelis, Britain makes them pugnacious. The British, more than anyone else, insist the Israelis, created this problem. They convinced the Arabs they would win. The British even tried to help them win so they could come back as advisers and still control the pipeline at Haifa and the Mediterranean. They watched the Arabs flee, when they could have done something to help.

In answer to American criticism, the Israeli asks why is everyone so concerned about these 350,000 refugees, what about the 16,500,000 in the rest of the world? They point out that Israel had refugee problems in 1948 when 1,000,000 Jews from Arab countries had to leave their lands. Israel housed, fed, and integrated all of them. Why, ask the Israelis, aren't the Arab sheiks with their oil royalties as generous with their brothers as Jews with money are with fellow Jews?

There is no answer to the Arab problem, only a reply: unfortunately for the refugees, Arab sheiks with their oil royalties are not Jews, and unfortunately for Jews, as the poet Heinrich Heine remarked, we have to be twice as good to get half as much.

Neighborhood punishment

In Gaza, two Arabs armed with submachine guns loitered in the *shuk* during the noon hour until a Jewish shopkeeper returned from lunch. This Jew did a thriving business with Israeli military and official personnel and had a profitable sideline selling Arab shawls, tapestries, and rugs to tourists. As he opened his door, the Arabs walked by and machine-gunned him to death.

In another Arab town, Hulhul, a young terrorist waited inside a small drugstore for the Israeli military police to pass by. He had chosen this particular location because he knew the jeep always slowed at the intersection, as it honked to clear the Arab donkey drivers and pedestrians from the road. As the jeep stopped, the terrorist threw the grenade. His timing was bad. The jeep started up and the grenade bounced past it into a cluster of Arab women.

Within twenty-four hours, Israeli soldiers blew up eight houses in the Gaza neighborhood where the two terrorists had staged their ambush. In Hulhul, the Israeli soldiers blew up the drugstore before dark.

They blew up the houses in Gaza to punish the neighborhood for not warning the Israeli authorities about the killers who had waited openly to kill the shopkeeper. They blew up the drugstore in Hulhul because the druggist had given a terrorist aid and shelter. On occasion, the Israelis have not only blown up a house in which they have discovered a cache of weapons, but the houses of the owner's relatives as well. The Israelis call this policy "vicinal" or "environmental" or "neighborhood punishment." It is not a subtle policy. It does not admit many contingencies. Two Gaza schoolteachers who were in their classrooms when the terrorists attacked found there is no appeal from the military commander's judgment.

The Israelis give the populace of the Administered Territories three choices: they can fight the terrorists and tell the Al Fatah it is destroying their lives; they can help the Israelis fight the terrorists; or they can suffer the consequences.

In one of his press conferences in December Moshe Dayan called this policy "collective punishment," which moved the United States State Department to issue a statement deploring the practice. Said State Department spokesman Carl Bartch, "We strongly urge the strict application of the Fourth Geneva Convention which specifically prohibits collective punishment. We deplore violations of this Convention and sincerely hope that all Israeli actions will be entirely consistent with its principles."

This criticism produced a flap in the Israeli Cabinet and Knesset. Foreign Minister Abba Eban quarreled with Dayan and said the Defense Minister ought to choose his words more carefully. Gossip has it that Dayan retorted that if Eban didn't like the way he was running things, he could get himself another boy. Golda Meir told them both to cool it.

Dayan appeared before the Knesset in December, 1969, to explain the policy. "I believe," said Mr. Dayan, "that when a terrorist is caught in possession of weapons, either on his person or in his house which is blown up within twenty-four hours, his neighbor will think many times before agreeing to store arms in his house and very often does not agree to it."

He went on to say that since the end of the war, 516 buildings in the Administered Territories have been either demolished or sealed off. Of these, 265 were on the West Bank, 227 in the Gaza Strip, and 24 in Jerusalem. Seventy-one men and women have been deported from the Administered Territories, including Ruhi el-Khatib, who is now the chairman of the Rescue of Jerusalem Committee. Fifteen of the deportees asked permission to return but only one woman was allowed back, and she for humanitarian reasons.

Yosef Tamir, a member of Gahal, the opposition party, closely questioned Dayan on these matters. Tamir asked the Defense Minister for an interpretation of the Jordanian statement that it would refuse to accept deportees in the future.

Dayan said, "I am speaking on behalf of the government of Israel. If you want an answer to your question, you will have to approach another parliament."

As Dayan spoke, 200 high school and college students gathered on "Demonstration Hill," opposite the Knesset. For two hours they protested neighborhood punishment. They carried home-made placards which read, "The destruction of houses is the destruction of our future," and "Collective punishment knows no bounds." The Knesset authorities had originally authorized the presence of 40 demonstrators. When more appeared, however, they did not interfere.

Later in the week, six Israeli border policemen surrounded a house in Jenin whose owner, Sheik Hassan, they suspected of helping the Al Fatah. They ordered Hassan to come out. Hassan burst from the door, followed by two men armed with Kalach-nikov rifles, who began firing. They killed police officer David Dahud and wounded another. Police returned the fire and killed Hassan and one of the terrorists. The third escaped.

Searching the house, the police found a dozen rifles, 1,000 rounds of ammunition and, cowering in the back room, Hassan's wife and seven children, all unhurt.

They blew this house up, too.

The Acre terrorist

BEFORE HE became notorious, Fawzi Ahmed Nimer was a hard-working, thirty-three-year-old Haifa taxi driver. He lived in the Arab section of nearby Acre with a Jewish wife who had renounced family and tradition to become a Moslem.

After the Six-Day War, Nimer was able to visit relatives in Nablus in the Administered Territory. He hadn't seen his brothers since he was a little boy whose mother had stayed in Haifa when father, uncles, and older brothers fled Israel in 1948. Nimer boasted to his brothers and his cousins how well he lived, how he moved about freely, how he enjoyed equal rights with Jews.

They listened sullenly. They charged he had sold his Arab soul.

When he asked what choice did he have, they said he had the choice of becoming a hero, a hero, they said, being a man who fights to save his national and religious identity. Nimer said a few grenades were hardly going to topple Israel, to which his brothers replied that a hero does what he can.

Nimer became a member of the Al Fatah, the heroic movement in the Arab world, though certainly the Israelis and many others question the heroism of sabotaging civilian rather than military objectives.

This would-be terrorist was an invaluable recruit. He spoke Hebrew and could pass for a Jew. He was a family man not noted for political intemperance and was, therefore, inconspicuous. He could command a car whenever he chose, for he had access to the Jewish taxi service where he worked. He was as familiar with the geography of Haifa as he was with his own front room. Lastly, he was smart and persuasive and able to convince five others to work with him.

Mohammed Moussa was another taxi driver who joined

Nimer. Nimer next recruited Fat'hala Saka and Abed Hazbouz, fishermen whom the Israelis allowed to go out at night. They were integral to the intrigue, for it was they who salvaged from shallow water along the deserted coastline the sealed explosives and weapons sent down from Syria by the Al Fatah. Ramaz Halifa, a house painter, and Yussef Khir, a carpenter, agreed to help make the bombs and to store the weapons in their shops.

They made these bombs of plastic explosives packed into the common jerry cans with which the Israelis carry kerosene. On a June night Nimer and Moussa crawled under the fence which surrounds the installation at Kishon Harbor and planted bombs under the oil pipes. Two nights later they destroyed a section of railroad track near Hahotrim. They blew up an electrical transformer at Shenkar, then another oil pipe near Kiryat Haim, the water pumps in Kfar Hassidim, and the oil pipes near Hadera. The bomb they planted on Tantoura Beach went off but did not kill any of the holiday vacationers.

They had become experts, and their expertise in smuggling and operating put them in contact with other terrorist groups in Jerusalem, Hebron, Tayiba, and neighboring Madj el-Krum. Nimer had become a hero to the Al Fatah and a source of desperate anxiety to the Israel police, who know the Israeli Arab is a far superior terrorist than the Fatah member from Jordan or Syria.

In October, Nimer started to bring the war home to the Israeli public. He decided to blow up apartment houses in Haifa, selecting five, all of them at busy street corners in various parts of town. He chose buildings where as many people as possible, especially tourists, could see the results. Chemically delayed-action detonators set off the charges at four-hour intervals over the next twenty hours in Haifa on October 22, 1969.

The blasts killed two Israelis, maimed seven, and injured another twenty-four. All of the apartment houses were so badly damaged by the explosions that the tenants had to leave them, and two were near collapse.

The act made headlines in the world press. Nimer determined upon another five explosions in November.

Military surveillance in the area was intense and unremitting and in November turned up Kassem Hathara. Kassem Hathara ran ammunition and explosives to the shallow waters of the north coast where Nimer and others retrieved them. Hathara, in his ten-foot speedboat, was the Fatah navy. On the night of November 4, as he made for the shoreline, an Israeli motor torpedo boat spotted him. Hathara sped for the shallow water, knowing that the MTB couldn't follow him along the shoals and that in the darkness he could elude its searchlight.

Before he made it, the MTB rammed him on his portside, knocking one of the twin 85-hp motors into the sea.

Hathara, like most of the terrorists, proved a compulsive talker when the police interrogated him. He told his interrogators the names of all his contacts, his accomplices, where they lived, where they could be found. That captured terrorists literally reveal every secret they know has convinced the British that the Israelis torture suspects, but that is far from true.

Israeli police arrested Nimer, Moussa, Saka, Hazbouz, Halifa, and Khir. In Khir's carpentry shop, police found three kegs of Czech-made plastic explosives, four chemical and eight mechanical British-made timing devices, a Russian-made antitank grenade and fifteen hand grenades, and two pocket-size cannisters of United States-made mace.

Nimer, too, recited the names of all the Fatah and Popular Front terrorists he knew, and the police began rounding up all of them. In turn, they, too, told everything.

A day before his seventeen-year-old daughter was to marry, Hathara, the gun-runner, committed suicide in his cell by hanging himself.

Nimer's Jewish wife was arrested but subsequently released. She was unaware that her husband had become a terrorist.

The local Arab councils of Jat, Jaljulia, Tayiba and Tira, as well as Knesset member Diab Oubed, publicly deplored the terror acts and called upon the Arab population to disassociate itself from such activities. Local councils in Galilee and Triangle and the Moslem trustee committees in Haifa, Lod, Jaffa, and Ramle also denounced the Acre terrorists.

Israel does not execute convicted terrorists, but these criminals can expect to spend a good portion of the future in the Nablus prison.

Part X
Our Man in the Middle East

Funny, you don't look Jewish

AT KIBBUTZ Ayelet Hashahar in the Galilee, I met Tobaiashi-san, a columnist for the Tokyo daily *Asaki*. Toby was in Israel reporting on life in the kibbutz.

Curiously, there are three or four kibbutzim in Japan, modeled after the Israeli template. Every year, forty or fifty Japanese students come to Degania Bet to study and work. Last year twenty of these Japanese decided not to go home at all, even though their nation was staging its first World's Fair.

Toby wasn't enthusiastic about the kibbutz. Why it should flourish with so many immigrants who surrendered their children at night was aberrational to him.

On the day of my visit, the work at Ayelet Hashahar had ended at 1 P.M. because of the heat. Toby said the kibbutzniks were goofing off. The Japanese, he said, worked very hard. The truth was that Toby wasn't particularly interested in the kibbutz. He felt it did not represent Israel. The future of Israel, he insisted, belonged to the United States, who should direct the Israelis to compromise on the Administered Territories.

Toby was drinking saki, which he had thoughtfully brought along with him, while I was drinking Israeli beer. So Toby began to believe in his own foreign policy pronouncements strongly. America's problem, he told me, was Okinawa, for whose repossession the Japanese were suing. On behalf of the American

261

constituency, therefore, I gave him back the island forthwith—
thereby topping Richard Nixon.

Our type

STANDARD AND POOR'S man in Tel Aviv is Leo G. Sheldon.
Gray-haired, portly, with slightly protuberant eyes, Leo has
the broad, confident smile of an eminently successful security
analyst. In fact, for twenty-five years, Leo Sheldon was just that
for Standard and Poor's. The only worthwhile tip I've had in
the last decade came from Leo: he told me to buy Dravo at
35 and it went to 74 and split. Leo put this great skill behind
him because he wanted to live in Israel. Standard and Poor's
thought if he was leaving after all these years, it ought to go
with him.

Standard and Poor's Corporation, of course, is the world's
largest financial publisher and investment counseling organization. It has established a branch office in Tel Aviv because it
suspects the Israeli economy, growing at a fast rate, will make it
the center of investment and finance for the entire Mediterranean area. Sheldon chose to open offices in Tel Aviv because
Israel's stock exchange is located in that city, and four American
brokerages operate there as well. Eventually, foreign investors
will want a stake in a rapidly expanding economy, and the one
practical way for a non-Israeli to invest in the country is through
the purchase of stocks of publicly traded companies. But investors will not buy securities in significant quantities unless they
have sufficient information on which to make sound financial
judgments.

Which is not to say Leo Sheldon has an easy time of it.
Standard and Poor's does not advise portfolios with less than
$100,000. Israelis with that much money are few and far between.
By law, the government limits the amount of money that a
citizen may invest in foreign securities although, as Sheldon
points out, "There are Israelis walking around Tel Aviv with
money in Swiss bank accounts who need counseling as much as
any other man."

Native Israelis, if they wish to purchase American securities with Israeli pounds, however, must do so through a bank by the purchase of investment dollars. Under the present official rate of exchange, 3.5 Israeli pounds buys one American dollar; 4.2 Israeli pounds buys one investment dollar; and the black market rate, published in the daily press, fluctuates between 3.7 and 3.9 Israeli pounds for the American dollar.

There is a pool of investment dollars created by the continuing flow of reparations from Germany, one-third of which is available for Israeli investors. All dividends and interest income, as well as profits realized on securities, also become investment dollars. The price of these investment dollars also fluctuates according to supply and demand. Several months ago, believing the pound would be devalued, Israelis paid almost 5 pounds for an investment dollar.

When an Israeli makes an investment in an American security, explained Lee, he is actually speculating not only on the securities but also on the price of the investment dollar at the time he sells. It is possible for a stock to go down, but because of an advance in the investment dollar, an Israeli can still realize a profit in Israeli pounds. Conversely, the investor can also sell stocks which have gone up but lose on the transaction because of a price drop in the investment dollar.

But Sheldon anticipates most of his business in Israel will come from corporations which must invest their profits in both Israeli and foreign stocks. The newspaper *Ma'ariv* runs half-page, two-color advertisements in Hebrew proclaiming the never-failing accuracy of Standard and Poor's judgment.

The main obstacle Israel has in attracting foreign investment capital is the battle which rages on the front page of the New York *Times* and the *International Herald Tribune* convincing many foreigners that the whole country is a garrison. To many of us, the image of a bombing raid involves the formation of hundreds of planes. But an Israeli bombing raid usually requires no more than three or, at the most, five planes.

Actually, Israel is willing to make many concessions to attract foreign capital, among which are loans at relatively low interest rates, a sheltered tax position and, in some cases, a guarantee of a minimum return.

"It sounds a lot harder than letting a few pals in on Dravo,"
I said.

"It is," said Sheldon. "It's a lot harder. But I wanted to be
on the team." *

William Craig is a six-foot-four Irishman from Boston, Massachusetts, with a splendid beard which makes him look like one
of his ancestral Tara kings. Years ago, Craig had a tryout with the
Boston ball club, and he still gets a tear in those clear blue eyes
when he describes what his fast ball and slider could have done
for the Sox during the lean years if only he hadn't turned to the
creation of living literature. Craig is the author of the best-
selling *The Fall of Japan*, of which Dial Press has published
three editions and which has been translated into seven other
languages, including Japanese and Spanish.

What brought Craig to Israel was the research he needed for
his new book which will recount as popular history the battle
of Stalingrad. He has spent several years compiling the recol-
lections of the survivors of the battle. He has traveled through
Russia three times, interviewed Italian and Rumanian veterans,
and lived for a year in Germany, where he learned that there
was a veterans organization in Israel composed of Russian Jews
who had fought at Stalingrad.

The Israeli embassy in New York put him in touch with Yad
Vashem in Jerusalem and Yad Vashem in Tel Aviv, with Kibbutz Yad Mordechai and Kibbutz of the Ghetto Fighters, from
whose registers Craig found the names of Stalingrad survivors
living in Israel.

His work was tedious, first because Craig does not speak
Hebrew and second because most of the people he needed to
speak to did not have telephones, which are generally in short
supply in Israel. This meant Craig's translator, college student
Liora Kedem, had to go, say, to Nazareth in the daytime and
ask a veteran's wife if Craig could talk to him that night.

In Israel, Craig found a Red Army nurse who had endured
the battle, a Russian sniper, a woman doctor who had tended
the front-line wounded, a commando officer, and others of vari-

* Sadly, Standard and Poor's and Leo had to throw in the sponge six months
later. The war on the Suez Canal didn't help and a nose-diving American stock
market helped even less.

ous ranks who fought in and around Stalingrad. All of them were cooperative, some of them, at first, hesitant but then anxious to reveal a part of their lives which had been submerged for the last twenty-five years.

"The striking experience," Craig told me, "and it happened in Russia and in Germany and in Israel, is that some of these men start to cry. They break down remembering what they went through. In Israel one of the men I wanted to interview apologized but said his psychiatrist absolutely forbids him to discuss Stalingrad. Another Israeli who said he'd meet with me had his son killed on the Canal the day I was to talk to him."

He liked the Israelis, admired them, and felt the book would be improved by these interviews. He talked to a bank clerk who was the surviving officer of a Stalingrad commando regiment. This fellow and his wife kept offering Craig and his interpreter tumblers of vodka, which they tossed off at one draft.

Craig confessed he was hard put to keep his wits about him. They offered him dinner. Through the meal, either the husband or the wife would ask the translator in Hebrew if Craig was Jewish. Liora kept replying it wasn't a question she could ask her boss.

"I can't understand why they asked," Craig said. "You know what dinner was? Cold pork hocks. That and the vodka were pretty hard to handle."

Nor could he handle the Sabbath. He sputtered on his first Saturday, "You told me about the Sabbath, I admit, but you didn't tell me I couldn't buy cigarettes."

Harry Araten is also a big bearded man, six-foot-four, but where Craig weighs in at two hundred, Harry weighs nearer three. Harry is an advertising man in Haifa. I learned about him by spotting one of the advertisements he prepared for Absorption Ministry. The ad shows a picture of Harry, in black-rimmed glasses and neatly buttoned sports jacket, flanked by his wife, Rachel, who isn't five-one in her high heels, and his three children, daughters Devra and Yael, six and seven, and son Gideon, just ready for kindergarten. The copy reads: "MY NAME IS HARRY ARATEN. I came as an Oleh from the United States together with my family. This is my story."

Harry told me he loved the United States. It gave him his education, his values, and living there had made him almost rich. He had worked for several years as an art director for a New York advertising firm whose billings were over $100 million, before establishing his own agency in New Jersey.

But he made the decision to bring up his children in Israel, in a complex-free Jewish atmosphere. Having made that decision, he acted upon it, liquidating his business, selling off his house and cars, getting passports for the family.

Harry chose not to emigrate through any of the Israeli Immigration Agencies but to come alone with his portfolio, which he showed to the Tel Aviv, Jerusalem, and Haifa advertising agencies. Each one offered him a job. He chose an agency in Haifa because he liked the look of the city, which mounts from the Mediterranean over steep hills and much resembles San Francisco. Then he brought his family to Israel.

Israeli advertising isn't a lead-pipe cinch, Harry told me. Hebrew has no capital letters, which often makes package design a truly imaginative chore. And the agency has to submit many of its proposed advertisements to the rabbinate, who can prove obdurate about some subjects.

"One of our ads for a food product showed a wife sitting in her husband's lap. The rabbi said no. We redrew it so it showed the husband and wife holding hands in the kitchen. It made the rabbi no happier. I thought we'd have to put two married people in solitary confinement to get his okay, but he finally settled for a soulful glance decorated by a valentine heart."

Harry Araten boasts he is a happy man. I believe him. Immigrating to Israel from America does not always make men happy. Many of the Americans who settle in Israel are often the odd-man-out at home. Sometimes they are people who cannot find their place in the sun; sometimes they are Socialists or anti-Socialists, idealists too easily discouraged by the rawness of a developing state, utopians who really believe there is a utopia. Sometimes they have been slum shopkeepers and are fleeing the anti-Semitism of the black ghetto; sometimes they are young boys and girls who have given up ever curing the Establishment's hangups.

Ten percent of these immigrants return home. There is

nothing unusual about this. As far as mass migration goes, ten percent is a low percentage of loss. Some leave because of the climate, others because they despair of mastering the intricacies of Hebrew, and some leave because Israel is a country for the young or the workingman, but it is no paradise for the middle class.

The Americans over thirty here sometimes strike me as disappointed people. Invariably they ask why am I not settling in Israel as they have. I feel that they have confused a social problem with personal problems. There are neighborhoods in our cities which are uninhabitable. The country is rent by a divisive war in Southeast Asia. Sons do not always respect their fathers. America is competitive. These are social problems; as we say, they are nobody's fault. But some of the folks feel guilty about them. And a minority of these come to Israel, only to discover that, while they have left one set of social problems behind, they have picked up another.

The American influence is obvious in the miniskirt, the cars, the movies, the new buildings and hotels, the music—it is what I call the Los Angelesization of the world. Which, in its way, explains why many Americans become disappointed and unhappy.

No country is without its tensions, certainly not a country filled with Jews. You can walk the streets at any hour of the night in Tel Aviv, but a man must serve thirty or forty days every year in the Army until he is fifty-five. A man can set up a business here, but the market is only two and a half million people and there are many competitors. For some skills there is no market at all.

In Rishon le Zion I met new settlers from America. The middle-aged husband had worked in retail lumber, for which expertise there is a zero demand in Israel. Though he could have proved an efficient office manager, for he had run his own business, his Hebrew wasn't fluid enough. He had found work as a fork lift operator. When I suggested that he had a tough row to hoe, Tommy Lapid told me to stop worrying. Tommy said, "He has a good job in industry and his wife works for the Women's International Jewish Organization and the daughter is a physical therapist. That means they have an income of over

2,500 pounds a month and in Rishon le Zion it is impossible to spend 2,500 pounds a month."

The most relaxed Americans I met were young men who were studying to become rabbis at Kfar Habad, a Hassidic yeshiva just outside Tel Aviv. One of these boys told me he had been a graduate student in archeology at Princeton here in Israel on a dig, when impulsively he walked into the yeshiva, wearing his Bermuda shorts, to see what it was all about. Now he stood before me with a beard, his hair in ringlets, a black broad-brimmed hat shielding his face. Another was a physicist from Rutgers, and when I asked if he would pursue physics or theology, he replied, "It is up to the Rabbi," meaning the Lubevitcher Rabbi in Williamsburg, Brooklyn. I saw over one hundred of these young men in a large room, each with a prayer book opened before him on his desk, all of them chanting and praying, their heads bobbing without unison, their voices animated by the knowledge of God.

The American who comes to Israel leaves the States as a pioneer, a hero, at least to his rabbi and his neighbors back home. After all, he is giving up something which his Jewish friends are not and, therefore, they tend to idealize his spirit of sacrifice.

When the immigrant family arrives at Lod, invariably a representative of the Jewish Agency or the Ministry of Immigration meets them, escorts the family to a car, and drives them to their apartment, where they find flowers on the tables and window sills, food for two days in the refrigerator, and a welcoming committee made up of other tenants.

The neighbors leave. The family is alone in a small house in a strange land, the rooms lit probably by a single light bulb hanging from the ceiling like a damaged nerve.

Sometimes it is even harder for the immigrants from the satellite countries who have no experience at all in competing in a democratic society for work. Communist and Socialist countries always provide jobs, and the fact that an employer in Israel is free to hire or not at his own discretion is almost a hallucinatory experience for these people. They cannot go home, while the American can. Some Americans stay. The challenge, the excitement of the country, the knowledge that everyone you speak to that day from the girl in the corner flower stall to the industrial baron is Jewish keeps them. As Leo Sheldon says, "It's a good feeling to be on the team."

Some boys and girls from the Windy City

TWENTY-EIGHT of them disembarked from the jet at Lod, 13 adults and 15 children, most of the children quite young. All of them came originally from Chicago. They had flown to Israel from Liberia, where they had been living for the past two years. All of them were Black. Their leader, Mr. Ben Ami, who was formerly Ben Carter (he said they changed their names from the slave days), told the airport police all of them were also Jewish.

The officials at the Ministry of Absorption said they needed a little time to think the situation over. These 28 Blacks had American passports and needed no visas to enter as tourists. But they announced their right to settle in the Jewish state under Israel's Law of Return. It was up to the Minister of the Interior to decide whether these Chicago Blacks were or were not Jews.

Rabbi Hananiah Der'i of Jaffa, who has ministered to many groups seeking to return to the fold, sped out to the airport. Sensibly enough, he saw to it the children got breakfast.

Ben Ami told Rabbi Der'i that he and his followers ate only kosher food, circumsized their male children, spoke passable Hebrew, and wore the traditional prayer shawls. It was good enough for Rabbi Der'i, and he went to Jerusalem to argue the case with the Interior.

Ben Ami was leading the pioneers of a group of Blacks numbering almost 400 who, on their own several years ago, converted to Judaism. Though they lived in a Chicago slum, all of them were high school graduates and some had finished college. Mrs. Ben Ami is a highly trained radio and television technician and Mr. Elhanaan Ben-Israel, a certified life underwriter.

Three years ago, Ben Ami convinced his followers to leave Chicago and to immigrate to Liberia, where Blacks were free people and where they could prepare themselves for the final homecoming to Israel.

In Liberia they lived in a forest in what can only be called austere circumstances. But they considered this hard life a trial, just as the Israelites faced the trial of wandering in the wilderness before coming to the land of milk and honey.

"We left America for Liberia," Ben Ami said, "in the hopes of living without discrimination. But in Liberia it is not easy to be Jewish and we want to be Jewish. We have been in exile from Israel for the past four hundred years, held in slavery for much of the time, and now we are home."

The new arrivals waited patiently for the decision of the Ministry of Interior. It came within twenty-four hours. The Ministry issued these 28 Jews visas and provided a bus to transport them to the desert town of Dimona in the Negev, where the authorities even had ten new apartments available. Dimona's mayor, Israel Navon, met the dusty bus, attended by the school-children of Dimona, anxious to see Jewish Blacks. The boys and girls from Chicago were a sensation, to put it mildly.

The Dimona Labor Exchange provided a job for each, most of them in the knitting mills.

These new immigrants have three months in which to petition the rabbinate for final recognition as "completely Jewish." They will be right behind the Bnei Israel—the Indian community of Dimona—whose petition is being processed now for the rights and privileges of Jews in the homeland.

Dual citizenship and the Arabs

THE UNITED STATES Supreme Court recently ruled that it was unconstitutional to deprive a man of his citizenship for serving in the army of another country not hostile to American interests. This ruling prompted the State Department to announce that American nationals who had served or were serving in the Israel Army still retained their United States citizenship. The Egyptians made this front page news.

After several conferences, Egyptian and Arab ambassadors charged that this policy constitutes "naked American aggression against the Arab countries." Though the State Department insisted it does not encourage Americans to serve in the Israeli Army, that most who do are conscripted, the Egyptians argued that any American living in an Arab country could be in the service of Israeli intelligence, that an American passport could camouflage an Israeli agent, "since the United States considers Israel an extension of its territory."

Perhaps 10,000 Americans have immigrated to Israel and renounced their American citizenship to become Israelis. As Israelis they must accept their military responsibilities—one month of duty every year until they are fifty-five. In case of war, they are called immediately to their regiment. A larger number of Americans who live in Israel have not renounced their United States citizenship. They are called "permanent residents." They enjoy what is, in effect, dual citizenship.* They are not subject to conscription. To force the issue of military service upon them might send them home, and they are valuable to Israel as settlers, if not as soldiers. Whatever the number of Americans serving in the Israeli Army, their presence does not materially affect that Army's efficiency.

A Cairo Radio dispatch, however, announced that the Supreme Court decision meant America had entered the war against the Arabs. The Lebanese press warned that "a new American-Israeli aggression against the Arabs is not far off."

No one in Israel thinks the Arabs have grown more panicky than before. There are two reasons for the Egyptian emphasis on the matter of dual American citizenship. First and foremost is the Egyptian persistence in trying to link Israel and the West to disguise the bitter truth that it was Israel alone who routed the Arab armies in the Six-Day War in 1967. A second reason is that, while there has been no progress in United States-Soviet discussion of a Middle East settlement, one day there will be. The Arabs will not want to enter those discussions unless some way is found for Israel to have lost the Six-Day War. The Arabs would like to inform world opinion that they cannot enter into talks sponsored by sworn enemies, like the United States.

I rather suspect the U.S. State Department wishes the whole subject had not surfaced.

* An Israeli born in the United States is an American and an Israeli citizen, as is an American born in Israel. Both have two passports.

The Jewish Baptists and Pastor Lindsey

THERE IS a congregation of twenty Baptist Jews in Jerusalem. Their pastor is Robert Lisle Lindsey, chairman of the Baptist Convention, who has lived in Israel for the past thirty years.

These Baptist Jews lived originally in eastern Poland. They were simple, unlettered rag pickers, coal peddlers, or draymen. During the holocaust, they found refuge with a community of Polish Baptists and converted. After the war, they emigrated from Europe to Israel.

"Why do you call them Baptist Jews?" I asked.

"After you have been in Israel awhile," smiled Mr Lindsey, "you will learn there are many kinds of Jews."

Pastor Lindsey is in his early fifties. There is no trace of gray in his hair, and I will bet he still has all his teeth. He is a farm boy who was graduated from the University of Oklahoma and was ordained at the Southern Baptist Theological Seminary. He came to Palestine in 1939 to learn Hebrew. He said he knocked around the country and worked on a kibbutz until he saved enough for tuition at the Hebrew University.

When the United States entered the war, Lindsey went home but returned as soon as it was over. Bob Lindsey is the father of six children, all of whom speak Hebrew, although they are more American than Israel oriented, since the Lindseys enjoy a stateside sabbatical every five years.

I asked him about his missionary work, and he answered disarmingly that the missionary is in greater danger of conversion than the heathen. Besides, the missionary impulse is not what keeps him in Israel. Though a member of an evangelical church, his primary mission is the administration of Baptist primary and secondary schools, for besides the 20 Baptist Jews there are over 200 Baptist Arabs in Jerusalem.

More than a school administrator, however, Bob Lindsey is a highly regarded theologian. He has recently advanced a revolutionary theory about the Synoptic Gospels in his *Hebrew Translation of the Gospel of Mark* which contains, in addition to the Greek and Hebrew texts, an introduction and a supporting foreword by David Flusser. The translation from Greek to Hebrew took Lindsey ten years, in the course of which he had access to some of the Dead Sea Scrolls.

Simplistically, the Gospel According to St. Mark has been the most unpopular of the Synoptic Gospels. St. Augustine called Mark a camp-follower and the lections for Sundays and saints' days in the Church of England Prayer Book, for example, show only three readings from Mark out of a total of seventy from the other three gospels. But scholars and theologians for the last fifty years have presumed that Mark served as one of the sources for Matthew and Luke. His gospel is ragged because he was the first to write about Jesus.

Lindsey argues that the basic reason for Mark's unpopularity is that this gospel was written by an early Jewish Christian who used the midrashic methods of the intertestamental rabbis, a process of homilizing history, bending it to a specific contemporary need. If this time locus is true, then Luke did not use Mark's gospel, but Mark Luke's and Matthew's. For Mark produced a gospel almost as much annotation and comment as the original story. Mark replaced half of Luke's mythopoeic authenticity with a variety of synonyms and expressions from the Old and New Testament, which Lindsey identified by consulting Greek and Hebrew concordance and the scrolls. This method resulted in the textual salad scholars excused as a beginning theology but which, more realistically, according to Lindsey, should be described as a fascinating but unskillful dramatization of the gospel story. Mark's midrashic methods, said Lindsey at a press conference well covered by commentators from the world's religious press, "is the first cartoon life of Christ."

Flusser's unequivocal statement is that Lindsey's research and translation has ended "in the most important and decisive correction of the usual view of Markan priority ever made."

Lindsey shrugged at my question about the problems of modern Israel. He said he feels he is part of the country and consequently he can enlighten me no more than any other Israeli.

"Perhaps," he said, "the problem with the Arabs is a result of our being so frightened before the war. I know I was frightened and all my Israeli friends were frightened. Maybe they weren't frightened of annihilation, but we thought Jerusalem would be shelled and ruined again and that the Egyptians would overrun Yad Mordechai and it would be a long and bitter war. Maybe the boys in the Air Force knew what they could do but no Israeli I talked to thought in six days the Army would be on the Canal at one end and on top of the Golan Heights at the other. I get the feeling that Arab weakness makes the Israelis ashamed of their worry. If they had thought Nasser was that weak, they would simply have knocked off his garrison at Aqaba."

"If there is anything wrong with Israel," I said to him when he left, "it isn't because you live here."

Good-bye to the Yemenite *mori*

THE YEMENITE *mori* is a combination witch doctor-social worker, part Mary Baker Eddy, part Harry Hopkins. In a country of refugees finding national identity, the *mori* is the displaced man. He started to lose his classic function when the Yemenite children went to schools established and financed by Israel; when judges appointed by the Ministry of Justice adjudicated disputes; when the rabbinate began to perform the marriages; and when the doctors and nurses began making their rounds of Yemenite settlements in mobile hospitals. The *mori* will be completely displaced when the Yemenite boys who have gone from the Army into the Hebrew University return to their villages and become the leaders of these communities.

I choose the *mori*, who dispensed magic charms and comforting advice to the sick and melancholy, as a singular example of how Israel is transforming its population of Oriental Jews, most of whom came from Syria, Iraq, Tunis, Algeria, Morocco, and Yemen. The Yemenites themselves number only 4 percent of the population, but within the decade probably 65 percent of the Israeli population will be Oriental Jews.

Of these Orientals, the Yemenites are not only the most interesting and the most studied, but they came to Israel first, as early as 1886, when Yemenite families settled in Jerusalem. Fifteen hundred came in 1911–15 and, in 1949–50, Operation Magic Carpet, in 378 flights, transported almost the entire

Yemenite community of 47,400 from the Yemen Peninsula to Israel.

Until Operation Magic Carpet, the Yemenites did not often mix with the Ashkenazim. They maintained their own schools and synagogues, married within their own group, and worked as cheap laborers. They are a small, fragile, dark-skinned people, whose men wear their hair in side curls and whose women wear embroidered trousers. But they are not as homogeneous as they appear. They come from both city and village, from northern, central, and southern desert areas, each group with its own practices, beliefs, and culture. They are superb silversmiths. Yemenite food is the most exotic in Israel. And the Yemenite INBAL Dancers are a world-famous troupe.

Once Yemenite children married between the ages of nine and eleven, and once the father ruled supreme over the family group. This situation no longer obtains, which makes puberty exceptionally difficult for Yemenite girls, because their mothers serve neither as an example nor as a counselor and the fathers find their traditional role weakened when their sons assimilate a new complex of attitudes in school.

Until the declaration of the state, the Yemenites were at a disadvantage in Israel. Their color sometimes provoked discrimination, masses of Yemenites were illiterate, and their primitive and unsophisticated life confined them to menial tasks. The Palestinian Jews were trying to build industry, which needs cities, and often Yemenites were shunted off to the dangerous border settlements, while new housing projects in urban residential areas were reserved for immigrants from Poland or Rumania.

Though there had been early Yemenite pioneers in Palestine, they were motivated by the idea of a return to the Jewish homeland, while the European settlers were motivated by a Socialist ideal. The Yemenites were awaiting the Messiah and the Europeans were building a workers' society.

But the Yemenites, and other Oriental Jews, have large families, and it was this salient statistic which, five years ago, attracted the attention of Moshe Eilat, a professor of Jewish history at the Hebrew University. Searching the records, Eilat found that only ten percent of Oriental Jews were registered in

the universities and almost all of these were the children of
Yemenites who had immigrated before World War I.

Unless the universities took remedial action, thought Eilat,
Israel, a developing society, faced the terrible inhibition of a
minority of professionals trying to support a majority of unskilled workers, at a large moral and economic expense.

Eilat presented his findings to the president of the Hebrew
University, Mr. George Harmon, who immediately authorized
him to found the Pre-Academic School of the university, in
which a selected faculty would prepare Oriental Jews for college
work. These graduates hopefully would become the leaders of
their towns and communities, in turn influencing the younger
generation.

The Army, which was crucial to the program, recruited the
first 55 students through a process of careful screening. It was
a protracted endeavor, because roughly only 1,000 out of over
1,000,000 of these Jews had finished high school. The next
year, however, the Army recruited 200. Eilat has hopes that by
1971 the Army will be recruiting 1,000 soldiers who will be
prepared by the Pre-Academic School for the regimen and
curriculum of the university.

Eilat told me these Oriental Jews are smart and ambitious
but they want the romantic work of a scientist or a lawyer. They
are not always practical. The great majority of Oriental Jews,
he said, know the Bible and related subjects by heart, having
learned it by rote, a skill which would equip each of them for an
immediate job teaching in the schools where religion is a
required subject. The job as a religious teacher has little attraction for these boys, said Eilat sadly. Though everything he needed
to know was at his fingertips, one Moroccan nodded no to
Dr. Eilat's suggestion that he prepare for teaching.

"They don't think religion is their thing," said Eilat. "They
say, 'It just doesn't go in this world.' "

Tel Aviv University, under the direction of its rector, Ben-Ami
Scharfstein, an American philosopher from Queens College, has
initiated a related though dissimilar program. It would have to.
There is a rivalry between the Tel Aviv and Hebrew universities
which is much more intense than the rivalry between Michigan

and Minnesota, only in Israel the two arch rivals are contending for the betterment of the immigrant not the Little Brown Jug. Tel Aviv University sponsors the Colleges of the Community which will number six, located at Tel Aviv, Hadera, Manashay, two in North Galilee, and Kiryat Shmoney. The university is establishing these colleges not so much to prepare people for the professions as to fill in cultural lags. One of these colleges, however, will offer degree courses in sea science and another in agricultural administration.

When I asked Dr. Scharfstein why Tel Aviv, rather than Hebrew University, was charged with establishing what will eventually be fifteen Colleges of the Community, he answered, "Because up in the hills, they are still discussing this in committee."

Let my people go

ONE OF the paradoxes of twentieth-century Jewish history is that affluence and religious freedom in the United States have diminished the American Jew's sense of identity as a Jew, while fifty years of proscription and suppression in the USSR have heightened the Russian Jew's. The American Jew by and large has confirmed his decision to be an American and a Jew, while the Russian Jew takes a daring chance to confirm his desire to immigrate to Israel.

There are 3,000,000 Russian Jews, at least 200,000 of whom have asked to leave, and there are probably many times that number who would go if they could. In the early winter of 1969, the Israeli government began officially encouraging this aliyah. It is a bold tactic to dictate to another government how it should resolve one of its internal affairs. Israel felt morally compelled to do so with Russia.

What prompted Israel was a petition submitted by Jews in the Georgian Republic to Prime Minister Golda Meir. The petition was signed by the heads of eighteen families and it asked the Prime Minister to dispatch two enclosed letters to the

United Nations Human Rights Commission and to have the letters also distributed to the UN General Assembly.

In part, one of the letters read:

> We ask you to help us to emigrate to Israel. Each of us, summoned by a relative in Israel, had received the necessary questionnaires from the proper organs of the U.S.S.R. and had filled them out. Each of us had sold his property and had resigned his job. However, long months have passed—and for some even years—and emigration has not yet been permitted. We have sent hundreds of letters and telegrams. They disappeared like tear-drops in the sands of a desert: we hear orally one-syllabled refusals, we see no written answers. . . .
>
> We shall wait for months and for years, if necessary for our entire lifetime, but we shall not renounce our faith and our hope because we do not ask for much—let us go to the land of our ancestors.

Before the Knesset, Golda Meir said Israel demanded, as an elementary human right, that all Soviet Jews who wished to settle in the homeland be allowed to do so. The USSR, she insisted, had no alternative but to realize it had failed after half a century and more to silence the Jewish voice. Because Russia's leaders are realistic people, she believed they would have the courage to admit their failure and let the Jews go. While her government had been advised by Jews and non-Jews alike to use quiet diplomacy on behalf of the Soviet Jews, she rejected this advice. Since the Russian Jews displayed supreme courage in submitting their petitions, Israel could not ignore them.

The subsequent debate in the Knesset was closed by a resolution phrased and supported by all parties, save the New Communists who could marshal only three votes against it. The resolution called upon the parliaments of the world to exert their influence to facilitate the immigration of the Jews in Georgia to Israel.

The Russian response said that "Thirteen of those who signed the petition were refused visas at once because they did not have close relatives living in Israel, as is required by the laws of the Georgian Republic for emigration. The remaining five never made official requests for going to Israel. None of the people who signed the appeal had sold their effects or quit their jobs. The Kutaisi rabbi has condemned the actions of his parishioners who applied to the United Nations."

Communist Russia has always been anti-Zionist even when it wasn't anti-Semitic, but the Six-Day War provoked an intensified anti-Israel campaign to demonstrate to the world and particularly to the Arab states unswerving Soviet support for the Arab cause.

At an unusual press conference, the Soviets produced forty high-ranking Jews in government and industry who monotonously intoned that Israel is dominated by Zionist imperialists who are as bad as the barbaric Hitlerites.

Shortly thereafter, thirty-nine Russian Jews submitted an open declaration to the Soviet Press Department which was released to Western correspondents. These Jews said:

> And it is the very preservation of the national identity of Jews that is the problem in the Soviet Union. No references to completely equal and joyful labor with Russians and no examples of a brilliant military or social career can divert our attention from the problem, for in this, Russians remain Russians and Jews cease to be Jews.

This is an emotional and poignant issue, but not on that account have the Israelis acted impulsively. The campaign, I believe, has been carefully thought out. The Israelis have not undertaken to play games with the lives of others out of a sense of national pride. Quite obviously, the Israelis expect the situation of the Russian Jews to worsen over the next few years. They expect it to worsen because they are in a position to know that the impasse with the Arabs either cannot or will not be resolved. If they are going to help their fellow Jews in Russia survive these consequences, now is the time to come to their aid. Mrs. Meir stressed that the Jews want to leave only to preserve their Jewish ties, not to embarrass or criticize the Soviet regime. The Israelis also undertook this campaign because nothing else has worked.

What's in a name?

"Let us speak plain. There is more strength in names than most men dream of," so say the Israelis. The Hebraization of names in Israel is epidemic. If you knew a Jew in the old country, you will have a lot of trouble finding him in Israel, because he probably will have chosen a Hebrew surname for himself and his family. Partly, this is an expression of willingness to start out in the homeland completely anew, and partly it is a resentment toward the old names, which were mostly German in origin.

In Biblical times, Jews were called by the names of their fathers—Meir ben Joseph was Meir, the son of Joseph—a custom which persevered until the Middle Ages. The Jew who achieved fame was honored with a nickname, as Maimonides was called "the Rambam." But to make the census easier and identification more complete, Gentile authorities decreed all Jews had to have a family name. A family which lived in a house decorated by a red shield became Rothschild, to cite the most famous example; the Rappoports are the descendants of Rofe miPorto, the physician from Porto; some Jews fashioned their names from their profession—the antecedents of the Sattlers were saddle makers or saddle merchants; or from their size—Klein or Gross; or from their favorite color—Braun, Gelb, Green, or Blau.

A Jew named Green was born in the Russian town of Plonsk. He immigrated to Palestine as a young man and became not only the leader of his people but the pioneer in Hebraizing family names. David Green became David Ben-Gurion. The succeeding Prime Ministers of Israel also came with different names. Moshe Sharet was born Shertok, Levi Eshkol was Skolnick, and Golda Meir was Myerson.

The most popular actress in Israel was a Roman Catholic born in Vienna with the name Eva Kerbler. She married a Jew, converted, and became so intoxicated with Judaism that after divorcing her husband she migrated to Israel alone and changed her name to Li-On.

The trend is encouraged by the government. The Hebrew Academy has issued a booklet which lists all the Hebrew family names from the time of the Bible and lists as well all the first names of the Biblical persona. Young couples spend nights leafing through the booklet to find an appropriate name for their expected child—perhaps the name of one of King David's generals if a boy, or the name of King Solomon's most beloved wife if a girl. It is matter of deep personal pride to find names fiercely Hebrew; in this endeavor, Tommy Lapid is the champion because Lapid means "Burning Arrow."

Changing an old family name is an easy matter. A man fills out the questionnaire, pays the clerk one pound at the nearest office of the Interior Department, and presto—he is no longer Morris Kolodny but Moshe Kol. To the despair of the Israeli police, criminals often resort to this tactic to disengage themselves from their past.

But the applicant need not necessarily select a Hebrew name. George Mikes, from whose book *The Prophet Motive* I have already quoted, tells the story of the Yemenite Jew named Yehuda Eliazar, a Jewish name to conjure with, who still felt it wasn't Jewish enough for him. So he changed his name to Shmuel Goldstein and proudly took his place with the Barkatts, the Ya'acobis, and the Zars.

How ya gonna keep 'em down on the farm?

In Tel Aviv, Zipora L. went to the district court to ask for an injunction which would keep David P., a new immigrant, in the country for a while. The judge asked Zipora why should his court keep a man in Israel who wanted to leave.

Zipora explained to the court that she was about to file a 10,000-pound suit against David for mental anguish and humility caused her by his disappearance when all the guests were gathered around the wedding canopy. Also, she demanded the return of 370 pounds in expenses for the time David lived in her house. And to top it off, he stole another 300 pounds from their joint checking account with which he purchased a motorcycle. Which explains, perhaps, why the reluctant groom has yet to be found.

To the editor of the Jerusalem *Post*

Sir:—I am a new immigrant from Mexico having come to Israel four months ago. Professionally, I am a cantor and am presently employed at the Bet Knesset Hagadol in Ramat Gan in that capacity. I left my position, not because of any problem, but because I wanted to settle in the Holy Land, the land of my fathers. Yesterday, I received a letter from a member of my former congregation in Mexico informing me that the position which I vacated is being filled by a cantor from Israel, Aryeh Brown, who has left Israel to settle in Mexico.

This bit of news has caused me great pain. One can imagine how shaken I am that I left the position to settle in Israel and a sabra took the opportunity to leave his homeland and occupy the pulpit of an immigrant. This type of action is certainly a big factor in the feelings of many a person who is considering settling in Israel.

The irony of it all is expressed in being a representative of a congregation praying before God: "May our eyes behold Thy return to Israel."

Cantor David Hagley

Ramat Gan, October 16.

Part *XI*

Only in Israel

Heading north

NORTH OF Tel Aviv is Natanya, the center of Israel's diamond industry. Natanya was built by the visionary Ben Ami, the Jew who later built the great southern port of Ashdod. Ben Ami hoped that Nathan Strauss, the famous philanthropist, would endow Natanya, hence its name—Natanya meaning "the gift of Nathan." Strauss had other ideas. By the time he said no, however, Natanya was in business. Ben Ami left it with the name Natanya to show other philanthropists he was a good sport.

Following the shoreline, the highway divides the land. To the right are the fields of the kibbutzim, to the left the Arab villages, the boundaries of each farm clearly laid out. On the right side there are acres and acres of blue bags, on the left house after house with blue windows. The kibbutzniks grow bananas here and cover the fruit with a plastic blue bag to protect it from the insects; the Arabs paint blue dados along their walls and around their windows, because the color blue has a religious significance. At least that is what the Israelis say, pointing out that the interior of mosques is always blue.

Not odd at all. The Virgin Mary is always robed in blue and blue is the predominant color in the stained-glass windows of the great medieval churches, because it was the one color whose depth and consistency the artists could control.

In fact, the interior of the old synagogues in Safed are also blue. Here in these mountains Rabbi Joseph Caro wrote his book *The Ordered Table,* which outlined the philosophy of the Cabala, the mystical branch of Judaism. *The Ordered Table* defines the discipline for every moment of the day: what prayers to offer upon awakening, how to conduct business, how to go to shule, what blessing to invoke before sleep. In the Joseph Caro Synagogue, which is over 400 years old, the parishioners sit in pews which circle the walls, as though they are watching theater in the round. In the center of the synagogue is the raised platform from which a rabbi still leads the service, circling constantly to face the worshipers.

Today, Safed is an artist's colony. Israeli writers, painters, and sculptors used to go there for the fresh mountain air. They moved into the abandoned Arab houses which the government leased to them. Safed is filled with art galleries, though making one's way from one to the other is hard, because some of the streets are tilted at a 45-degree angle.

Blue is the predominant color, too, of the Church of the Beatitudes, which overlooks the Sea of Galilee from the north shore. On these grassy, tree-filled slopes, Jesus delivered the Sermon on the Mount to Jews who assembled below him.

The Church of the Beatitudes, which Mussolini built in 1937, is octagonal. It is ringed by marble walks and maintained by the Franciscan nuns of an Italian hospice who excitedly describe that it was in this very pew that Pope Paul, Il Papa, stopped to meditate when His Holiness visited Israel.

This is the land called the upper Galilee, the most fertile land in Israel, to whose lush valleys the first kibbutzniks came to start their settlements. This is the land Jesus trod and hallowed for Christians through all time. It is a land where Arab life in the small villages goes on much as it went on in Biblical times.

The brown and purple Golan Heights stretch southward to the right. To the left, the road curves toward Tabigha, where Jesus multiplied five loaves and two fishes into food for the multitude. A restored Byzantine basilica, the Church of the Multiplication, re-creates the event. The floor is mosaic work from the fourth century. John Goldhurst somehow pried loose one of these colorful tiles, to the distress of his father and the absolute alarm of a Benedictine priest.

Not far from Tabigha is Capernaum, the site of the synagogue where Jesus preached and performed His miracles. Israeli archeologists have uncovered the foundation of a second- or third-century synagogue, probably built over the first-century original.

Farther south is Tiberias, whose warm mineral baths were first exploited by Herod Antipas, seeking their recuperative powers as he plotted his salacious way to share Salome's sack. He built the first bath houses, as well as the conduits, and named the spa after his emperor, Tiberius. The baths are still thought to make the rheumatic agile and the barren fruitful. Even the Talmud subscribes to the importance of the therapy, for it lists special provisions for bathing in Tiberias on the Sabbath.

It was in Tiberias that fifth-century rabbis invented two vowel signs for Hebrew, which up until then lacked any vowels. The vowel signs were "God" and "Lord" and were inserted between the letters YVHW, the initials of God's name, too holy for pronunciation. From this late insertion comes the name of God, Jehovah.

From a curving stone pier in the north end of Tiberias, a fishing fleet still sets out in the late afternoons. It numbers perhaps ten longboats, powered by small outboard motors, each manned by two fishermen who carry their midnight meal in a miner's lunchpail. The catch is sardines and St. Peter's fish, named, of course, after the big fisherman, who sailed from this shore too. St. Peter's fish is a white fish, a member of the perch family, delicious when broiled and served with lemon.

Tiberias is below sea level, hot and muggy, and the night is filled with droning mosquitoes as large as any ever bred in the New Jersey swamplands. The warning to guests in the Ginton Hotel is to secure all windows. In the deserted lobby, Richard and I learned from the two-line filler in the Jerusalem *Post* that the Mets had won the World Series. As we waited for dinner, two tourist buses drew up and discharged 100 Americans, all of them members of Temple Sinai in Philadelphia, where a few months before I had delivered a lecture. They were accompanied by Rabbi and Mrs. Korn. So that evening in Tiberias, I gave them the same lecture all over, but this time for free.

The king of the *felafel* is dead

THE *felafel* is stuffed *pita*, a Middle East hero sandwich. The Arabic *pita* looks like two pancakes soldered together, except this bread has the consistency of Italian pizza dough. The sides of the *pita* can be separated and into the sack then formed a vendor stuffs balls of mashed chick-peas fried in oil until they are crisp, along with diced squares of pickled cucumbers, onions, green tomatoes, and cauliflower, over which he ladles a gummy hot sauce.

Arabs ate the *felafel* for centuries, but it took a Jew named Moshe Elnatan to make the *felafel* as popular among Israelis looking for a quick lunch as the sauerkraut-laden Sabrett hot dog is among New Yorkers.

Elnatan was a Persian who came to Israel in the early 1930's and set up a popular café in Tel Aviv. During the war he served in the RAF, and when he was discharged, he opened a stand on Pinsker Street which he called "The King of the Felafel." He boasted he sold the best stuffed *pitas* in Israel, a challenge some Jerusalem vendors disputed but could not disprove.

During the years of austerity, from 1948 to 1953, Elnatan's restaurant thrived. The *felafel* was cheap and nourishing and he himself was a distinct personality. He was a moustachioed *bon vivant* with a poetic flair. His place was decorated with his own paintings—gay desert flowers, visions of Jerusalem, the Temple Mount, as well as proto-pop portraits of Theodor Herzl, Chaim Weizmann, and David Ben-Gurion.

Unfortunately, he did not trust his true talent. He wanted recognition as a great painter, not realizing the *felafel* was his vocation and his supreme art.

He sold his stand and opened a studio on Rehov Hanevi'im. Though admitted to the Jerusalem Artists Association, financial success and recognition eluded him. He died broke, in a cheap furnished room in Tel Aviv. Like King Lear, he had given up a kingdom as a roundabout way to happiness and, like Lear, he was embittered by the realization that sacrifice does not of itself bring man fame, love, or gratitude. His *felafels* were delicious but his canvases were stale. R.I.P.

Right on!

THERE ARE few demonstrations on Israeli campuses and little dissidence. Some years ago when Konrad Adenauer, Chancellor of West Germany, visited the Hebrew University, a few students paraded with placards which expressed nasty anti-German sentiments. Unwisely, as you will see, university officials asked the police to disband these demonstrators lest they provoke an incident.

Policemen the world over swear they never use their clubs except in case of a tie. On this day the cops and the students were caught in a Mexican standoff. The cops, as is their wont, began to bang a few heads to make their point. A professor told me that the nearby classrooms suddenly emptied, and within minutes students were chasing the policemen down the hill toward the Knesset.

It could never happen in America. The police may be only the reserve guard of the campus, but once they appear, they are invincible. The reason it happened in Israel is that the students are the officer and noncommissioned officer corps of the Army. Ninety percent of these young men had already completed their initial military service and these ex-paratroopers, tankers, and commandos knew more about using a stick than the cops did about using clubs. In the melee, however, Konrad Adenauer came and went unsullied by picketing students.

Fortunately for the ivory towers of Israel, this was the only demonstration in which anybody raised his voice. The reasons are obvious. Israeli students are all older. They are beginning their education at an age when most Americans and Frenchmen are finishing theirs or ruining the academy in the process. Israeli students are more mature, and maturity makes a great difference in what demands these students make of the faculty and administration.

Students here *do* make demands and not always wise demands but at least negotiable, unamnestied demands. Often the Israeli complains that the student from Africa, of which there are a surprising number, usurps the seat of a sabra. Students ask for more business and marketing and accounting courses and they want a larger concentration upon practical living than upon theory. They do not want to study ancient, medieval, or romantic philosophers, they want to study contemporaries. They win a great many of their points.

The universities have some things going for them. University involvement in the war effort is not *prima facie* evidence of immorality. Everybody is involved in the war effort. The university is the only place where soldiers can develop certain skills to help guarantee Israel's security.

Education is expensive in Israel. A large majority of the students must live at home and must work to afford their degrees. Although there are campuses, beautiful campuses in fact, there is little campus life, as Americans since the days of F. Scott Fitzgerald have termed a college education. Americans here for a year at Tel Aviv or Hebrew University are disappointed. One American asked me, "Why are they always in the library? Everybody knows the library inhibits thought."

Perhaps the last reason for the tranquillity of the Israeli campus is that the university is populated by Jews who have traditionally placed a high value on education. Nor has the country become stratified or automated so that the student feels he has no choice but to conform or drop out and destroy.

I do not mean to insist there are no demonstrations in Israel. Indeed there are. Throughout history, students have been shouting on street corners even before there were street corners.

Yeshiva students Dov Berber, Haim Epstein, and Shmuel Shmueli were charged with disturbing the peace by trying to disrupt a conference of pathologists at Tel Aviv University. These three had splattered the street leading to the conference hall in red paint with the slogan, "Driver beware—the pathologist is hungry."

Facing the judge of the Magistrate's Court with dissidents Dov, Haim, and Shmuel were Modechair Edelstein, Moshe Yarkoni, and Moshe Rotholtz. They had decorated the conference building itself also in red paint with the demands, "Down with heart transplants." "End autopsies now!"

While these six tried to convince the judge that prayer was not a disturbance of the peace, another hundred of their Orthodox fellow students from the Yeshiva sat in the courtroom muttering and wailing for their friends' deliverance. But it didn't work this time. The judge said, "Sixty pounds or thirty days."

Arabs and Communists demonstrated in front of the United States Embassy on Vietnam Moratorium Day and I saw American hippies demonstrate outside Bethlehem on Christmas Eve.

In most of Israel, Christmas is just another day, but not in Jerusalem. On Christmas Eve, Monsignor Alberto Cori, the Roman Catholic Patriarch, flanked by Teddy Kollek, the mayor of Bethlehem, and the military governor of Jerusalem, leads a procession of Christian pilgrims from St. Stephen's Gate in the Old City to St. Catherine's in Bethlehem, there to celebrate midnight mass.

Choirs from all over the Christian world sing carols, as these worshipers wend the five miles from Jerusalem to Manger Square. Among these choirs were two from the United States.

With the appearance of these two choirs, a group of Americans suddenly broke out placards reading, "Get Out of Vietnam Now," and "Up Against the Wall." They also shouted unpleasant sentiments about the American establishment.

Unbeknownst to our SDSers, the entire line of march was guarded by a regiment of Israeli soldiers, rifles at the ready, to discourage attacks by Arab terrorists. A platoon descended upon the Americans with explicit directions on how to get to the paddy wagons.

When the Americans complained that their right of free speech was being abridged by militaristic fascists, the Israeli lieutenant said, "You don't understand. This is a *Christian* holiday."

In the Rubinstein Forest

On MY way back from the Kennedy Memorial, which takes the shape of the base of a huge fallen tree, I passed a hillside outside of Jerusalem where several workmen were raising a small bronze monument, not four feet high. When they set it upright, I read that it marked the Artur Rubinstein Forest.

Rubinstein had concertized the week before, once in Tel Aviv and once in Jerusalem. He had concertized, as he himself remarked, "for free," to help the Jewish Agency raise money. Rubinstein has concertized many times in Israel—as have many of the world's leading musicians, from Leonard Bernstein to Yehudi Menuhin. But the Israelis have a special affection for Artur Rubinstein, partly because he is Jewish and partly, of course, because he has lent his prestige and his fame to Israel's cause, but mostly because he is the premier pianist in the world today. The Israelis are devoted to music. They are as knowledgeable about classical and serious music as they are about the Bible. They love music so much they gave Artur Rubinstein a living hillside.

When I arrived in Tel Aviv, Tommy Lapid confessed it would be hard for him to arrange interviews with Golda Meir, Abba Eban, and Moshe Dayan, because they were so busy. And it was impossible to get me tickets for any of the performances or concerts at the Mann Auditorium.

This ultramodern concert hall on Huberman Street in the center of Tel Aviv is the home of the Israel Philharmonic. During the season, the Philharmonic, under several conductors, will present three or four programs every week, for which all tickets have been sold by subscription years before. The cashier in the box office is there to tell the tourist or visting dignitary or new Knesset member that there isn't a chance for standing room let alone a seat.

There have been several Solomon-like decisions by divorce court judges who award contesting husband and wife each one half of the subscriptions they owned as a married couple. Some Tel Avivians conscientiously read the obituaries every day in the hopes of recognizing the name of a casual acquaintance who might have held tickets in life. Tickets for the Israel Philharmonic are at such a premium, so highly valued, that there are no scalpers.

But the devoted music lover can hear the Philharmonic and the other orchestras which visit Israel by repairing to a kibbutz when these organizations make their usual tour of the kibbutzim, almost all of which have their own Lewisohn Stadium. And there are several opera companies, the largest of which is the

National Opera on Allenby Street. The repertoire of Israeli tenors is between fifteen and twenty roles, compared to the eight or ten a Metropolitan Opera regular must know.

A long-playing record is a luxury for most households. Yet in several homes I saw shelves and shelves of them. Tommy Lapid had two, mind you, two recordings of Beethoven's 33 *Variations on a Theme by Diabelli*, which until this visit I not only had never heard but never suspected even that there was a Diabelli.

Popular music apparently appeals to the Israelis little. In the time I spent, not once did Kol Israel, the radio station, play through a complete song. The announcer kept talking until the song hit its first release, and he resumed talking as soon as the melody began to repeat. Of course, the disc jockeys gossip in Hebrew, so I had no idea whether he was condemning the song or touting a product.

There's no -ism like chauvinism, and the one time the Israeli chauvinism becomes arrogant is when they begin to tick off the names of the great chess players and violinists, almost all of whom are Jewish. From the Israelis I did not learn the name of the world's greatest tympanist because he probably comes from Naples, but I learned the name of the world's greatest flautist, Mme. Suzanne Bloch, the daughter of the famous Jewish composer. Pablo Casals' artistry they have to concede, but they insist they have adopted him anyway. I never heard an Israeli mention the names of Wanda Landowska or Yella Pessl, so I can only conclude either that Mmes. Landowska and Pessl are not Jewish or that the Israelis are coming late to the delights of the harpsichord.

Receiver of complaints

NINE SCANDINAVIAN countries, two American states, and three Canadian provinces employ an ombudsman. So, too, does Jerusalem. An ombudsman is a government official empowered to mediate between the citizenry and the bureaucracy. Since 1967, Jerusalem's ombudsman has been Shlomo Kadder, who for many years was Israel's envoy in Prague and later inspector of the Foreign Service.

On a typical day, Mr. Kadder will demand that the Ministry of Religion immediately furnish tap water to a Jerusalem Arab whose cistern one of the Ministry's archeological teams mistakenly tapped while excavating for an old buried road; defend an impoverished peddler sent to jail for nonpayment of fines; and intercede on behalf of the nuns of the Sisters of Mercy Hospital with the Municipal Sanitation Department, Kadder indignantly shouting, "Would you dare dump junk near Hadassah?"

His services have proved so successful that the Knesset has recently passed a law establishing a national ombudsman who will serve as a "receiver of complaints and defender of the 'little man.'"

Prisoners 108061 and 108062

JOSEPH FOXENBRAUNER, an air conditioning engineer in Tel Aviv, had just set down his lunch in a cafeteria. He pulled his chair closer to the table to let another man pass. He caught a glimpse of a number tattooed on the man's left arm between elbow and wrist, the numbers carried by the survivors of the concentration camps. The number was 108062. Immediately, Foxenbrauner rose and went over to the man's table and bared his own arm. The two stared at each other in silence. Foxenbrauner's number was 108061. Bruno Fink, an electrical engineer, had been the man behind Foxenbrauner when they were tattooed at Auschwitz.

Both Jews had been arrested in Krakow, Poland, on May 15, 1943. Not only did they discover they had spent the same time in the Krakow jail without knowing each other, but they had been students together at the same technical institute in Brno, Czechoslovakia, before the Nazis. This was the first time the two had met—here in a Tel Aviv cafeteria, with dozens of other diners hustling by unconcernedly and busboys scooping silverware and plates from the table.

Both men had survived the first Nazi roundups by forging papers which identified them as Christians. But the Nazis became more efficient in their checklists. Carrying forged papers was a capital crime and the Nazis took several pseudo-Christians out of the Krakow prison a few days later to execute them. Foxenbrauner and Fink were in a truck which broke down on the way to the execution grounds and their guards deposited them instead at the Jewish prison near the railroad yards.

On the 25th of May both men were shipped in cattle cars with hundreds of other Jews to Auschwitz. They remained in the cars for three days without food or water, for the guards at Auschwitz fed no inmate until they had tattooed and registered them.

The men waited in line for the infamous "selection"—to the right, hard labor; to the left, the gas chambers. The Nazi doctor signaled both to the right. Foxenbrauner and Fink surmised that the Germans, with their love for order, had put them in successive order because their surnames began with the same letter.

Foxenbrauner was transferred the next day to the coal mines at Ibishowitz, a working camp a day's walk from Auschwitz. His younger brother, Munik Foxenbrauner, remained at Auschwitz and was one of the inmates who later tried to blow up the ovens and was killed by the guards. At Ibishowitz, Foxenbrauner was eventually assigned to constructing the power station for the mining camp because of his engineering background. He managed to filch the several parts he needed to build a radio receiver and could then report to the other inmates about the Allies' sweep through Europe and the Russians' push from the east. The Russians freed Krakow in January, 1945, and the Nazis herded 2,000 Jews from Ibishowitz toward Buchenwald. They marched for over a week without food. Foxenbrauner was 1 of 200 who survived.

In Buchenwald, a Christian who was also interned helped Foxenbrauner pass as a Gentile. As such, the Nazis assigned him to a group of engineers. This time Foxenbrauner stole not only the parts to construct a radio but also a transmitting unit. He made contact with Patton's headquarters in April and maintained it for a week while the Americans sped toward Buchenwald. The Germans heard the radio call but could not locate the set.

After the war, Foxenbrauner returned to Krakow and, in 1949, emigrated with thousands of other Jews to Israel.

Fink had a harder time of it. He was transferred to Birknau and assigned to the sick bay as a medic. He watched thousands of Jews from Salonika die from disease and debilitation. Then he was transferred to a correction camp, where he carried sacks of cement all day. The hard work killed the men almost as quickly as did disease, and Fink ran away, hiding in the main camp until he got the chance to volunteer for factory work in Silesia. He worked with 3,000 other slave laborers assembling cars and, like Foxenbrauner, was marched out in January, 1945, when the Red Army came close. The workers were shipped in sealed cattle cars to Mauthausen in Austria. Fink worked in Gonez-Kirchen in an underground factory, this time assembling Messerschmitt airplanes.

The Americans reached Gonez-Kirchen on May 6, 1945, and found hundreds of living skeletons living in rude sheds in the forest. Fink weighed 88 pounds. At first, the Americans couldn't believe the Nazis had simply arrested and punished millions of innocent people. They kept asking these survivors if they'd been arrested for dealing with foreign currency. When he recovered, Fink went to Vrotzlaw and stayed there until 1957, when the Polish government permitted the Jews to immigrate to Israel.

These two new friends told their story to reporter Isaiah Aviam of *Ma'ariv*. "Do you know," said Foxenbrauner, "on the day I met Fink, a big truck splashed me on my way home and I noticed its license plate—108061."

Jerusalem's worldwide trial

MICHAEL DENNIS ROHAN, the Australian sheepherder who set fire to the Al Aksa Mosque, was the beneficiary of one of the most brilliant defenses ever presented to a court of justice. Rohan's lawyers convinced the judges their client was crazy and, instead of a long prison term, Rohan was sentenced to an indeterminate stay in one of the mental hospitals to undergo therapy. The mechanics of his arson were not at all crazy. He wasn't crazy when he soaked the rags in kerosene, when he found a way into the mosque, when he lit the match, or when he escaped undetected.

Rohan set fire to the wooden pulpit. The flames did not do appreciable damage. Workmen completed repairs within a week. The fire left no scars on the exterior of Al Aksa. Its beautiful, globular minaret still dazzles visitors with reflected sunlight. But some of the beautiful mosaic work on the interior dome was burned badly.

What Rohan could have done was set off a riot in Jerusalem. Moslems were sure a Jew had desecrated their holy place which, along with its neighbor, the larger Dome of the Rock, from which Mohammed ascended to heaven for a day, are all that occupy the Temple Mount in breathtaking splendor.

The Jews were sure an Al Fatah provocateur had set the blaze. The fire was serious enough to interrupt a Cabinet meeting and for the chief of police in Jerusalem to put every cop on a twenty-four-hour alert.

The police arrested Rohan the next day. He was living on a kibbutz where he attended an *ulpan* and was bragging about his accomplishment. Rohan had set the fire to destroy Al Aksa so that the Second Temple could be rebuilt in which he would be crowned king of Jerusalem. Al Aksa is directly above the Wailing Wall. Jews as they approach the wall can see the gleaming minaret and at sundown hear the *muzzein* over loudspeakers call Moslems to prayer.

After a four-week trial, Rohan's lawyers had convinced editors, policemen, citizens, and judges that the Arab guides were to blame first, and after them the Israeli Ministry of Religion. Rohan seemed a supplementary figure in the proceedings.

He had gained access to the mosque by distributing lavish tips for several days to the Arab guides. On the morning he set the fire, a guard was preoccupied elsewhere. But it is true that guides are simple fellows, not handsomely rewarded in this life, and a 50-pound note isn't something they see every day.

The world press charged that the Israelis should have been more careful. The Temple Mount is an irreplaceable treasure—only the Taj Mahal compares to it for exquisite architectural beauty.

But it is also true that the security forces of Israel are unable to prevent the incursion of Arab terrorists. Why would the Israelis suspect demented Christians were also making incursions?

When it was Rohan's turn to testify, he mesmerized the court, the psychiatrists, and the reporters with his story of divine revelation. One could almost hear those voices urging him on. But is true that any defense which did not bring a religious motivation before the court would have meant Rohan would never see daylight again.

Only Moslems are allowed into Al Aksa and the Dome of the Rock today, although the mount is open to visitors. Stationed around the walls, from which one can look over to the Mount of Olives where the Messiah will appear and from whose crest Jesus ascended, are armed Israeli sentries.

Odd men out

THE ODD MEN out in Israel are the Jewish atheist and the interfaith Jew.

The atheists are in a bad way, although the country is filled with them. The unanswerable argument the Israelis offer to the world is that God gave them this land. That indeed they have repurchased much of it, have fought for it time and time again, is offered, too, but it doesn't have the weight of God's dispensation. God makes Israeli priority simpler to understand and, as Israelis insist, He wouldn't have it any other way.

There is an interfaith movement in Israel. Earlier I discussed the work of the Rainbow Group in Jerusalem. But the interfaith movement in Israel differs greatly from the interfaith movement in America.

In Israel, the Jews are an overpowering majority and there is no theological confrontation. Christianity is not theologically important to Judaism, although Judaism is important theologically to Christians.

The movement in America gains its impetus from the desire of the Jew to preserve his civil rights and share in all the advantages of his Christian neighbors. The interfaith Jew in the States is out to prove he is no different from Gentiles except in the way he worships. He has a social motive. The interfaith movement hopes, say, that Jew and Christian can unite in the attempt to abolish poverty.

This situation does not obtain in Israel. There are hundreds of thousands of Israelis who probably have never met a Christian. The Christians in the Holy Land are usually either Arabs or clergymen. The Jews interested in the interfaith movement are intellectuals and the Christians who are interested are a small number of the same. The Jews in Israel are a living presence. The interfaith Jew is dedicated to helping Christians understand that the Jewish religion and the Jewish state are one and the same thing. The movement has a political motive.

But there is one day in the year which is an interfaith day which would make an American Jew turn green with envy. That is New Year's Day when the President of the state, now Shalman Shazar, holds a reception for all Christian and Moslem clergymen. A good time is had by all, including Israel's President, who is a Hassidic Jew.

Every daily is a national paper

WITH A population of 500,000, Tel Aviv incredibly supports two dozen daily newspapers.

There are reasons for this proliferation. With the exception of the English language Jerusalem *Post*, Tel Aviv represents the entire Israeli press. Israel isn't much larger than Massachusetts, which makes regional newspapers unnecessary. Every paper is a national paper.

Then, too, only half of the newspapers are published in Hebrew. There are newspapers published in French, Yiddish, German, Hungarian, Polish, and Arabic, and there is even a Bulgarian daily, an ethnic group famous for nodding when they mean "no" and shaking their heads when they mean "yes."

This diversity of language represents the melting-pot nature of Israel, some of whose population has yet to melt into the Hebrew culture. For every Jew who lived in Israel on May 14, 1948, there are four today, which gives the reader an idea of the magnanimity of the "ingathering of the exiles," a process still going on.

But how can two dozen daily papers survive in such a small market?

The answer is they can't.

All but three are subsidized by the political parties. These dailies range from *Hamodia*, financed by the ultra-Orthodox, to *Kol Haam*, the official organ of the tiny Communist Party. Some of these papers sell barely 1,000 copies a day, but their publishers persevere. A political party in Israel isn't worth its slogans if it doesn't have a newspaper.

The three which do make money are *Ha'aretz*, *Yedioth Achronoth*, and *Ma'ariv*, which are politically independent, liberal newspapers.

While most newspapers in the United States are corrupted by advertising interests, the corruption in Israel is purely political. Advertising pressure is unknown there: the party papers carry scarcely any advertising and the profit makers depend more on sales than on advertising revenues. No advertiser in Israel is immune from editorial attack, but the editorial and political pages are almost never objective.

Ha'aretz and *Ma'ariv*, however, are probably two of the finest newspapers in the free world. No newspaper of similar circulation makes efforts comparable to *Ma'ariv*'s to provide accurate and timely information to its readers. No American newspaper with a circulation of 100,000, or even several times 100,000, keeps three staff members permanently abroad. *Ma'ariv* has its own men in Paris, London, and New York. It has stringers in another twenty countries from Japan to Argentina. It uses the services of the AP, UPI, Reuters, the French Telegraphic Agency, the Israeli Telegraphic Agency, and the news services of the London *Observer* and the *Daily Telegraph*.

Like the famous *Le Monde*, *Ma'ariv* combines the swift, easy journalism of an evening paper with the dependability and seriousness of the morning paper. Half its front page and at least half its features are foreign material, which reflects, I suppose, traditional Jewish cosmopolitanism as well as the outwardness of a small country depending in many ways on the doings of the giants. And the giant with the closest coverage in the Israeli press is Uncle Sam.

Pay the man the $2

MY GUIDE was Shimon Yazon, a small, dapper Berliner who came to Israel in 1933. He took me all over the country in his beautifully groomed Mercedes Benz. My stay was drawing to an end on the day Shimon returned me to Jerusalem from Hebron, where the bones of my ancestors, Abraham, Isaac, and Ruth, are buried.

To the left was Rachel's Tomb, a large crowd of the Orthodox waiting to go inside to chant their prayers, and to our right was a young Army lieutenant. Shimon slowed to take aboard this hitchhiking soldier.

As we slowed, suddenly an Arab cop charged from his station in front of Rachel's Tomb and planted himself in front of Shimon's car. He pointed agitatedly to the signs, which in Syrian, French, Arabic, Hebrew, and English said, "No Stopping in Front of Rachel's Tomb."

Shimon yelled that he only stopped to give the soldier a lift—the soldier by this time having melted away. The Arab cop kept shaking off Shimon's expostulations as he wrote out the ticket. When Shimon yelled in Arabic, "You're exceeding your authority," the cop slapped it to him.

The fine for stopping in front of Rachel's Tomb is 15 pounds, which would buy a kilo of meat.

"This is not only a bum rap," yelled Shimon to the retreating policeman, "but it is a bum rap handed out by an Arab."

It is customary, explained Tommy Lapid, at the end of one of these extensive trips, to offer a government guide a small but appropriate gift (only American tourists tip in Israel). As I was taking my leave of Shimon, I said that as a small remembrance for his efficient services I wanted to pay the fine.

Shimon would have none of it. He was innocent. Who knew that better than Harry Golden?

Therefore, I have filled out and still fill out depositions in triplicate to the Jerusalem Traffic Authority explaining that Shimon had not come to a halt when the cop stopped our passage. I have explained that Shimon did not interfere with the duties of a police officer; he just gave the police officer a little lip, certainly a motorist's prerogative.

Shimon, I am perfectly willing to fill out another set, but I have a distinct prescience that the Traffic Authority is going to make the ticket stand up.

Earl Warren said it straight

To SAY Israel is the country of limitless possibility is untrue. It is a poor country and it is hard to become rich in it. But the people make a decent living, and there is, at the moment, absolutely no unemployment. By American standards, however, they don't earn much. Taxes are high. So are interest rates.

But there are infinite possibilities for a career. A large part of the framework of this quickly developing state is filled by newcomers, immigrants who become in no time directors of the banks and managers of the corporations or high government officials or university presidents or influential journalists. They have to master Hebrew and prove their talent, but after that, the sky is the limit. In this sense, Israel is an open society, highly mobile, more so than America.

Retired Chief Supreme Court Justice Earl Warren said of it, in an interview on his last visit, "This country is very much like California in the time of my father."

Anecdotes in closing

ON MY WAY to Lod, where I would catch an El Al jet to London, Tommy Lapid and I passed several gangs of hitchhiking soldiers. We were constrained to go on because the back seat of Tommy's Toyota was filled with my luggage and typewriter.

Tommy stared in the rearview mirror at the receding image, turned, and said, "Know why everyone has a good time in this country? Because everyone does his duty. Nobody is ever guilty about Israel. El Al public relations is going to serve us a delicious breakfast because you are a departing VIP and I am going to enjoy myself and not worry one bit about the boys going to the Sinai because when it's my turn, I go to the Sinai and let the others enjoy the eggs."

These Israelis have already built up a substantial school of humor about the Six-Day War. They tell of Nasser's cable to Kosygin, "Israeli aircraft attacks Cairo. Send help."

No reply.

Another telegram, this one, "Israeli soldiers have entered Cairo and are raping our women."

This time Kosygin answers. "*Mazeltov.* Twenty years from today you'll have a good Army."

With these jokes, however, another school of humor has disappeared. An actor who emigrated from Poland always opened his skit with the laugh-getting "Two Jews were walking down the street when two anti-Semites came along. 'Let's run,' said one Jew to the other, 'there are two of them and we are alone.'" But it never draws a laugh from an Israeli audience.

Everyone in Israel has known a St. Crispin's Day, and the experience makes them relish everything else all the more. They relish their work, their country, their homes, and their children—and even their disappointments.

I remember talking to a blue-eyed, blond soldier to whom I offered a lift to his kibbutz in the Galilee. This young fellow told me he was on the Israeli Olympic handball team, a fact I received with appropriate praise.

Quickly, he interrupted me. "What I really love," he said, eyes glistening, "is basketball. I wish I could be on the Olympic basketball team, but it will never be. We can never beat the Americans. You have to be a eunuch to grow big enough to beat the Americans."

Watching him run into his kibbutz, rifle and pack banging against him, I had the feeling he wouldn't trade this Sabbath weekend for Israeli victories *in perpetuum* over Wilt Chamberlain and the Lakers.

This zest for the daily event is infectious. In Hebron, I stopped at an Arab shop to buy silver earrings for a grandniece. The shopkeeper produced a tasteful pair for a seventeen-year-old who has yet to have her ears pierced, and I asked how much? He said 100 pounds positively. I put the earrings back on the glass counter as much in surprise as in outrage.

"All right, all right," said the Arab. "To save time, 12 pounds. It's my first," the very words I heard fifty years ago on the Lower East Side of New York from Jewish peddlers exhorting the patronage of housewives. The first sale of the day is a good luck omen and the seller promises a bargain.

As I said in the beginning, the war hasn't changed them as much as time has. It has, of course, changed them somewhat. On my first trip to Israel, everybody came to the Sheraton to see me, but on this trip it was understood I would go to see everybody, which at least got me out and around the country.

Take Tommy. Years ago when I first met him he was a working newspaperman running back and forth across Tel Aviv in search of the day's big story. Now he is a recognized playwright, an influential editor, and an author who commands the largest advances paid by Israeli publishers. Last summer he traveled through 19 countries in Europe writing a travel book because 100,000 Israelis go abroad every year.

Perhaps the true miracle of Israel's survival is that the people have let time and events change them as time and events should. They have not outgrown their first purpose, because they have always found new ones.

The Six-Day War had its effect. In the Sabbath schools during Purim, when the teacher recites the story of the saving of the Jewish people, whenever the name of Hamen or Ahasuerus is mentioned, the kids shoot off cap guns and boo and when Esther and Mordechai prevail, the kids wave Mogen Davids and cheer.

Causerie on the death of Nasser

TWO CURIOUS circumstances attended the death of Gamal Abdel Nasser, President of Egypt and leader of the United Arab Republic.

The first of these was the nature of his death which was attributed to a heart attack. This in itself was surprising because Nasser had survived dangers far more perilous than ill health. For one, he had survived three losing wars, in the first of which he was the commander of a beleaguered battalion. In the second and third wars for the same cause he was the leader of a country as decisively beaten as any country in the sad, empirical history of warfare. He survived the infighting of a palace revolution to emerge the strong man. He survived handily the decision of one John Foster Dulles not to build the Aswan Dam and survived even more handily the decision of the British Empire to recall the pilots who guided the ships through the Suez Canal.

It is possible ill health did him a favor. Few leaders, if any, have ever survived a geometric growth in population accompanied only by an arithmetic growth in industry and agriculture. Every year there are two million more Egyptians. If the Israelis treated Nasser roughly, it was child's play compared to what the Malthusian theorems would have done to him.

The second curious event was the way the American press treated Nasser's death. A segment of the American press and television treated Nasser to the tributes they might bestow on the death of an obnoxious and cantankerous pope. It is true the Egyptians venerated Nasser as a demi-God. The Neapolitans venerated the Borgias, but the Borgias didn't do to Italy what Nasser did to Egypt. The Suez Canal, once one of the major arteries of world trade whose traffic supported a large segment of the Egyptian economy, is inoperative. When again it does accommodate ships, it will be as a convenience for smaller cargo vessels. The Mogen David flies over the Sinai. Twenty years ago, there were almost 500,000 embittered refugees in Gaza and they are still in the camps and more embittered than ever. That is a large constituency for a Brother to neglect. And Egyptian sovereignty has been compromised by the installation of Soviet missiles and the investment along the Suez and in Cairo of Soviet technicians.

Demagogues are usually bad news and Nasser was bad news for the Egyptians, the Jews, and the West. What concerned most observers, of course, was what would emerge from the vacuum Nasser's death created. Or let's say it concerned most observers except Israel's Foreign Minister Abba Eban, who explained that the Israelis were not interested in the composition of cabinets in Cairo or Amman, just in the cabinet in Jerusalem. But the Israelis knew the enemy was Egypt, and Russia, not Nasser or, for that matter, Sadat. The Egyptians might believe a modern God has died, but the Russians do not play in games where a kid can break up the team by taking his baseball home.

The question is: If there had been no Nasser, would there have been a Six-Day War? Professor Sidney Hook once argued persuasively that without Lenin there would not have been a Bolshevik Revolution. There are scholars and historians who might well argue that Nasser, a singular figure, awakened Arab pride and the intimations of Arab potential.

The more significant question is: If a more extreme militarist should follow in Nasser's place, will there be an Israel?

But you know my answer.

A Short Glossary

Administered Territories: Israeli euphemism for territory taken from the Arabs at the end of the Six-Day War. These territories include the Golan Heights in the north, the West Bank of the Jordan in the central region, and the Gaza Strip and the Sinai in the south. It does not include Jerusalem, which was formally annexed in 1967.

aliyah: Immigration. The word in Hebrew means "ascent."

agora: One-tenth of an Israeli pound, worth 2.8 cents.

Ashkenazim: In Israel, the Jews who immigrated from Europe.

Bank Leumi Le-Israel: The national bank.

Bedouin: Nomadic Arabs indigenous to Palestine.

bet: Home or the French "chez."

bris: Ritual circumcision.

Cabala: The Jewish mystical tradition which dates from the seventh century and reaches a peak during the Renaissance.

Chanukah: An eight-day festival falling in December which celebrates the victory of the Maccabees over the Syrians in the second century B.C.

dunam: A measure of land; roughly one-third of an acre.

Druse: An Arab who is a member of a Moslem splinter sect.

Habimah: Israel's national theater.

Haganah: The underground army the Jews mustered during the British mandate. *Haganah* means "defense."

Halakah: The Jewish laws and ordinances which have descended from the oral tradition.

Hassidim: A Jewish mystical sect who celebrate work, zeal, and joy.

"Hatikva": Israel's national anthem.

307

Histadrut: The general organization of all labor in Israel.

Irgun: The Jewish terrorist organization which hanged British sergeants and blew up the King David Hotel during the mandate.

Israeli pound: Twenty-eight cents; 3.5 £ = $1.

Keren Kayemet: Jewish Fund Raising Agency.

kosher or kashruth: Food prepared according to ritual.

Knesset: The Israeli Parliament which convenes in Jerusalem.

mandate, British: The League of Nation's directive which let the British post troops and settlers in Palestine after World War I.

menorah: The traditional candelabrum of seven branches. The Chanukah candelabrum has nine branches. The colossal menorah stands outside the Knesset, a gift to Israel from the British Parliament.

Mogen David: The six-pointed Jewish star, the signal of King David's regency.

mohel: An ordained rabbi who performs circumcisions.

moshav: An Israeli cooperative village whose profits are divided among the inhabitants every year.

Municipality: Town Hall.

Orthodox: Jews who keep the strict letter of religious law.

Palmach: The kibbutz wing of the Haganah.

partition, United Nations: The vote by the General Assembly in 1947 which divided Palestine so that Jews could declare statehood in one of its parts.

Pesach: Passover, the celebration of the Jews' escape from Egyptian bondage.

piseta: One-tenth of an *agora*—worth nothing.

Reform: Jews who understand the religious tradition prescriptively rather than descriptively.

rehov: Street.

Sephardim: In Israel, the Jews who immigrated from Arab and Eastern countries.

Talmud: The collection of writings which outline Jewish civil and religious law.

Torah: The first five books of Moses; also called the Chumash.

ulpan: A school for immigrants offering an intensive course in spoken Hebrew.

Uzi: The light, automatic rifle of the Israeli Army.

Zionism: The political movement founded by Theodor Herzl among European Jews to found a state in the homeland.

A Very Select Bibliography

The two best novels about Israel are *Who? Me??* by Yoram Matmor, published by Simon and Schuster, New York, 1970; and *Gore and Igor* by Meyer Levin, also published by Simon and Schuster, 1967. Matmor is an Israeli and Levin an American. They are more than interesting books and more than books about Israel. They are literature. Read them even if you are not going to Israel. Read them even if you're Jewish, because we Jews can do some marvelous things with sentences.

There are an endless number of books about the Six-Day War, about the Sinai Campaign in 1956, and about the War of Independence in 1948. The most interesting of these have yet to be published—Dayan's memoirs, Golda's letters, or Ben-Gurion's history. The American syndrome is for a general to become a corporation president or a diarist; the Israeli syndrome is for a general to become a Cabinet member or an ambassador.

The following are the books I read just prior to my trip. They are revised yearly. You should read them, too, pilgrims:

Bazak Israel Guide. New York, Toronto, London, Pitman Publishing Corporation. This book is subsidized by the Israel Ministry of Tourism and republished annually.

Facts About Israel. Jerusalem, Publication Service Division, Israel Program for Scientific Translations. A paperback, the book is available in large bookstores everywhere in the United States.

Fodor's Israel. New York, David McKay Company.

Holiday Magazine's Guide to Israel. New York, Random House.

Israel and the Holy Land. New York, Golden Press.

Israel on $5 A Day, by Joel Lieber. New York, Arthur Frommer, Inc., distributed by Pocket Books, Inc. More likely it is $10 a day now.

Nagel's Encyclopedia Guide to Israel. New York, Cowles Education Corporation.

And, of course, the Old and New Testament in any version.

Index

ISRAEL

CEASE-FIRE LINES, JUNE, 1967

N

Mediterranean Sea

Dead Sea

Jordan River

BEIRUT

LEBANON

Sidon

Tyre

Nahariya

Acre

HAIFA

Hadera

Netanya

TEL AVIV Jaffa

Rishon Le-Zion

Ashdod

Ashkelon

Yad Mordechai

GAZA

El Arish

Nahal Sinai

Port Fuad

PORT SAID

DAMASCUS

Kiryat Shmona

Quneitra

GOLAN

Safed

S Y R I A

Degania

AMMAN

Galilee

Tiberias

Nazareth

Jenin

Nablus

Samaria

Ramallah

Jericho

JERUSALEM

Bethlehem

Lod

Ramle

Rehovot

Hebron

Ein Gedi

Judea

Masada

Arad

Dimona

Sodom

Beersheba